THE WARING SCHOOL

The Spread of Islam

D. LANCELOT
CH. BARBANT. sc

The Making of the Past

The Spread of Islam

by Michael Rogers

ELSEVIER·PHAIDON

Advisory Board for
The Making of the Past

John Boardman
Reader in Classical Archaeology, University of Oxford

Basil Gray
Former Keeper of Oriental Antiquities, British Museum

David Oates
Professor of Western Asiatic Archaeology,
Institute of Archaeology, University of London

Series Editor Courtlandt Canby

Managing Editor Giles Lewis

Editor for this volume Graham Speake

Picture Editors Polly Friedhoff, Andrew Lawson

Design Edward Gould

Index Griselda Taylor

Visual Aids Dick Barnard, Roger Gorringe

Frontispiece: the minaret of Khwāja ʿAlam at Iṣfahān, probably late 14th century, destroyed in 1934. After Dieulafoy.

ISBN 0 7290 0016 8

Elsevier-Phaidon – an imprint of Phaidon Press Ltd,
Littlegate House, St Ebbe's Street, Oxford

Planned and produced by Elsevier International Projects Ltd, Oxford,

Origination by Art Color Offset, Rome, Italy

Filmset by Keyspools Limited, Golborne, Lancs.

Printed in Belgium

Contents

Preface to the series

This book is a volume in the Making of the Past, a series describing the early history of the world as revealed by archaeology and related disciplines. The series is written by experts under the guidance of a distinguished panel of advisers and is designed for the layman, for young people, the student, the armchair traveler and the tourist. Its subject is a new history – the making of a new past, uncovered and reconstructed in recent years by skilled specialists. Since many of the authors of these volumes are themselves practicing archaeologists, leaders in a rapidly changing field, the series is completely authoritative and up-to-date. Each volume covers a specific period and region of the world and combines a detailed survey of the modern archaeology and sites of the area with an account of the early explorers, travelers, and archaeologists concerned with it. Later chapters of each book are devoted to a reconstruction in text and pictures of the newly revealed cultures and civilizations that make up the new history of the area.

Titles already published in the series

The Egyptian Kingdoms
The Aegean Civilizations
Biblical Lands
The New World

Titles to appear in 1976

The Spread of Islam
The Emergence of Greece
Barbarian Europe
Man before History
The Greek World
The Rise of Civilization

Future titles

The First Empires
The Roman World
Ancient Japan
The Persian Revival
Ancient China
The Kingdoms of Africa
Rome and Byzantium
Prehistoric Europe
India and Southeast Asia
Archaeology Today

Introduction

Islam is remarkable above all for its rapid territorial expansion. From its origin in 622 with Muhammad's flight from Mecca to Medina, within two generations it reached the Atlantic on one hand and Central Asia on the other. It is no less remarkable for its subsequent grip upon all these lands so quickly conquered (with the exception of those in Europe) as well as its later expansion in south Asia and Africa south of the Sahara. Throughout its history it has included within its ambit many different peoples with varied traditions, customs and languages, and it is fair to ask whether there is a common culture and art which might rightly be called Islamic. This book tries to answer that question by surveying the sites and monuments that survive from the first 800 years of Islam's history in the light of the literary sources and by studying the buildings themselves, their planning, style and decoration. In spite of recent work, much remains to be done in the way of excavation, and the principal material available to the Islamic archaeologist is the standing monuments. However, modern scholarship can now deal fairly with the evidence from a wide range of sources available to the specialist but not yet to the general reader, to recreate the medieval Islamic past.

There are inevitably limits: archaeology tells us what the buildings were like; but the institutions they housed did not always develop congruently with them. Institutions must be interpreted from the historians or the lawyers; for Islam is such a deeply conservative religion that much can be learnt from the condemnation of innovation. Ideally the legal and historical sources should complement the extant monuments and their inscriptions. However, for Baghdad, which till 1258 was the seat of the ʿAbbāsid Caliphate, virtually nothing remains but medieval topographers' descriptions; and few of the great cities of the Eastern Caliphate (the Mashriq) – Shīrāz, Nīshāpūr or Merv – are in any better state. For Qayrawān in Tunisia on the other hand, the greatest medieval city of Western Islam (the Maghrib) after Cordova, the historical sources for its many monuments have not yet been exploited.

There remain 13th- to 15th-century Egypt and Syria, 13th-century Anatolia, and 14th- to 15th-century Persia and Central Asia, where the richness of the documentation and the many standing monuments make detailed investigation particularly fruitful. Elsewhere, the monuments without the sources or the sources without extant monuments have been used with much more caution. The approach is inevitably partial, but the material upon which it concentrates is typical of its period or culture.

The material has also determined the temporal limits of this book. Under the Umayyads (632–750) and the ʿAbbāsids (750–1258) there occurred not only the major conquests of Islam but also the evolution of Islamic political institutions and administration, theology, law and the sciences. This has often led Western Orientalists to conclude that after this Classical Age of Islam there was only decline, and, sometimes, to regret that Islam had no renaissance. There was, indeed, no Islamic revival contemporary with the 15th-century Italian Renaissance; hence my consistent use of the terms "Middle Ages" for the period 622–1171, and "Later Middle Ages" for the period following. However, although the Arabic historians saw the destruction of the ʿAbbāsid Caliphate at Baghdad in 1258 as the ultimate catastrophe, the process of disintegration had set in long before; nor did progress come to a sudden stop. Even if the semblance of political unity was lost, the legacy of the Great Seljuks was a state in 13th-century Anatolia, which was succeeded by the birth of the Ottoman Empire. The Mongol invasions in Persia and Central Asia, though undoubtedly destructive, were of crucial importance in their development as separate states, and the far more destructive campaigns (1370–1405) of Tīmūr (better known as Tamerlane) were followed by a brilliant cultural flowering under his 15th-century descendants.

However, by the late 15th century these successors of the ʿAbbāsids were generally in decline. Persia and Central Asia were overwhelmed by tribal or dynastic warfare. The Mamlūk state in Egypt and Syria was seriously weakened by internal faction and economic decline. Granada, the last Muslim enclave in Spain, fell in 1492. And the Ottoman conquest of Syria, Egypt, Iraq and much of North Africa in the early 16th century then established Turkey as the dominant Islamic power.

I am deeply indebted to many friends and colleagues, in particular to M. Henri Abdelnour, Mrs Layla ʿAlī Ibrāhīm, M. and Mme Jean-Charles Balty, Mme Yolande Crowe, Dr and Mrs Norman Daniel, Mlle Sophie Ebeid, Fr Peter Levi SJ, Professor Muhsin Mahdi, Professor V. L. Ménage, M. André Raymond, Professor G. J. Toomer and Professor and Mrs Magdi Wahba. But I am above all indebted to Basil Gray, whose constant interest has encouraged me and whose generous criticism has saved me many errors. To him and to his wife, Nicolete, I affectionately dedicate this book.

Note on Dating

For editorial convenience dates have been given according to the Western calendar. Islam uses a lunar calendar dating from the Hegira (the flight of Muhammad from Mecca to Medina in 622 AD). Persia uses a solar calendar, which was introduced by the Seljuk Sultan Malikshāh, likewise dating from the Hegira, but with a confusing difference of about 40 years. These calendars rarely coincide and the Western equivalents therefore are not always exact.

Note on Transliteration

For Arabic, Persian and Turkish names or technical terms I have wherever possible used current English forms. Otherwise I have transliterated them according to the system recommended by the *Encyclopaedia of Islam* (but with *q* for *ḳ* and *j* for *dj*), which works well for Arabic, adequately for Persian but rather badly for Turkish. Transliteration is useful to both the professional and the ordinary reader, since it reproduces the original form fairly exactly and saves much time in consulting standard works of reference. Place-names raise different problems. Many medieval Islamic capitals still exist and have standard English equivalents. Where they do not, I have employed the following system: Turkish place-names are given as they would appear on a modern Turkish map; but Persian, Syrian and Egyptian names are strictly transliterated. For place-names in the Soviet Union I have compromised between the modern name, the best-known name and the medieval name, when that can be identified, with alternatives given in cases of doubt.

Chronological Table

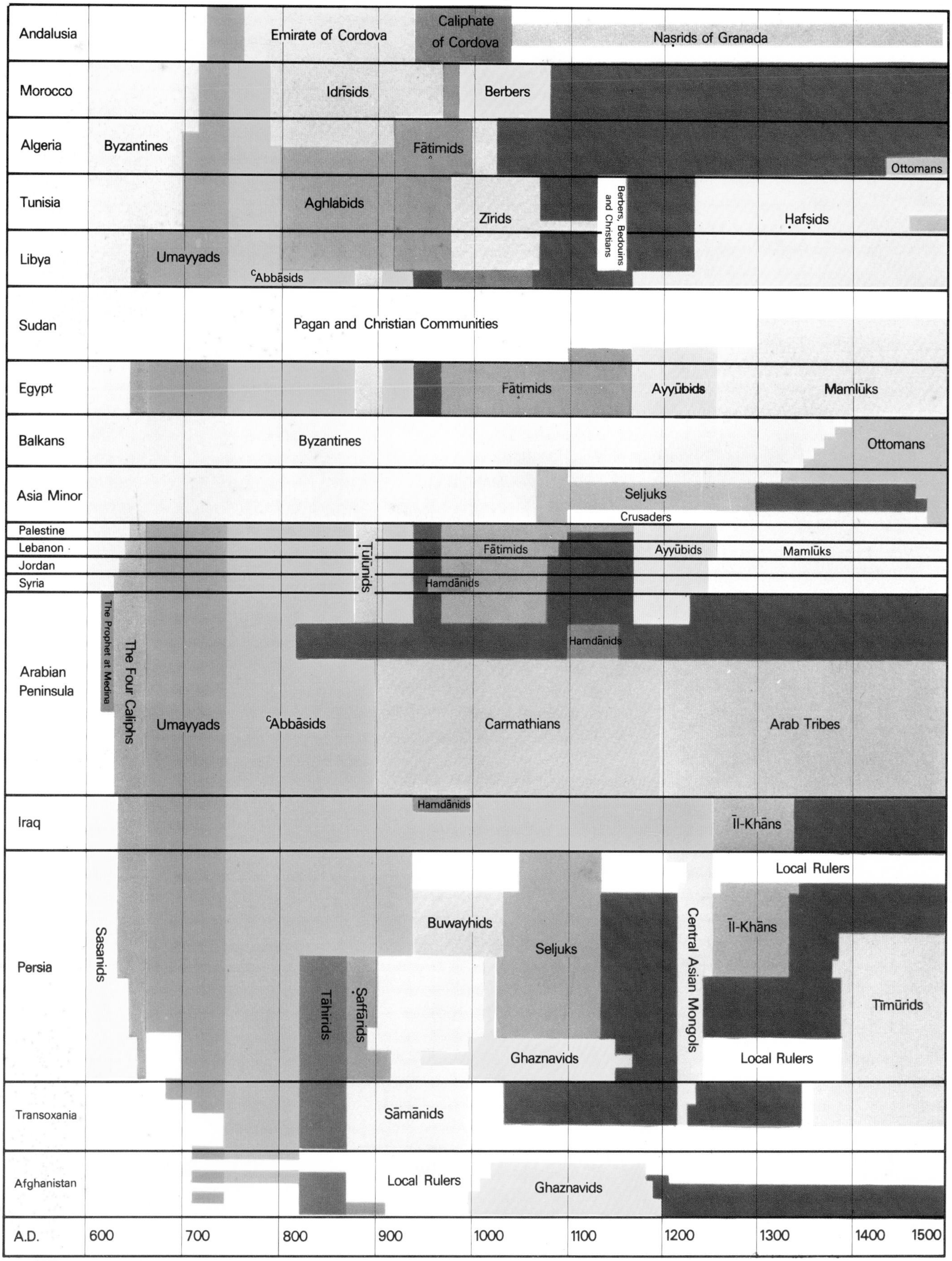
Andalusia
Emirate of Cordova
Caliphate of Cordova
Naṣrids of Granada
Morocco
Idrīsids
Berbers
Algeria
Byzantines
Fāṭimids
Ottomans
Tunisia
Aghlabids
Zīrids
Berbers, Bedouins and Christians
Ḥafṣids
Libya
Umayyads
ᶜAbbāsids
Sudan
Pagan and Christian Communities
Egypt
Fāṭimids
Ayyūbids
Mamlūks
Balkans
Byzantines
Ottomans
Asia Minor
Seljuks
Crusaders
Palestine
Lebanon
Jordan
Syria
Ṭūlūnids
Fāṭimids
Ayyūbids
Mamlūks
Hamdānids
Arabian Peninsula
The Prophet at Medina
The Four Caliphs
Umayyads
ᶜAbbāsids
Hamdānids
Carmathians
Arab Tribes
Iraq
Hamdānids
Īl-Khāns
Persia
Sasanids
Local Rulers
Buwayhids
Seljuks
Central Asian Mongols
Īl-Khāns
Ṭāhirids
Ṣaffārids
Tīmūrids
Ghaznavids
Local Rulers
Transoxania
Sāmānids
Afghanistan
Local Rulers
Ghaznavids
A.D.
600
700
800
900
1000
1100
1200
1300
1400
1500

1. The Lure of Islam

Study of the numerous and varied standing monuments of Islam is just as effective as excavation as a means of bringing Islamic institutions and their developments to life, even if it lacks the glamorous discovery of a "buried" civilization. In any case, although Islamic excavation and the analysis of its monuments have now moved beyond the stage of unorganized curiosity and treasure-hunting that characterized most archaeology until the late 19th century, they are still behind European studies in prehistory, Egyptology and the Classics.

Antiquarianism. This antiquarianism and treasure-hunting, crude as they were, did at least often betray a genuine interest in the reconstruction of the past. Muslim antiquarianism certainly lacked the Italian Renaissance appreciation of the antiquity of an object as being itself an intrinsic value. However Muslim historians were not, as has sometimes been asserted, wholly unconscious of their past, and Islamic antiquarianism, if one may call it that, often took the form of a certain patriotic veneration for places or for buildings important in history or legend. Persepolis, the famous ceremonial palace of the Persian kings, first became important in Persian Islamic national sentiment when the Buwayhids usurped power in the 10th century. Being commoners, they had to establish their royalty, particularly in the eyes of the ʿAbbāsid caliphs at Baghdad, spiritual rulers of Islam. To do this they revived the Sasanian (pre-Islamic) conception of charismatic kingship, already accepted by the ʿAbbāsids, which included ceremonial visits to places sacred in the Iranian tradition like Persepolis, or the ancient rock carvings of Persia, where they read their predecessors' inscriptions or added their own. The problem of establishing themselves as orthodox clients of the Caliphate was insoluble and the Shīʿī Buwayhids assumed control of the orthodox Caliphate.

The continuing importance of Persepolis after the Buwayhids is attested by inscriptions there commemorating ceremonial visits by virtually every Muslim dynasty from the 12th to the 19th century. Even the Mongols frequented Persepolis and other Persian sites some years before their official conversion to Islam in 1296 – possibly because it had already become identified in popular legend with the "throne of Solomon" and Solomon was a

Koranic as well as a Biblical prophet. This tradition remained strong and successive dynasties describe themselves in the inscriptions they left at Persepolis as "heir to the Kingdom of Solomon."

For the most part these inscriptions repeat one another in emphasizing the ruler's kingly attributes. However, one ruler (of Shīrāz) recorded in 1339 that he had "visited in state this strange place and these marvelous buildings," which suggests that he was impressed not only by the historic associations of Persepolis but by its architecture as well.

The unbroken associations of Persepolis with the Iranian-Muslim tradition of kingship explain, incidentally, its preeminent attraction for European travelers from the 17th century, when they first began to visit it, to the present day. Of course they also knew the legend of Alexander's feast at Persepolis and the destruction of the palace at the whim of a courtesan; but from a distance its ruins are unimpressive and their enthusiasm must have been prompted by their local interpreters' accounts.

Moreover, by the 18th to 19th centuries, when Islamic antiquities began to arouse aesthetic attention in Europe, their utility as historical documents was ignored, for Classical antiquarianism, initially a source of cultural inspiration, was frowned upon by historians as unsystematic, historically useless and a pursuit fit only for amateur collectors.

However the essentially Renaissance antiquarian attitude did persist well into the 19th century, particularly in the works of two connoisseurs, Reinaud and Michelangelo Lanci, the founders of Islamic iconography. Lanci was the first of many Europeans to attempt to explain Islamic epigraphy and decoration in allegorical terms, as if the objects he described were talismans or Renaissance emblems, allegorical compositions to test the viewer's erudition. His old-fashioned approach is shown not just by his rather primitive and sometimes naive explanations but also by his choice of iconography in the state of Islamic studies at the time. He was, however, typical of his generation. The minor arts of Islam also came increasingly into European favor in the 19th century, but were treated mostly as objects of beauty or curiosity without any relevance to the society that produced them.

Antiquarianism has, therefore, set the tone of Islamic archaeology. It owes its advances to the development of various associated pursuits: topography, from haphazard travelers' notes to the drawing of large-scale maps; illustration, from the *Stadtpläne* (conventionalized and often

Opposite: the dome over the *miḥrāb* of the Great Mosque at Yazd in Persia. The dome was built by 1316 but the exterior is a recent restoration.

Below: an 18th-century view of the ruins of the Achaemenid palace at Persepolis (destroyed in 330 BC). After Niebuhr.

inaccurate town views) of medieval and Renaissance Europe to archaeological drawing where accuracy is the prime consideration; historical geography, using both Muslim and European sources to identify medieval ruins; chronology, using inscriptions, the literary sources or the architectural evidence of a standing monument to determine its date, place it in series, and date similar monuments accordingly; and finally modern techniques of site surveying, using surface-sherding, brick-types or the evidence of disused irrigation systems as a means of determining when or how intensively a site was inhabited. Although these are now taken for granted by any digging archaeologist, the first archaeological survey in which material from Islamic sites was recorded and classified was made in 1905 in Mesopotamia by Sarre and Herzfeld and the methodology of such surveys is still under discussion.

Geographers and historians. Topography relies upon both Muslim and Western sources. It is often assumed that the difference between them is that the former fail to distinguish fact from fiction and are only interested in "travelers' tales." But up to the 19th century *all* geographers are fairly undisciplined and it is easy to cite examples of Islamic accuracy and European credulity for even the most accessible monuments. Jerusalem, like Mecca and Medina, may have attracted exceptional attention because of its importance as a place of Muslim pilgrimage. Nevertheless, for the Middle Ages, we learn far more of the Christian shrines from the Muslim sources than we do of the Muslim shrines from the Christian.

The Islamic historians tend to be especially reliable when it comes to recording inscriptions. I only know of one downright invention, but this culminates a tirade by Yāqūt (just prior to 1220–21) against the contentiousness, the heresy, the adultery and the general debauchery of the inhabitants of Iṣfahān. On a caravansaray at Idāj, just outside Iṣfahān, there is, he says, the following inscription: "Woe to those who travel by Idāj to earn their living in Iṣfahān! And may God cover with ignominy those who once having been there dare to return!"

But this "signpost to Sodom" would have been recognized by any of his contemporary town-historians as rhetorical device, not basic epigraphy. On the contrary they record inscriptions with conscientious accuracy, and make full use of older foundation documents or chancery documents, either the originals or notes of them in the registers accessible to them in the archives.

Particularly valuable are histories of Islamic capitals, for example Damascus (by Ibn al-ʿAsākir (died 1178 AD)), Aleppo (by Ibn Shaddād (died 1235), and the 15th-century historians, Ibn al-Shiḥna and Sibṭ ibn al-ʿAjamī), Cairo (Maqrīzī (died 1427) and many others) and Jerusalem (Mujīr al-Dīn, 1496): all of these give ample evidence of having used inscriptions among their sources and often attempt to reconcile inscriptions of different dates on the same building. This is all the more remarkable in that the scripts they had to read were often archaic and often so placed that they were difficult to see, let alone decipher.

However, there is a perceptible difference in the Muslim attitude towards architecture; unlike that of the pharaohs or Gothic Europe it was not "built for eternity" but, on the contrary, was envisaged as inherently impermanent. This attitude is expressed in a saying attributed to Muhammad, "Nothing so much wastes the substance of a believer as architecture"; the saying is almost certainly spurious, but the attitude it suggests is real enough. Most surviving early Islamic buildings are associated with religious institutions maintained by pious endowments, where the building is less important than its organization (or its constitution).

Travelers and explorers. The great age of the Muslim geographers was from the 10th to the 15th century. Subsequently, European travelers are more useful. I have mostly chosen my examples from Persia, Turkey and Central Asia because these routes were well traveled and give us a continuous series of memoirs. However, the results of four centuries of travel along the great eastward route via Erzurum, Tabrīz, Iṣfahān and Shīrāz to Hormuzd on the Persian Gulf are miserably inadequate to our purpose, and it would be mistaken to suppose that other areas, Egypt or Syria for example, were better served. The earliest European traveler to describe even contemporary Islamic monuments in any detail is Clavijo, who headed a Spanish embassy to Tamerlane (in Persian, Timūr) in 1403–04, and who gives valuable descriptions of what he saw of Samarkand and Shahr-i Sabz. A century later an anonymous Venetian described the Hasht Bihisht (the Eight Paradises), a no longer extant palace of Uzūn Ḥasan outside Tabrīz. In plan it appears to have been much like the Çinili Köşk, built by Meḥmed the Conqueror in Istanbul in 1473, but it was set on a rectangular terrace with a channel into which water gushed from enormous dragons' mouths at each corner, in a garden containing summer houses, a vast harem and other buildings, filled with jasmine and

The great *īwān* or portal of the palace of Chosroes (early 7th century) at Ctesiphon in Iraq. After Dieulafoy.

The walls of Cairo. The Citadel, dating from the early 13th century, is here seen from the east.

roses, fountains and swans. Inside the palace the central area was covered by an enormous circular silk carpet, and the dome and the walls were painted with scenes of battle, real and legendary, hunting parties and receptions of ambassadors. Only in the 17th century do travelers regularly mention Ṣafawid monuments, and even then in nothing like such detail, partly because they were chiefly impressed by their flashiness and partly because, while appreciating Persian developments in town planning, they found them inferior to Europe and sometimes downright decadent.

This chauvinism is prominent in French memoirs. Chardin, who visited Persia in the 1670s, devotes a whole chapter to the badness of Persian painting (in all fairness Ṣafawid painting was by this time fairly bad) which he says, for religious reasons, utterly fails to follow European taste (viz. Poussin and Claude)! In general he was appreciative of the urbanities of Persian architecture but his contemporary Thévenot, whose description of a building at Mosul (probably the Great Mosque) is the first European notice of Mongol stuccowork, expresses his praise patronizingly.

Some Muslim shrines, like the Umayyad Mosque at Damascus and the Ḥaram al-Sharīf at Jerusalem, were inaccessible to non-Muslims up to the mid-19th century and therefore pass unnoticed in European memoirs. However, travelers were unsystematic and very rarely read either the early geographical compilations (like Dapper's, 1681) or their predecessors' accounts. There are few exceptions. J. B. Fraser, who set off in 1821 with, apparently, the idea of making a geological survey of eastern Persia, an area in which he had conspicuously few European predecessors, disapproved absolutely of all Persian architecture from the 16th and 17th centuries up to his own time.

However, he thoroughly approved of the brick architecture of the Seljuks and Mongols in Persia, and it is our good fortune that his route to Mashhad included Ribāṭ Zaʿfarānī, a Seljuk caravansaray (c. 1100) of which there is now no trace. From his careful, even systematic, description it has been possible to reconstruct its plan in detail, and his remarks on its construction and decoration justify the accuracy of his dating. The reasons for his interest in earlier Persian Islamic architecture and its chronology, which runs against the traditional English admiration for gaudy Ṣafawid architecture, are unknown: in this he was certainly 50 years ahead of his time.

At this point it is perhaps relevant to consider illustration. Even in the European Renaissance, faithful representation of architecture is extremely rare, and views of towns are generally conventional plans with no pretensions to accuracy. There is one striking exception, Gentile Bellini, though his influence was impermanent. Summoned to Constantinople in 1481 to paint Meḥmed the Conqueror's portrait, he may have returned to Europe via Alexandria, since a painting of *St Mark preaching at Alexandria* in the Brera Gallery in Milan has a background very similar to the interiors of 15th-century Cairene Mamlūk *khān*s, and this must be the Venetian *fondaco* (factory) at Alexandria. Even more interesting is a painting

A painting attributed to Gentile Bellini of the reception of a Frankish delegation by the Mamlūk governor of Damascus. Musée du Louvre, Paris.

ascribed to his studio, which has often been said to represent the reception of the Venetian ambassador, Domenico Trevisano, at the Citadel of Cairo in 1512 by the Mamlūk Sultan al-Ghūrī. Sauvaget has convincingly shown, however, that the building in the background is indubitably the Umayyad mosque at Damascus with its western minaret as it was restored in 1488. From the architectural details it is even possible to localize the point from which the paintings or the sketches for it were executed. The bath, the domes of which appear in the middle distance, is probably that founded by Nūr al-Dīn in 1169–70, now at the southeast corner of the 17th-century Palais ʿAẓm. In the same neighborhood Watzinger and Wulzinger noted in their survey of Damascus (c. 1910) an old European trading house. This might well have been the Venetian *fondaco* in Damascus, which was certainly nearby, and if this was so the painter most probably worked from there.

Strikingly enough, there is an Ottoman work, probably finished in 1537, by Naṣūḥ al-Ṣalāḥī al-Matrāqī with an invaluable series of topographical illustrations. They are influenced by European *Stadtpläne* and Western cartography, and they must have been intended to serve partly as maps, since they illustrate an account of the campaigns of Selim I and Süleymān the Magnificent in which Naṣūḥ participated. Nevertheless the sketches must have been made on the spot, and in many instances show buildings which have disappeared. He made, for example, a series of detailed illustrations of Constantinople from which, despite the lack of stereometric projection, its appearance in the early 16th century can easily be recreated.

After 1650, even if travelers ignored the Islamic buildings of the East, their interest in the more ancient monuments – Persepolis, Babylon and Baalbek – grew, and with it the idea that they should be accurately recorded. One might expect, therefore, that later Islamic monuments would have benefited from this new desire for accurate recording. So they probably would, but for the disastrous effects of the Romantic revival, in particular the cult of exoticism and the picturesque.

The immediate effect of the Romantic emphasis upon individual psychological reactions was to turn travelers away from accurate description or depiction and in upon themselves, for example Delacroix's *odalisques* or *fantaisies*. It also encouraged writers to think of illustration as superfluous, discovery overriding description, enthusiasm knowledge, brilliance accuracy, and impressionism meticulous analysis.

This typically Romantic attitude towards architecture was shared by a more famous traveler, Sir Richard Burton, who made the journey to Mecca and Medina in 1853 disguised as a Persian-speaking Indian doctor touring the shrines of Islam. His interest in the architectural history of the Holy Places runs in his account to a chapter on each, though without any attempt to relate the historical data to the buildings he visited or made sketch plans of. As for Islamic architecture, his views could not be more insular,

Sir Richard Burton in Arab dress. Disguised as a Persian-speaking Indian doctor, he toured the shrines of Islam.

egocentric, choleric and prejudiced.

The miserably slow progress in architectural description and illustration is demonstrated by European memoirs of the Mausoleum of the Mongol Īl-Khān Öljeytü at Sulṭānīye which lay on the main route south from Tabrīz and was so conspicuous from a distance that even the least interested traveler needed no excuse for visiting it. It fared even worse at the hands of illustrators. Naṣūḥ al-Matrāqī's illustration of Sulṭānīye (c. 1537) is not only the first but also, all things considered, the best. It clearly shows the mausoleum in a state far removed from its present ruin, part of a rectangular stone-walled enceinte, a second mausoleum and a large building with a pair of minarets at its entrance. Olearius' sketch of Sulṭānīye is sheer fantasy, but he admits that his draughtsman died during the travels and that he therefore had to do it himself; the same misfortune evidently had befallen Pietro della Valle, none of whose letters is illustrated. Morier's view (1808) is adequate, though very small in scale, but thereafter draughtsmanship passes into the hands of professional illustrators, working up sketches made on the spot into picturesque compositions.

They were no Orientalists, so inscriptions were beyond them, and their working methods, not suprisingly, meant that the final product was often far from reality. Among them are Flandin (1851, though he traveled in Persia ten years earlier), Coste (1867) and Texier (1841). None of their drawings tally, but Texier took what to us must seem unpardonable liberties, inventing decorative motifs and adding inscriptions wherever he thought fit. We have, therefore, no reliable drawing of the Sulṭānīye mausoleum till Dieulafoy's plan and section (1883) and Sarre's architectural details (1890s), many of which are particularly valuable as they are of fragments which have since disappeared.

The Romantic movement encouraged travel and exploration, "the lure of knowing what should not be known." But it could not free travelers from the domination of their Classical and Biblical education, and the attempt to relate their experiences to the Classics or the Bible left them with no time to treat the Muslim monu-

Naṣūḥ al-Matrāqī's view of Sulṭānīye (c. 1537) from a manuscript in the Istanbul University Library. It clearly shows the mausoleum in a state far removed from its present ruin.

The Mausoleum of Öljeytü (1310–16) at Sulṭānīye as it appears today.

ments with equal care. Morier's *Journey through Persia* (1812) is so full of quotations from Xenophon and the Old Testament that he appears to have gone on his travels with Xenophon in one hand and the Bible in the other. A similar preoccupation is evident in the memoirs of almost all travelers in Syria and Palestine up to the late 19th century. This is perhaps one reason why, although Jerusalem was visited and described hundreds of times before, the first representation of the Dome of the Rock occurs in Bernhard of Breydenbach's *Peregrinationes in Terram Sanctam* (1486) after Edward Reuwich of Utrecht. Their Biblical or Classical preoccupations satisfied, however, travelers tended towards social observation of Muslim customs rather than to monuments or inscriptions.

Early archaeologists. The striking development of European descriptive geography in the mid-19th century and the gradual application of inscriptions and Muslim chronicles to the monuments themselves were not, therefore, simply the culmination of a process but a by-product of political interest in the Middle East generated by the concern of the European powers in the decline of the Ottoman Empire. The impulse was first given in Egypt where, although Napoleon's occupation of the country lasted only three years (1798–1801), a brilliant team of scholars attached to his expeditionary force collected information on most subjects from pharaohs to fleas but including Islamic antiquities. This was written up over the following 20 years in the *Description de l'Égypte*, an encyclopedic work very much in the spirit of the French Enlightenment.

The scholarly success of Napoleon's expedition to Egypt prompted imitation. When, after the treaty of Finckenstein in 1807 between France and Persia, General Gardane was sent out on a military mission, he took with him a team of surveyors and draughtsmen. However, one drawing of an Islamic monument emerged from this, that of a facade at Sulṭānīye, clearly c. 1340 but no longer extant, by Michel-François Préault, which is probably to be identified with the two-minaret construction of Naṣūḥ al-Matrāqī's *Stadtplan*.

The attitude of the French towards the monuments of Islam was later conditioned by their occupation (1830) of Western Islam (the Maghrib) for more than a century. However, the interest in the Islamic monuments of Egypt aroused by the *Description de l'Égypte* was permanent. Initially, illustrators like Coste (1839) were not sufficiently concerned with accuracy, but to two of his successors, Prisse d'Avennes (*L'Art arabe d'après les monuments du Caire*, 1877) and Bourgoin (*Précis de l'art arabe*, 1892), we are indebted for the earliest corpus of Islamic ornament.

The Napoleonic occupation of Egypt also taught one very important lesson. By the early 19th century virtually the whole Muslim world, from Tangier to Samarkand, had disintegrated into local despotisms, whose conduct ranged from the capricious to the brutal and who were in any case unable to guarantee travelers' safety outside the towns they controlled, leaving the countryside and the sea to be ravaged by brigands and pirates. Only a victorious army could properly deal with such nuisances, and whereas fanaticism or orthodoxy might normally exclude foreigners from shrines, like that of the Imām Riḍā' at Mashhad, little could be done to prevent the entry of a triumphant conqueror. Armies, moreover, have the means to carry out surveying and detailed cartography, and it is not surprising, therefore, that we should owe some of the most useful guides to the antiquities of the East to military intervention.

Equally important has been European imperialism – expansionism in the quaint belief that one is doing the inhabitants good by occupying their territory. This is particularly well shown in the gradual Russian penetration of the Caucasus and Central Asia from the later 18th century to the 1880s. The relatively slow rate of expansion enabled Russian scholarship in Islamic history and Oriental languages to keep pace with it and provided a corps of scholars ready to follow up any Russian advance. The first "systematic" Russian excavations of an Islamic site were Veselovsky's at Samarkand in 1885. The preeminent attention still given to the Islamic period in Russian Central Asia has indisputably put Soviet archaeologists to the forefront in study of the eastern provinces of Islam.

German interest in Islamic archaeology developed almost as rapidly as Russian and under rather similar conditions. In the 1890s, as the collapse of the Ottoman Empire appeared imminent, Germany, like some other European powers, decided to turn the situation to her advantage and the choice fell upon Turkey in Asia, the Baghdad Railway and its ensuing complications, and a campaign to establish German ascendancy at the Porte. Once again the military were in the fore: Von Moltke, the Chief of Staff in the Franco-Prussian war, set up a military mission to reorganize the Ottoman army and strengthen the eastern frontiers of Turkey against further Russian encroachments; consuls, many of them distinguished Islamic scholars, were appointed to the larger towns of Anatolia; and in 1898 Kaiser Wilhelm II paid a state visit to ʿAbdü'l-Ḥamīd, as Emperor of the West, before making a triumphal progress to Jerusalem.

Wilhelm II's visit has sometimes been treated as a picturesque but insignificant episode in the final years of the Ottoman Empire. But its archaeological consequences were important. In return for the gift of a remarkably ugly green marble fountain erected on the Hippodrome in Istanbul outside the Mosque of Sultan Ahmed I and an inscribed marble slab intended to replace the 12th-century wooden cenotaph inside the tomb of Saladin at Damascus, ʿAbdü'l-Ḥamīd was generous beyond all expectation. Among the caravans of spoils which followed Wilhelm on his return to Berlin and which half-filled the newly created Imperial Museum was the facade of the unfinished Umayyad palace of Mshaṭṭā in Transjordan. European Orientalists were for the first time face to face with one of the masterpieces of early Islamic architecture, and a flood of speculation was unleashed, terminated only by Creswell's authoritative attribution of it to al-Walīd II in 743–44 AD.

The German archaeologist Sarre worked initially in Anatolia in the 1890s. His marvelous accuracy as a draughtsman is shown in the three volumes of his *Denkmäler persischer Baukunst* (1901–10). As both Orientalist and epigrapher, he was a pioneer in the joint interpretation of the architectural history of the monuments he surveyed, their inscriptions and the elaboration of a chronology for comparable but undated monuments.

In 1905 Sarre and his collaborator Herzfeld embarked on a detailed archaeological survey of Mesopotamia, emphasizing Islamic sites and the standing monuments, with plans, records of the sherd types collected and an epigraphic supplement, published as *Archäologische Reise im Euphrat- und Tigris-Gebiet* (1911–20). This was followed by seasons of excavation at Sāmarrā on the Tigris which were brought to an abrupt end by World War I.

One final tribute is owed to German archaeological activity in the prewar period, the patronage of the early career of the Swiss scholar Max van Berchem. He had already begun to work in Egypt and from 1903 onwards he devoted himself to the collection and publication of Arabic inscriptions in stone in Anatolia, Syria, Palestine and Egypt (the *Corpus Inscriptionum Arabicarum*). At his death in 1921 Anatolia remained unfinished and his notes on north Syria were later written up and published by colleagues, including Herzfeld.

The British contribution to Islamic archaeology during the 19th century was principally in India. Where the study of Islamic history and archaeology went together, the

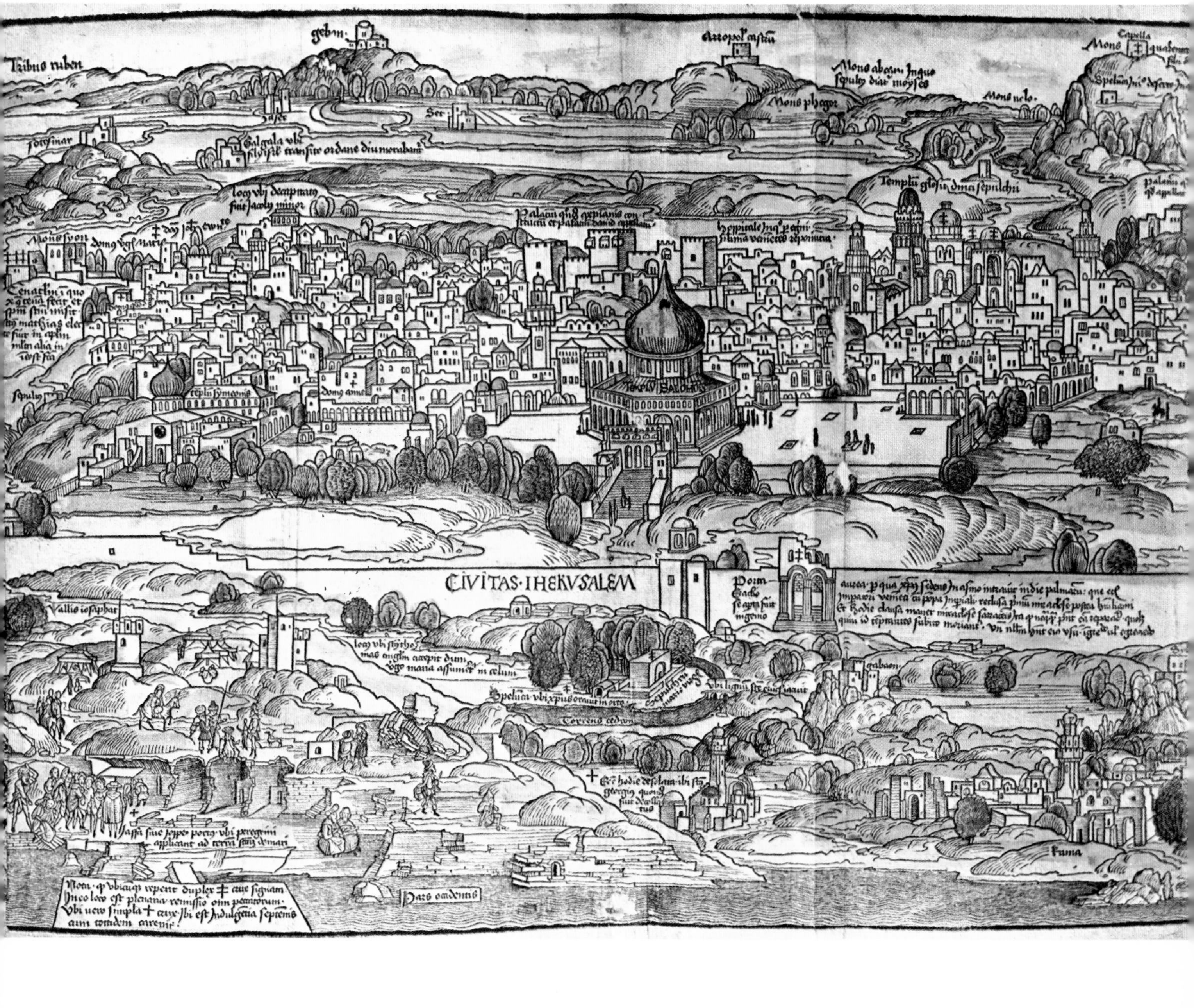

A 15th-century view of the Dome of the Rock, Jerusalem, from Bernhard of Breydenbach, *Peregrinationes in Terram Sanctam*, after Edward Reuwich of Utrecht.

Above: the Umayyad fortress of Qaṣr al-Kharāna, Jordan.

Left: a detail of the facade from the palace of Mshaṭṭā (*c.* 740), Jordan. Islamisches Museum, East Berlin. This facade was among the spoils which followed Kaiser Wilhelm II on his return to Berlin in 1898.

principal contributions made by British scholars in India were related to the Mogul monuments.

The German exploration of Mesopotamia also stimulated British interest which had previously been limited to the pre-Islamic period. It was Gertrude Bell whose travels in Syria and Mesopotamia at this time were most fruitful for Islamic archaeology. Among her studies of early Christian, Byzantine and Muslim monuments is a detailed monograph (1914) on the early ʿAbbāsid desert castle of Ukhayḍir in Iraq (785 AD).

But a near contemporary, K. A. C. Creswell (1880–1974), remains the outstanding figure of Islamic archaeology. With singular perseverance he traveled all over the Near East between 1910 and 1930 to produce a massive two-volume corpus of the Umayyad and ʿAbbāsid architecture (*Early Muslim Architecture*). This combines meticulous survey of the standing monuments (backed up on occasion by trial excavations) with a concern for their chronology, and is the basis of any work on the architecture of the early centuries of Islam. Later he was to produce two equally important volumes, *The Muslim Architecture of Egypt*, containing all the extant monuments of Egypt from 950 to 1326. Comparable publications of the monuments of Turkey, Persia, Central Asia, Iraq or even Egypt in the later Middle Ages exist only as scattered monographs. Monographs, rather than a corpus, are probably the form in which monuments will be published for the foreseeable future: but even these will build upon the foundations of Creswell's work.

Samarkand in the 15th Century

VISUAL STORY

Samarkand has always been the chief town of Central Asia, controlling the valleys of the Zarafshān and the Kashka Daryā. Though captured and sacked by Alexander the Great, it remained the capital of Soghd continuously from 500 BC up to the Arab conquest of 712 AD. Henceforth it was known as Afrāsiyāb, the name of the legendary ruler of Turan who in Firdawsī's *Book of Kings* was the inveterate enemy of Iran.

Samarkand, like Bukhārā and Merv, is a large oasis irrigated by canals from the Zarafshān. The oasis was enclosed by a wall, possibly pre-Islamic, 27 miles long, surveyed in 1903, which went by the ominous name of the Wall of the Last Judgment (Divār-i Qiyāmät).

From the early 7th-century Chinese Buddhist pilgrim Hsüan Tsiang/Ch'ang we learn that Afrāsiyāb was full of Buddhist monasteries (*vihārās*), Zoroastrian fire-temples and Christian (probably Nestorian) churches, and even had a synagogue. On the Muslim conquest in 712 AD the chief of these (whichever it was) became the first Great Mosque. Afrāsiyāb then consisted of an inner citadel (*quhändizh*), which originally contained the Muslim governors' palace and a prison; and an inner walled town (*shahristān*) containing the 9th/10th-century Great Mosque, government offices and the notables' palaces.

In the 11th and 12th centuries the town center shifted south to occupy the *shahristān* and a new Great Mosque was built. But on the Mongol invasion (1220–21) Afrāsiyāb was destroyed and never rebuilt.

In 1912–13 the remains of an early palace at Afrāsiyāb came to light: the decoration, interesting evidence for the persistence of local, pre-Islamic traditions, included panels of carved stucco, a small room with a *miḥrāb* which was doubtless a private *masjid* and a wall-painting representing a young man and a girl enthroned. The style led Bartol'd to characterize it as *Buddhist*; but it is actually closer to the 7th/8th-century Soghdian paintings at Pyandzhikent. Material from excavations by Vyatkin (1912 onwards) is on exhibition at the Hermitage and in the Samarkand Museum, and his short report (1926) is more a guide to the museum than to the site.

After the Mongol invasion Samarkand remained derelict for nearly a century. In accordance with the simple, brutal Mongol custom, it resisted and suffered accordingly: the walls were razed, the city sacked and the first of several deportations of thousands of craftsmen took place, which effectively deprived Samarkand of its male population. In the reign of Tarmāshīrīn Khān (1326–34), the first Muslim Mongol ruler of Samarkand, the town began to recover. Ibn Baṭṭūṭa (1330s) comments on the absence of walls or gates and the ruined palaces still to be seen, but he also remarks upon its size and splendor, the many water-wheels (*naʿūras*) on the Zarafshān and the promenades by the river.

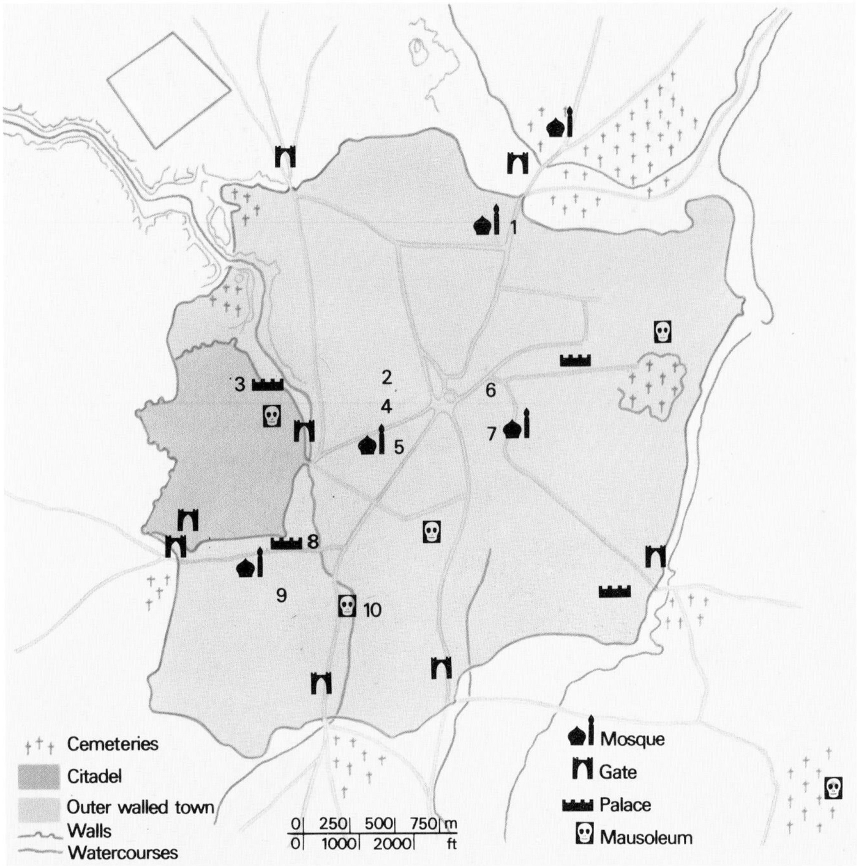

Tīmūrid Samarkand. The best literary source for Tīmūrid Samarkand (1370 onwards) is the charming Memoirs of Bābur, the first of the Great Moguls. Most of the palaces and gardens he mentions have disappeared without trace, though the mosques and mausolea of the period show how grand they evidently were. Of Tīmūr's first palace there, the Göksarāī (3) (the Blue Palace), we know only that it was four-storied and unpopular. None of the town palaces can have been on the scale of the Āqsarāī at Shahr-i Sabz, for lack of building space. Outside the city the gardens, if not the buildings, were more extensive.

The plan (*left*) shows the relative positions of the Bībī Khānum Mosque (1), the Mirzāī caravansaray (2), the Göksarāī (3), the Madrasa of Ūlūgh Beg (4), the Masjid-i Muqaṭṭaʿ (5), the Khānqāh of Ūlūgh Beg (6), the Mosque of Göñüldāsh/Alīke Kukeltāsh (7), the Palace of Muḥammad Sultān (8), the Khānqāh of Muḥammad Sultān (9) and the Gūr-i Mīr (10). After Pugachenkova and Rempel.

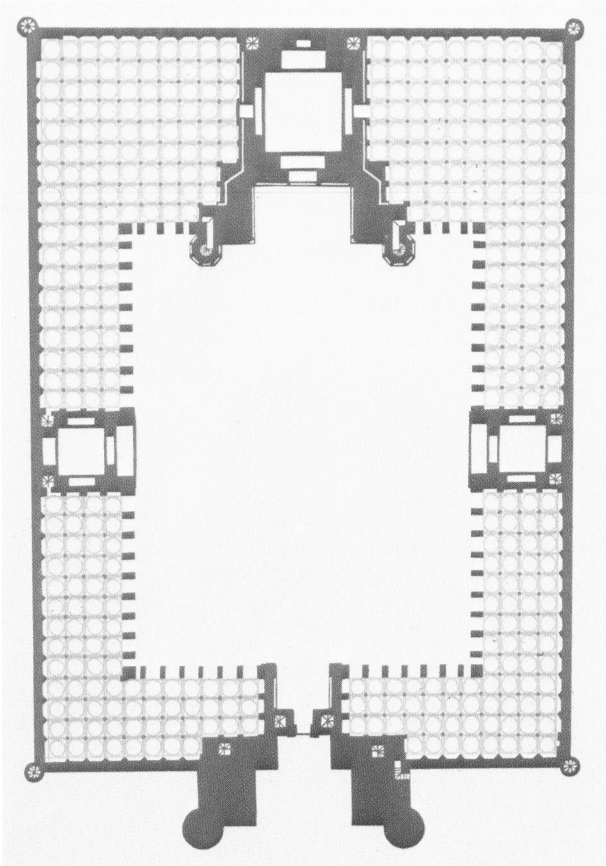

The Bībī Khānum Mosque. Samarkand already had a Great Mosque when Tīmūr proclaimed himself ruler of all Transoxania in 1371. But he celebrated his triumphal return from India in 1399 by building a new one near the North Gate of Samarkand, opposite the *madrasa* of one of his favorite wives, Sarāī Mulk Khānum, naming it Bībī Khānum (literally, Lady Lady). The enormous building (its courtyard measured 74 meters by nearly 64) was cruciform, with a minaret at each corner, a domed prayer hall on the axis of the building fronted by a massive *īwān* flanked by smaller minarets, and smaller domed chambers fronted by *īwāns* on the cross axes of the courtyard. The area between appears to have been occupied by low arcades on stone columns, 480 in all, bearing shallow brick domes. Plan after Ratiya.

On Tīmūr's return to Samarkand in 1404 he found the porch too unimpressive: he ordered it to be demolished and rebuilt higher. New foundations were immediately dug but work was interrupted by the onset of winter and Tīmūr died in February 1405. The mosque remained unfinished. The entrance (*right*) projected from the facade, 18 meters wide and probably nearly 30 meters high, flanked by buttress-like minarets (*left*). The doorway, inset in a twisted arch, had a marble frame bearing a stalactite canopy which collapsed in 1897. The brickwork was inlaid with a curious mixture of thin bands of ceramic decoration or carved stone plaques in the form of 5- or 8-pointed stars.

The entrance porch and the axial *īwān* were strikingly similar in plan and decoration to a facade drawn by Michel-François Préault in 1808 (*right*), perhaps the "Inner Mosque" which Tīmūr so much admired when he first occupied Sulṭānīye in 1385 (see p. 16). It is highly probable that Préault's building was the prototype of Tīmūr's Bībī Khānum mosque and that Tīmūr's architect was inspired by it.

There are two surviving elements of the original furniture of the mosque. The first is a massive marble Koran desk (*above*) on nine elephantine feet with tracery designs resembling leather book-bindings of the period for open Korans to rest against. This is not sheer pretension. In Mamlūk Egypt and in Mongol and Tīmūrid Persia there was a fashion for enormous Korans, usually in two volumes.

The other survival is a vast bronze basin (1399) probably intended to stand in the center of the courtyard of the mosque instead of a fountain pool. The technical problems raised by casting the basin (rim diameter 8 feet; weight about 2 tons) were enormous. Nevertheless two similar bronze basins were made – for the shrine of Aḥmad Yassawī which Tīmūr restored in 1397 and for the Great Mosque at Herāt.

The Gūr-i Mīr. Tīmūr, heartbroken at his son's death in 1403, ordered a splendid mausoleum for him. This was the Gūr-i Mīr (His Majesty's Tomb). The rubble and mortar foundations, which go four meters deep, bear solid brick walls and a drum crowned by a ribbed dome, with an inscription like that of the Bībī Khānum mosque, two meters high. Later Tīmūr himself was buried there. Plan after Polupanov.

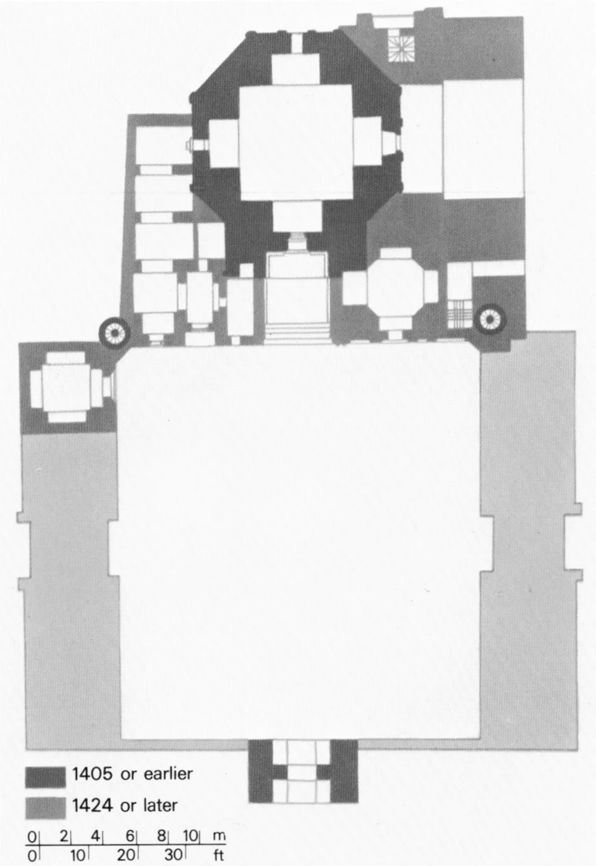

The works of Ūlūgh Beg at Samarkand.
The great central square of Samarkand, the Registān, owes its original form to Tīmūr's grandson, Ūlūgh Beg, and is the first known ornamental square in Islamic town planning. The west side is wholly occupied by the facade of his *madrasa* (*above*) (completed 1420, but with inscriptions also of 1417 and 1419), where astronomy probably formed an important part of the curriculum and the idea of his famous star tables (the Zīj-i Gūrkānī) developed. On the north was the Mirzāī caravansaray, which he built as an endowment for the *madrasa*. On the east side he founded a *khānqāh*, a richly decorated bath and a 12-sided covered bazaar (*chahār-sūq*). And on the south he built the Masjid-i Muqaṭṭaʿ (decorated with exotic designs of carved wood), while one of his emirs, Alīke Göñüldāsh/Kukeltash, built a mosque in the 1430s on the site of a ruined congregational mosque. Of this first period only the *madrasa* of Ūlūgh Beg survives.

Ūlūgh Beg's *madrasa* was originally two-storied with four *īwāns* on the axes. Beyond the main *īwān* was a single-storied prayer hall or winter mosque, the modest dimensions of which suggest that, as in Seljuk Turkish and Ottoman *madrasas*, prayers were probably said in his *masjid* next door, the Masjid-i Muqaṭṭaʿ. All four corners of the building, probably, were occupied by lecture rooms (*darskhānes*). The facade consists of a central enormous *pīsh-ṭāq* with a minaret crowned by a stalactite cornice at each end.

On rising ground NNE of Afrāsiyāb are the remains of Ūlūgh Beg's observatory (reconstruction *below left*, after Leonov; basement plan *below right*, after Kary-Nyazov). It is described in some detail in Bābur's Memoirs, and trial excavations by Vyatkin (before 1914) and later by Soviet archaeologists (1941) have enabled its basement plan, built some 11 meters into the hillside, to be restored. Its main entrance cannot be determined and even the location of the staircases is hypothetical. But excavation revealed a double sextant, used for observations of the sun, moon and planets (but not the stars) lodged in a circular building, 48 meters in diameter. The sextant is calibrated in degrees, indicated by engraved bronze plates; its angle of curvature gives a radius of nearly 40 meters, which amply confirms Bābur's observation that it was three stories high. The observatory was completed by 1428–29, and the star tables, which were a fundamental contribution to Renaissance astronomy, were completed there by 1437. The smaller rooms in the basement doubtless housed the library and rooms for the mathematicians employed in calculating the star tables, as well as some of the larger instruments – astrolabes, armillary spheres, sundials etc., which were doubtless used from the roof.

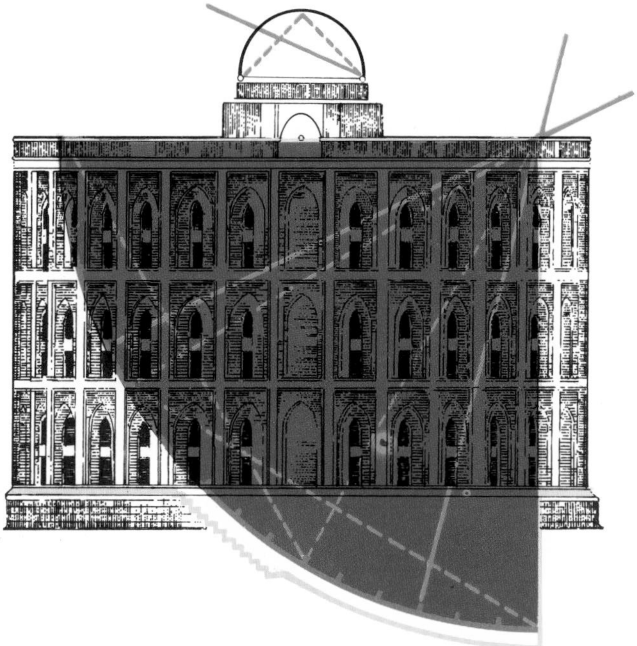

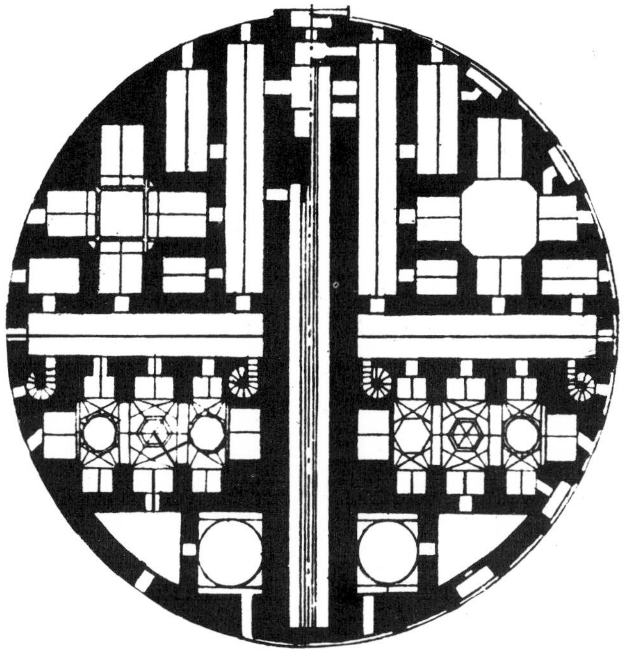

2. Islam: The History of a Religion

Islam is a living religion with a very rich political and cultural tradition. The changes resulting from the rise and fall of the Ottoman Empire and its inveterate enemy, the Ṣafawid state of Persia, since 1500 make it dangerous, therefore, to read back much of modern Islam into the Middle Ages, when it was virtually impossible to distinguish between state and religion. There are many excellent studies of early Islam, from its origins as a religion in 7th-century Arabia to its height as a world power and its subsequent transformation into a series of separate states which could absorb even the Mongols (Buddhists, Christians or even pagans) who swept over the Middle East in the 13th century. The details are out of place here, and the present sketch is merely a background for the monuments and institutions to be considered in this book.

Chronology fails to take into account the survival of dynasties long after they had lost power as the result of a decisive battle, and their own historians and even their coinage, often struck at mint cities which were no more than temporarily occupied, give conflicting accounts of the extent of their domains, so that sheer political history also explains relatively little. Theological history rapidly becomes abstract theological exposition. And even national or racial consciousness, particularly in Persia, while important for literature, political theory and court ceremonial, is difficult to trace in institutions and their architectural forms.

First conquests. The inevitable distortion, however, does not prevent broad generalizations, nor an exposition of the amazingly rapid expansion of Islam in the century following Muhammad's death (632). It was initially on two fronts – against the Byzantine Empire into Syria, and against the Sasanians into Iraq. Damascus capitulated (635) without much resistance, and the defeat of Heraclius' army on the Yarmuk, a tributary of the Jordan (636), led to the conquest of Palestine and the occupation of Jerusalem (638). There ensued a campaign against Egypt, the granary of the Byzantine Empire, culminating in the foundation of the military encampment (*amṣār*) of Fusṭāṭ on the Nile (641) and the fall of Alexandria (642). By 661 most of Byzantine Africa (Libya and Tunisia) was in Muslim hands: Carthage fell in 669, and the *amṣār* of Qayrawān was founded a year later. By 700 the Muslims controlled the whole of North Africa and crossed via Gibraltar into Spain in 710–16. Cordova was captured in 712 and most of Spain occupied in the few years following. Advance into northern Europe was halted by the defeat of the Muslim forces by Charles Martel at Poitiers (732), but the conquest of Constantinople was only abandoned (after two abortive attempts, in 673–77 and 716–18) in 747 when the Byzantine fleet defeated the Arabs in a naval battle.

On the Sasanian front the Muslim victories at Qādisiyya (637) and Nihawand, south of Hamadān in Persia (642), gave the Arabs control of the Sasanian capital of Seleucia-Ctesiphon, though after sacking it they established *amṣārs* at Baṣra and Kūfa (641), and then of Azerbaidzhan (643), Khurāsān (651) and Seistān (653). By 670 they had reached the Oxus, though the area was not completely subdued till 708, and Transoxania in 714. Muslim domination was then assured by a victory east of Samarkand (750) against a confederation of Chinese and Turkish troops, one consequence of which was the capture of Chinese craftsmen who introduced paper into Islam, though vellum or papyrus long continued to be used in the chancery.

After the mid-8th century the pace of conquest slackened, though the ʿAbbāsids continued the campaign

Opposite: the castle of Isḥaq Pasha at Doğubayazit, eastern Turkey. Though an 18th-century foundation, it is built in the style of a medieval Seljuk fortress.

Right: the siege of Jerusalem by the Crusaders in 1099 from Jacob van Maerlant's *Revenge of Jerusalem* (1332). University Library, Groningen. Jerusalem is portrayed as a contemporary 14th-century castle.

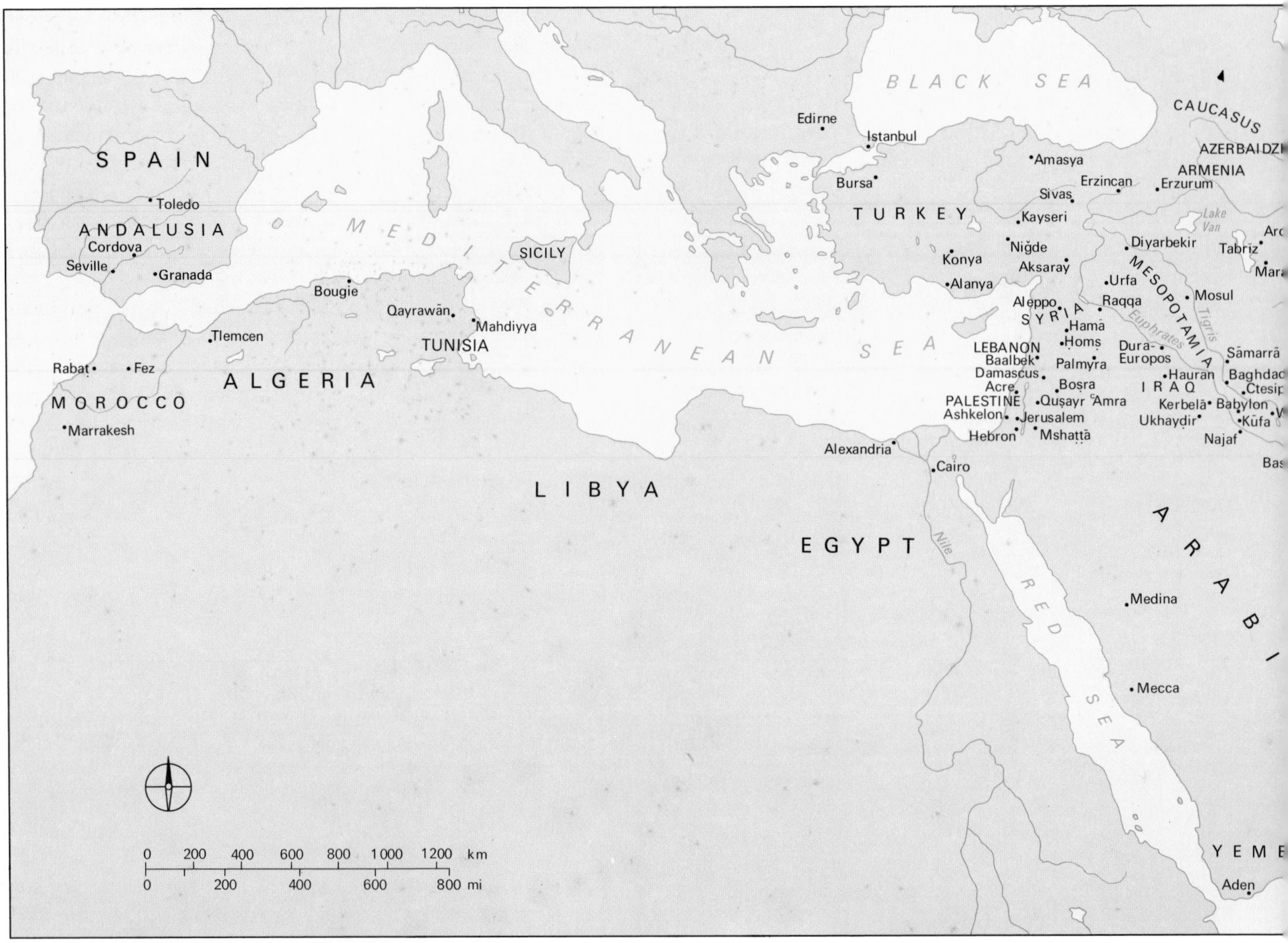

against Byzantium, occupying most of the eastern Mediterranean, including the southern coast of Asiatic Turkey, and winning a signal victory at Amorium (833); and in the early 11th century the Ghaznavids invaded India, paving the way for the Muslim states of the 12th to 14th centuries in northern India. Perhaps the most significant victory of this period, however, was that of the Seljuks over the Byzantine Emperor, Romanus Diogenes, at Manzikert in eastern Turkey (1071), since Seljuk forces reached as far west as Nicaea/Iznik, established themselves there temporarily and created the basis of a Seljuk state in Anatolia, which was to be succeeded by the Ottomans.

But by this time Byzantium was no longer the principal enemy: the Normans recaptured Sicily (1061–91); the Christian kingdoms of Spain, encouraged by the disintegration of the Caliphate of Cordova, were embarking upon the Reconquista; and Syria and Palestine were menaced by the first Crusades. The Mongol invasions of the 13th century, though they left little mark in the long run, and the campaigns of Tīmūr, or Tamerlane (1336–1405) were as destructive to Islam as they were to Europe or Byzantium. But whereas the steady attrition of the Balkans in the 14th and 15th centuries by the Ottomans could well be construed as anti-European and not just anti-Byzantine, the early Muslims, in spite of European contemporary chroniclers, show few signs of conscious opposition to the West.

These early conquests were to some extent inspired, nevertheless, by the idea of a *jihād* (Holy War) and a distinction arose between those provinces that voluntarily submitted (Dār al-Islām) and those subjugated by force (Dār al-Ḥarb), whereby in theory the latter had no choice between compulsory conversion or enslavement. Intertribal feuds in Arabia and the ill-treatment Muhammad received from the merchants of Medina doubtless account for some of the belligerent utterances of the Koran, but by the 9th century the *jihād* was recognized as a duty incumbent not upon the individual but upon the community as a whole. The Shīʿī Ḥamdānid rulers of Aleppo in the late 10th century, who were perhaps the last Islamic dynasty to rally the Bedouin to their cause, presented their campaigns against the Byzantines as a *jihād*, as did Maḥmūd of Ghazna (997–1030) his Indian campaigns, though the latter was more probably motivated by zeal for booty, a useful by-product of any war. Even the Seljuks and the early Ottomans in Anatolia, whom the 15th-century Turkish

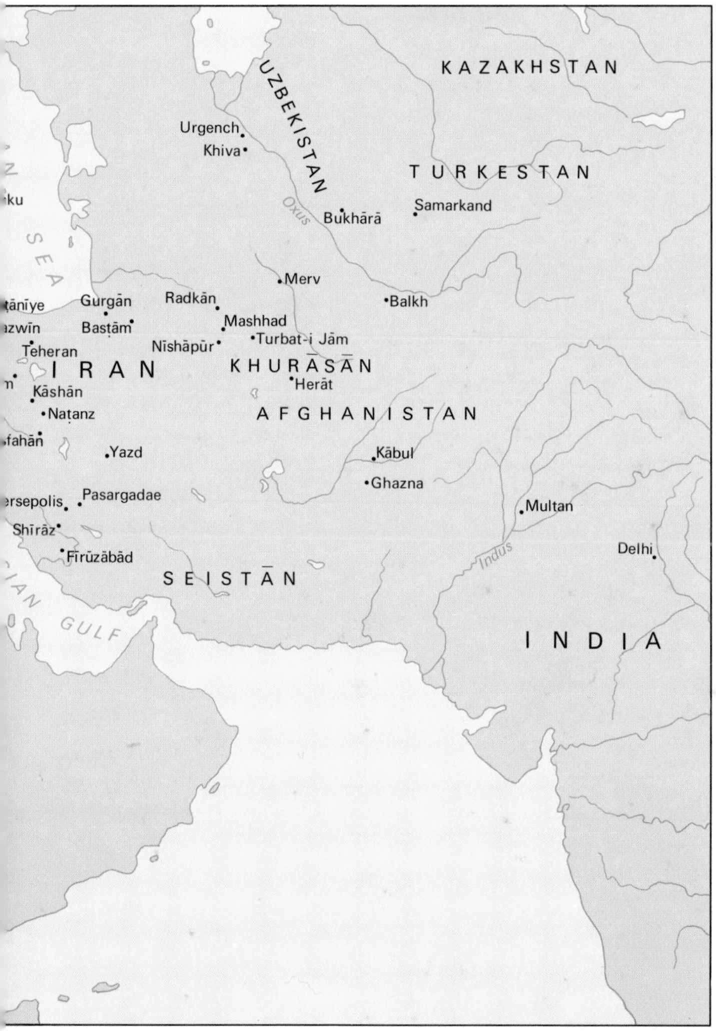

The Islamic world.

historians present as fighters for the faith, were probably not motivated by any systematic desire for the *jihād*, and whereas many rulers grandly include references to it in their personal titulature, the grandeur is often in inverse proportion to their actual efforts. The Counter-Crusade in 12th-century Syria is a more difficult case: Saladin himself hoped ideally for the union of all Islam against the Infidel and saw his crushing defeat of the Crusaders at Ḥattīn (1187) as a vindication of this. But he was evidently exceptional, since in 1229 his cousin, al-Malik al-Kāmil of Egypt, surrendered Jerusalem to Frederick II of Hohenstaufen against certain minimal guarantees, and although the treaty was roundly condemned on both sides, it gave the Latin Kingdom of Jerusalem a further 50 years of life.

The rapidity and ease of the first conquests of Islam need little explanation. The Byzantine provinces were only partially Hellenized, taxation was onerous and enserfment common, and, particularly in Egypt and Syria, where most of the population was Monophysite (denying the humanity of Christ), the interference of the Orthodox Church was bitterly resented. By the time Islam was well enough known to evoke anathemas from Constantinople, most of the Islamic conquests, often with the active support of the local population, had already occurred. Much less is known of pre-Islamic Iran, but the Sasanians had not recovered from the defeat of Khusraw II by Heraclius at Edessa/Urfa and their vast and heterogeneous territories were subject to internal religious and social strife. In any case, Syria and Iraq in the 6th and 7th centuries were already considerably Arabicized, with native dynasties controlling large areas of them, the Ghassānids in Syria and the Lakhmids in Iraq.

Administrative developments. Initially the conquests changed little. The Umayyads confiscated abandoned lands to the state, but respected existing titles to land, left their administration to local officials and designated certain protected minorities, whose scriptures foreshadowed the Revelation of the Koran, in particular Jews and Christians, but also Zoroastrians and Sabaeans, the latter star-worshipers at Ḥarrān in Mesopotamia. They were allowed, with certain minor disabilities, to retain some of their places of worship, against payment of a land-tax and a poll-tax, and, initially at least, to be judged in their own courts. Conversion certainly took place, but the motives for it were generally not financial: indeed, eventually it had to be discouraged, since the convert could claim immunity to the land-tax, with a consequent drain upon revenue; the land-tax thus became exclusively territorial, irrespective of the owner's religion. There was a further disincentive. Converts were accepted as Muslims, but not as Arabs (which they of course were not), and were treated as inferior clients (*mawlās*). The Arabs established themselves usually away from the larger towns in new encampments (*amṣārs*), most of which later became important Islamic cities on their own, leaving the *mawlā* converts, who were largely of Iranian stock, to the towns. The tolerance preached by early Islam did not extend to lack of discrimination: the protected minorities were not in any position to protest; but the *mawlās*, who steadily grew in numbers and power in the 8th century, were a rallying point for the forces of discontent which led to the triumph of the ʿAbbāsids over the Umayyad Caliphate in 749.

The first three caliphs, all Companions of the Prophet, Abū Bakr (632–34), ʿUmar (634–44) and ʿUthmān (644–56), followed by ʿAlī, Muhammad's cousin and son-in-law (656–60), were as much concerned with the family and tribal feuds of their Arabian heritage as with governing the empire they had suddenly acquired. With Muʿāwiya (660–80) power passed to the Umayyad clan, and under his successors, particularly ʿAbd al-Malik (685–705), the beginnings of Islamic administration appear. Arabic was introduced to replace Greek (or Pehlevi and Syriac in the eastern provinces) in the chancery; a standard gold coinage (the *dīnar*) and silver coinage (the *dirham*) were introduced, with legends in Arabic bearing both the ruler's name and titles and the assertion of the unity of God; there was a more far-reaching standardization of weights and measures; improvements in the collection of taxes were attempted, probably on the basis of pre-Islamic tax-registers; and Byzantine monopolies like papyrus and the state looms (*ṭirāz*) were taken over. These administrative reforms did not greatly add to the expenses of the Umayyad court. However, with the slackening of the pace of conquest, the army, which previously had lived well off the four-fifths of the booty allotted it by right, began to demand further subvention, and military discontent could only be alleviated by increasing the burden of taxation upon the peasantry and landowners, Muslim and non-Muslim alike; the former protested most violently, since their duty of paying the lawful tribute (*zakāt*) soon came to be seen as a right to pay no more than that. The Umayyads may well have come to deserve the accusations of impious behavior launched by their enemies, but when in 749 a revolt in Khurāsān led by partisans of the Prophet's uncle ʿAbbās broke out, the Umayyads found no support. The ʿAbbāsids occupied Kūfa, massacred all the Umayyads save one, ʿAbd al Raḥmān, who fled to Spain where he established himself at Cordova by 756, and made their capital the new city of Baghdad (754).

The immediate result of the ʿAbbāsid triumph was the rise to power of the Khurāsānian *mawlās*; typical of these were the Barmecides from a priestly Buddhist family near Balkh, Arabicized and highly literate, for 20 years ministers of the Caliph Hārūn al-Rashīd (died 809). It is, however, easy to exaggerate the importance of this Iranian element. On Hārūn al-Rashīd's death the Caliphate was indeed split into an Iranian half and an Arabic half, but it was reunited four years later, and the Iranian element only assumed the dominant role with the advent of the Shīʿī Buwayhids from Daylam in north Persia who controlled the Caliphate from 945 to 1055. Still less are there any grounds for seeing the ʿAbbāsid revolution as necessarily opposed to Shīʿism; but rather it was principally under the ʿAbbāsids in the 8th and 9th centuries that Shīʿism spread into Persia, and the Caliph al-Maʾmūn even tried to heal the split by appointing the seventh Shīʿī Imām, ʿAlī al-Riḍā, as his heir, a scheme which was frustrated by the latter's sudden death in 818.

The ʿAbbāsids evolved a centralized administration under the caliph. They came to delegate much of the administration of the empire to a vizier who supervised the bureaucracy (*dīwāns*), some of the most important departments being those of the army, the chancery and communications. They controlled the expenditure and the revenue through provincial *dīwāns*, registered the land and calculated the taxes. These were extremely complicated, since they were levied on the basis of productivity, generally after the harvest, which entailed the use of a solar calendar and consequent discrepancies with the Muslim lunar calendar. In Persia hot lands (*garmsīr*), less productive than cold lands (*sardsīr*), were taxed at a fixed rate, whereas in Egypt, where the harvest depended upon the height of the Nile flood, the rate varied each year.

The administrative developments were not, however, without serious drawbacks. The expense of the *dīwāns* both at Baghdad and in the provinces made taxation steadily less remunerative to the caliphal court, which lived on a scale undreamed of by the Umayyads and which was in addition saddled with the high cost of maintaining a large standing army to suppress the frequent rebellions – of Shīʿī or Khārijī factions; distressed classes like the Zanj, Negro slaves employed in the harshest conditions on land reclamation near Baṣra whose revolt (869–83) threw Iraq into turmoil; or non-Muslim "heretics," mostly Persian and loosely classified as *zindīq* (Manichaean). Al-Maʾmūn (813–33) and his successors attempted to remedy this by employing armies of Turkish slaves imported from Khwārizm, whose only loyalty would be to them. It was a mistake. The Turkish troops were uncontrolled and often mutinous, making life in Baghdad so impossible that al-Muʿtaṣim was forced to move with them to Sāmarrā which he founded in 836. And their leaders constantly interfered in the running of affairs, adding to the disorder rather than suppressing it.

A further solution, designed first as a way of paying the army, but later as a means of removing recalcitrant troops to border provinces, was to grant them the revenues of provinces in lieu of salary against the obligation of military service, with the intention that local revenues should be spent on the spot. This was the origin of the *iqṭāʿ* (lands held by soldiers in lieu of salary or by high administrative officials during their term of office) under the Seljuks, and later under the Mamlūks in Egypt and Syria. Inevitably these border provinces made themselves independent. After 850 virtually none of the Maghrib beyond Tunisia even recognized ʿAbbāsid suzerainty; while from among the first independent Persian dynasties – the Ṭāhirids (821–73), the Ṣaffārids (867–900) and the Sāmānids (874–999) – there emerged the Daylamites or Buwayhids who from 945 usurped power in Baghdad itself. In principle, the loss of border provinces from the Caliphate should have been an economy. However, so vast were the expenses of the central administration that the loss of revenues from them had to be compensated for by higher and higher taxation.

Nationalism. In the 7th and 8th centuries it is accurate to speak of Islam as a single culture with Arabic as the language of religion, law, the chancery, the coinage and literature, uniting the subject peoples – Copts, Syrians, Berbers or Persians – regardless of their culture or national history. The supremacy of Arabic was rarely challenged, and a consequence of the central tenet of the uniqueness of the Koran was that while interpretation of it in other languages might be permissible, it could never be translated. However, in Persia the 9th-century dynasties began to move away from the ideal of Arabic culture. The Ṭāhirids (821–73) were the first to write Persian in Arabic script. The Ṣaffārids (867–900), though descended from a coppersmith, vaunted the Persian national tradition: they were

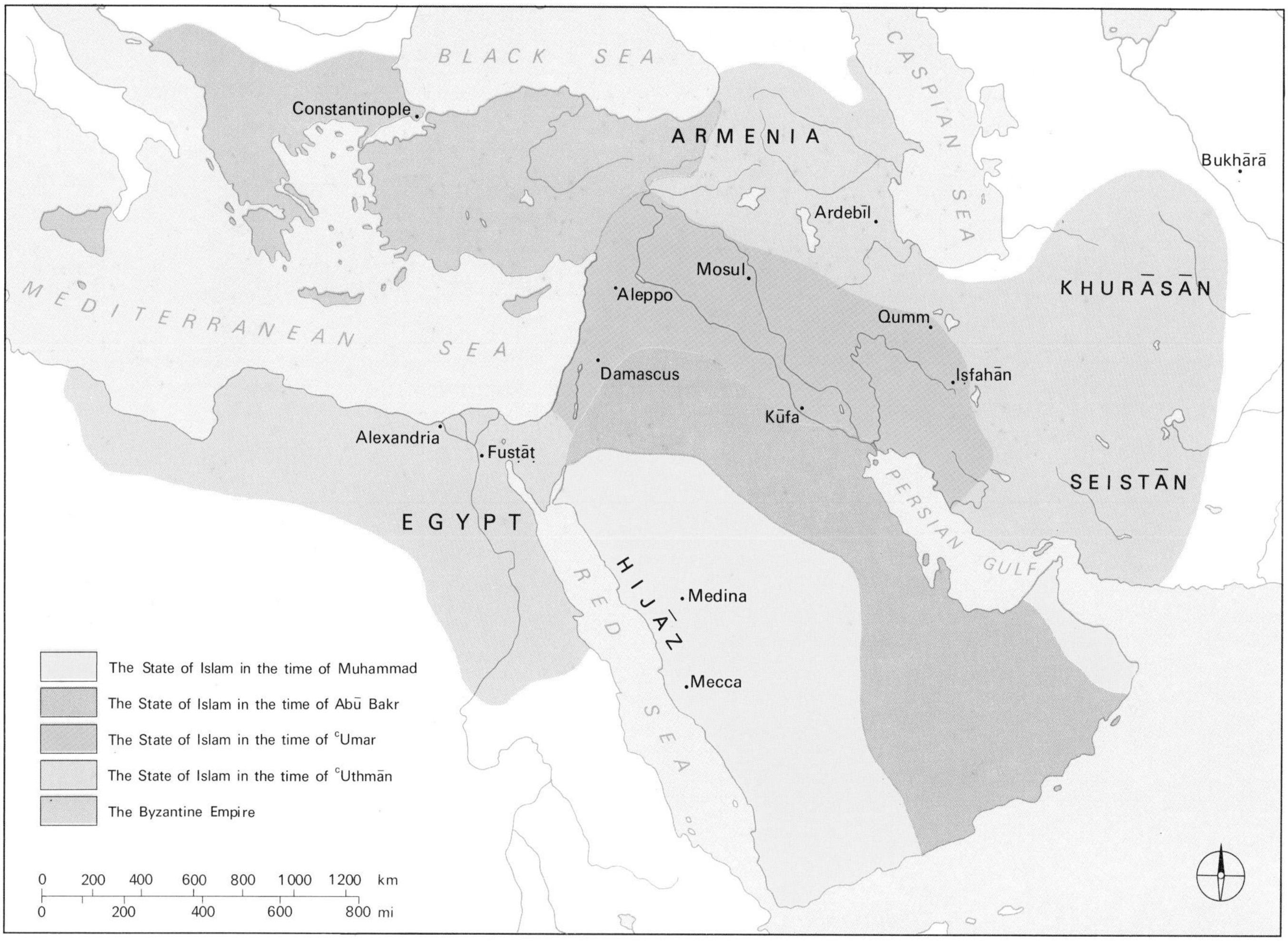

Above: Islamic conquests of the 7th century.

Below center: a gold dinar of the Umayyad Caliph Hishām (735). *Left and right:* obverse and reverse of a silver medal of the ʿAbbāsid Caliph al-Muqtadir bi'llāh (908–32). The ʿAbbāsid coinage bears only inscriptions, but many of the caliphs also struck medals in their name. Bibliothèque Nationale, Paris.

kings, they claimed, when the Bedouin (a standard jibe) were still eating snakes, lizards and mice. The Sāmānids patronized new Persian literature on a large scale (874–999), paving the way for the Buwayhid revival of Sasanian court ceremonial at Baghdad in the later 10th century. Thereafter the triumph of the Iranian tradition was complete. The Turkish Ghaznavids patronized the *Shāhnāme* (*Book of Kings*), a collection of national legends written down by Firdawsī, which was to become the Persian national epic; and the Seljuks adopted the Persian theory of the autocratic monarch expounded in the *Siyāset-nāme* (*Book of Councel for Kings*) of their Persian vizier, Niẓām al-Mulk (assassinated 1092). Even the Mongols, who established themselves as a dynasty, the Īl-Khāns, in Persia in 1256, were already under the sway of their Persian viziers, and after the conversion of Ghāzān Khān to Islam in 1296 were ready to have themselves presented as the heirs of the Persian tradition in their vizier Rashīd al-Dīn's *Jāmiʿ al-Tawārīkh* (*Collection of Histories*).

This movement was political, not religious, since all but the Buwayhids were Sunnī, acknowledging the authority of the ʿAbbāsid Caliphate in Baghdad and often posing as its champions. Its literary side is very pronounced. But it is unclear what influence Persian "national" ideas had in

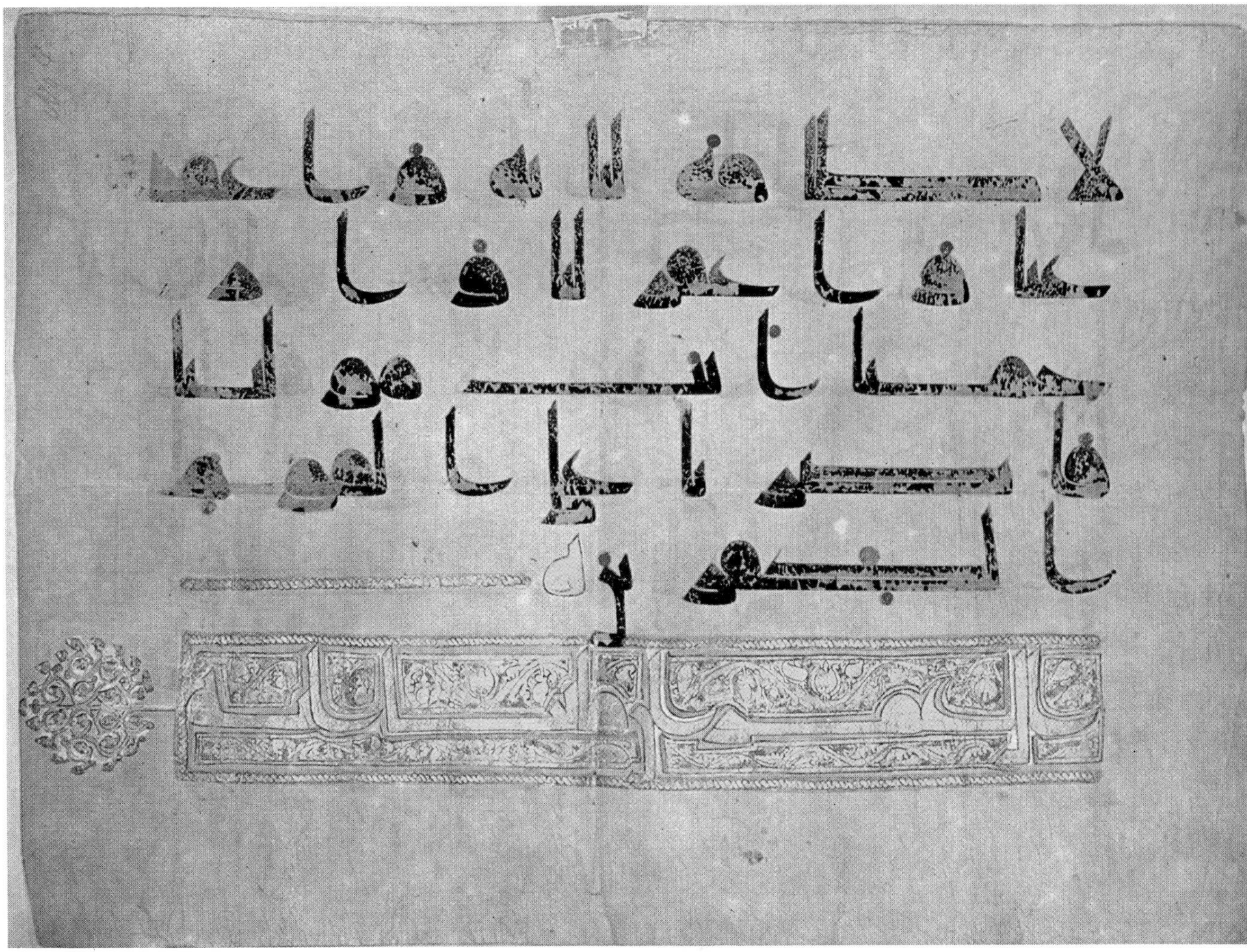

A page from a Koran in the so-called "ʿAbbāsid" Kufic script, 9th or 10th century from Syria or Mesopotamia. Black ink on parchment; the heading of the following chapter with the number of verses it contains is in gold.

the development of Islamic institutions in the 9th to 13th centuries. This is perhaps not surprising, since without careful adherence to the pronouncements of the Caliphate they could scarcely pretend to be its champions. It is curious, however, that there was no other appeal to the pre-Islamic past, either in Egypt, or Syria, or even in North Africa, where Berber and Berber history were not forgotten. Yet in the long run *shuʿūbiyya* is most relevant to this book as simply one special case of separatism. Dynasties, as they became independent, would imitate the traditions of the Caliphate more closely, in particular its architectural or institutional traditions, though with the reservation that the schools of law or rites (*madhhabs*) tended to concentrate in different parts of Islam – the Ḥanbalīs in 11th- and 12th-century Baghdad and then Syria, the Shāfiʿīs in Egypt, the Mālikīs in the Maghrib and the Ḥanafīs among the Turks – and may have tended to favor certain types of institution above others.

If there is little architectural evidence for national differences in Islam, there are nevertheless many local schools. Far too little is yet known for us to say that they represented the tastes of the ruling classes. On the contrary, the pre-Islamic traditions which often persisted for centuries, climate, building materials and local schools of craftsmen who imitated one another and remained often out of touch with developments elsewhere in Islam, almost certainly account for the most noticeable differences. Craftsmen are necessarily conservative, otherwise their buildings fall down, and it is only slowly that national schools evolve or become apparent. The Mamlūks in 13th- to 15th-century Cairo were less interested in ceramic mosaic than marble paneling as a means of interior decoration, though the few experiments in ceramic mosaic show that they could easily have adopted it had they wished. It may be that decoration was determined as much by the rarity of materials as by their splendor. Egypt, for example, was so short of wood by 1100 that it came to be prized for its value in architectural decoration, to be stolen, along with marble or bronze whenever the necessity arose and placed in someone else's building. Such differences strike the modern observer, but they are the product of chance and time, rather than taste.

Religion. One of the attractions of Islam to the Byzantine provinces, wearied by centuries of subtle theological distinctions to avoid grave heresy, was its obvious simplicity. The Koran, the word of God, transmitted by his Prophet, Muhammad, enjoined the simplest of duties – the affirmation of God's unity, prayer five times a day, fasting in the month of Ramaḍān, alms-giving and pilgrimage to Mecca – together with certain not very onerous dietary requirements, of which abstention from pork and strong drink was the most conspicuous. Yet religious divisions within Islam, almost invariably qualified as heresies, very soon arose. Indeed, it is probably even truer of Islam than medieval Europe that war was not politics but theology carried on by other means.

The causes of the first splits were only partly religious. One important factor, which has endangered almost all Islamic dynasties, was the lack of any principle of succes-

The bier of Alexander the Great, from the Demotte *Shāhnāme*, a dispersed manuscript, probably the most sumptuous copy of Firdawsī's *Book of Kings* ever illustrated; the present scene is characteristic of the Tabrīz school in the mid-14th century. Freer Gallery of Art, Washington, D.C.

Marble paneling from the mosque-*madrasa* of Sultan Ḥasan (1356–62), Cairo. No marble was quarried in Egypt after the Byzantine period and the scarcity of colored marbles encouraged the use of thin veneer. The extraordinarily complicated interlocking patterns of the *miḥrāb* arch could never have been possible if veneer had not been used.

sion. In confederations of tribes, like those of Arabia in Muhammad's time, neither primogeniture nor the primacy of any individual family was taken for granted, nor was descent through the female line accepted. There was, therefore, nothing strange in the fact that Muhammad's cousin ʿAlī was thrice passed over before he was finally made caliph in 656, and something quite exceptional in the claims of his followers after the death of his son Ḥusayn in a skirmish at Kerbelā in Iraq (680) that his descendants owed their right to lead the faithful to their descent from Muhammad's daughter Fāṭima. But the succession to Muhammad was also a religious matter: with his death, his followers held, Revelation ceased so that although the faithful needed a leader or guide (Imām) he could only be a vicar (*khalīfa*, caliph), who would gain his authority from being legitimately chosen but who could not be expected to be more perfect than any other man. It was over the qualities the Imām should have, no less than the succession, that ʿAlī was at odds with the first three caliphs, Abū Bakr (632–34), ʿUmar (634–44) and ʿUthmān (644–56), and although his followers, known as the Shīʿa (faction), were forced to compromise after a defeat at Ṣiffīn on the Euphrates (657), part of them, the Khārijīs (Secessionists), broke away, demanding that any successor to Muhammad must be perfect, otherwise he must be deposed by force of arms. Their influence was a considerable factor in the fall of the Umayyads, and they probably fomented some of the rebellions suppressed by the early ʿAbbāsids. They were always taken seriously, but, perhaps fortunately for the stability of the Caliphate, they tended to retreat in disgust at its corruption rather than rebel against it.

ʿAlī was assassinated in the Great Mosque at Kūfa (661) and his followers refused to recognize Muʿāwiya, the first Umayyad caliph, who had supplanted him a year earlier. After Ḥusayn's death in 680 there was a further split, when the Zaydīs, who affirmed that the Imām should be recognized by his warlike qualities, broke away preaching armed insurrection and actually founded small states on the Caspian (864) and in the Yemen (901). The Shīʿīs then continued to recognize Ḥusayn's descendants, till the sudden disappearance of the twelfth Imām (879), the young son of al-Ḥasan al-ʿAskarī (died 874), who would sometime return and complete Revelation. The Twelver Shīʿīs, as they are known, tended to accept the *status quo* under the ʿAbbāsids; since no Imām could be legitimate till the coming of the twelfth, it did not matter much who reigned in his stead. Even the Shīʿī Buwayhids, on their occupation of Baghdad in 945, did nothing: a Zaydī caliph, though doubtless more suitable in their eyes, would have seriously damaged their predominant political hold. The Twelvers were in any case counseled to practice prudence (*tāqiya*), which justified concealment, or even perjury, should they be accused of heresy. On the fall of the Shīʿī Ḥamdānids at Aleppo, for example, in the early 11th century the population of the town professed themselves Sunnī and Ḥanafī.

Much more radical were the Ismāʿīlīs, who recognized only seven Imāms, the last being a son of the sixth Imām, Jaʿfar al-Ṣādiq (died 765); he too disappeared but his progeny might at any time return and portend the Millennium. Ismāʿīlī states were founded in Syria and then in Baḥrein (10th century) by the Qarmatians, an egalitarian society which was sufficiently unorthodox to raid Baghdad and Baṣra and even remove the Black Stone from the Kaʿba at Mecca. At the same time an Iraqi missionary reached Tunisia, where ʿUbayd Allāh founded a Fāṭimid Caliphate (916), which occupied Egypt (969), then Syria, the Yemen and even Multan in India. In the late 11th century a further split led to the secession of the Nizārīs who established themselves in Syria and Persia with the Assassins and actually went so far as to announce the appearance of the seventh Imām in 1164.

Even the Ismāʿīlīs, repugnant as they were to Sunnī

Modern poster of the ascension of the Prophet. He was believed to have traveled on Burāq, a winged creature, half-human, half-horse. The building which appears here is a stylized representation of the Aqṣā Mosque in Jerusalem. The figure of Muhammad has been omitted, for reasons of respect if not of space. The event came to play a prominent part in the biography of Muhammad which was collected by the 9th century.

orthodox Islam, were still regarded as Muslims. The Shīʿī Sharīfs of Mecca, moreover, continued to be respected as the kinsmen of Muhammad. Sunnīs and Shīʿīs share a deep respect for Muhammad and ʿAlī and their descendants and both agree on the fundamental importance of the Koran and Tradition (*ḥadīth*) for the law and dogma of Islam, except that the latter reject opinions uttered by the first three caliphs. However, to justify the idea of the Imām as a God-guided Messiah, the Shīʿīs were forced to allegorical interpretation of the Koran, but in esoteric language, which the profane would not understand. Ismāʿīlī exegesis is also veiled in a thick mist of Neoplatonism, with stages of initiation to which only the chosen could be fully admitted. Such parochialism went against the basic Sunnī tenet of the community of all the faithful (*umma*). In its more revolutionary forms Ismāʿīlism preached an end to injustice, and the popular support it obtained is more evidence of widespread distress than a sign that it had gained more adepts of the higher wisdom. Understanding of these more esoteric trends has been hampered by the lack of sources, since any work supposed to be tainted with heresy was immediately burned. However, recent discoveries of Ismāʿīlī tracts may throw some light on their willful obscurity.

The Koran itself raised many difficulties, however, even for Sunnīs. It was transmitted in a series of dicta which were collected gradually and only arranged in series under the third caliph, ʿUmar. Its language was archaic and its meaning often obscure, although Muhammad himself during his lifetime often commented upon it; these comments constitute Tradition (*ḥadīth*) which was slowly collected together by the theologians. The universal recognition of its uniqueness, however, set the Koran as the model for the early grammarians and made it the ultimate authority even of those who read it allegorically. Arabic grammar was much advanced under its stimulus, particularly by writers like Sībawayh (died 793), who turned to the magnificent corpus of pre-Islamic Arabic poetry for the elucidation of its obscure points, and kept the Arabs' pride in their past alive. It was quite soon agreed which of the possible readings due to ambiguities in the original script were to be rejected. However, even the Koran, the *ḥadīth* and the grammarians left many problems unresolved and provided some justification for the esoteric meaning given certain passages by the Twelvers and the Ismāʿīlīs.

One natural reaction to this was the literalism of Ibn Ḥanbal which was proclaimed the official doctrine of the ʿAbbāsid Caliphate in 1017 but which declined markedly in 12th-century Baghdad. No theoretical arguments might be used to expand the body of theological dogma; since Revelation was complete no one could replace Muhammad and the duly elected caliph should be automatically obeyed. This was a response not only to Shīʿism but also to the Muʿtazilī controversy in 9th-century Baghdad. This controversy became famous not only for its claims – that God was transcendent and had created even the Koran and that the Imām had a duty both to command good and do it, otherwise revolt against him might be justified – but also for the official inquisition which al-Maʾmūn (813–33) set up to test the assent of the *ʿulamāʾ* to it. This created such disorder that in the reign of al-Mutawakkil (847–61) it was officially condemned.

The Muʿtazilīs were thereafter regarded as dangerously near to Shīʿism with their requirement that the Imām should be perfect, but the controversy left an important legacy: the appeal to reason in theology (*kalām*). This triumphed at Baghdad in the Ashʿarī school, which received the support of the Seljuk vizier Niẓām al-Mulk and then of the eminent theologian al-Ghazzālī whose works are a vindication of scholastic theology (1058–1111). The community should respect a legitimately elected caliph, but without losing sight of the transcendent importance of Muhammad and his Companions; the Koran was not created by God, since it was his word, but its ascription of human attributes to God was more than analogical, even if often incomprehensible; and though God is omnipotent, human beings have free will. It was a sort of *via media*, but its approach was even more important: rational argument, not devastation by polemic. To this extent Ashʿarism cuts across differences between Sunnīs and the Shīʿa. It won the approbation of orthodox theologians from Persia to the Maghrib. The Shāfiʿīs and most of the Mālikīs were won over; the Ḥanafīs subscribed to similar rationalizing trends, and only the Ḥanbalīs rejected it.

Extremism apart, the contrast between orthodoxy and heterodoxy often cut across the Sunnī-Shīʿī distinction. As a Persian Shīʿī apologist argued in 1160: if a Friday mosque was frequented only by Ḥanafīs and another only by Ashʿarīs, who also rejected each other's legal decisions (*fatwas*), the Shīʿa can scarcely be blamed for following their own way. If the Muslim community was one, then why was it divided against itself?

Law. The Koran and the *ḥadīth*, like the Old Testament, were also a manual of law, the Sharīʿa. Although the Umayyad caliphs claimed authority in law as well as dogma, they tended to leave judgments to the lawyers (*qāḍīs* under a Chief Qāḍī). In principle there must be unanimity on points of law, but even appeal to Revelation, exegesis of the Koran (*tafsīr*) or reflection (*ijtihād*) was often insufficient, and early legal practice shows much divergence, particularly because of differences in the customary law of the various peoples subject to Islam, who mostly continued to be tried by their own judges. Moreover, the Sharīʿa, though of universal validity, might vary in stringency with the circumstances. By the mid-8th century it had to be admitted that even the pretense of unanimity was impossible. There evolved, therefore, certain procedures to replace individual judgments, which were codified in a sort of case law by groups of lawyers forming schools or rites. They differed not only in their judgments in certain cases, but also in their approach to certain considerations, particularly equity and the extent to which they were prepared to admit law which did not originate from the Sharīʿa. By the 12th century there were two recognized Shīʿī schools, the Imāmī and the Ismāʿīlī, and four Sunnī – the Ḥanafī, Shāfiʿī, Mālikī and the Ḥanbalī, the former two being generally held to be the most tolerant and the last the least. They were all well enough entrenched by the 10th century for the early practice of reflection (*ijtihād*) to be abandoned in favor of corpora of decisions (*fatwas*) from which conclusions could be obtained either direct, by analogy or, if necessary, by legal expedients.

Although in principle the various schools were all ultimately in agreement, there were many disagreements of practice, and it was therefore usual to judge litigants' cases according to the school to which they belonged. No principles for avoiding conflict of law were ever evolved, and in case of fundamental disagreement or patent inequity the caliph or his legally appointed representative was required to give a personal judgment. With the development of financial and military administration under the ʿAbbāsids and the Seljuks, moreover, many regulations were required which could not be deduced from the Sharīʿa, even though they might be compatible with it. Against strong opposition from the Ḥanbalīs, who argued that public law must follow the Sharīʿa to the letter, there evolved the notion of public law (*qānūn*) promulgated by the ruler, for example to mitigate certain penalties prescribed by the Sharīʿa. The other schools generally agreed that *qānūn* law was by definition compatible with the Sharīʿa, though in cases of doubt appeal might be made to custom (*ʿurf*). These principles were canonized in a treatise of public law written by al-Mawardī (died 1058) at Baghdad.

There was also criminal law, generally called *siyāsa*, perhaps first under the Fāṭimids in Egypt, since their society contained many Berber elements, but much more conspicuously under the Mongols and the Mamlūks. It is best known from early Ottoman criminal codes, but it can clearly be read back into many earlier Islamic societies. It was principally to justify exemplary punishment – for treason, counterfeiting the coinage or burglary of the Royal Treasury, for example – and was executed by the ruler at his own will, hence the sinister use of *siyāsa* in Ottoman Turkish to mean execution. Justification, if called for, was generally found in the public good, and protests by the jurists against legislation by the ruler which is *ultra vires* are curiously rare. Nevertheless, the *ʿulamāʾ* often saw themselves as the guardians of the whole community against injustice by the ruler, so that arbitrary punishment must have been frequent.

Much has been said of the legal regulation of trade in Islamic societies. Careful provision was made in family law that all legitimate issue of a union, both male and female, should receive a specified portion as their inheritance. Since families were often numerous because of polygamy, which was encouraged under certain fairly strict conditions, vast fortunes might be broken up in the course of two or three generations. There was, therefore, an inherent difficulty in the accumulation of capital. In general the schools discouraged cut-throat competition as harmful to the community as a whole, and this also may have discouraged the exploitation of trade. However, the Ḥanafīs at least allowed partnerships, normally on a minor scale and only for the duration of a single enterprise, as a way for merchants to augment their capital. As in medieval Europe usury was prohibited. This is not to say that lending money at interest did not take place, since there are medieval contracts surviving specifying the interest to be paid on loans, though the intermediaries were generally non-Muslims – Christians or Jews.

Banking facilities, though limited to letters of credit, were in general adequate for the conditions of trade. There was no prohibition of capitalism as such, and it is impossible to explain why Islam, unlike early Renaissance Europe, did not profit more from the gains of its lucrative trade with China and India in spices, precious stones or metals and luxury objects which were re-exported to the West. In one respect, however, Islamic public law certainly was deficient: there was never any legal mechanism for the state regulation of prices in time of famine, except impromptu legislation against hoarding and speculation. The regulation of the just price was left to the official in charge of the markets, the *muḥtasib*, whose powers were almost unlimited in the Middle Ages. However, impromptu legislation was no substitute for forethought, and the periodic economic crises which swept over Islam were generally more severe in their effects for the lack of a consistent policy on the part of the jurists.

Political disintegration. This sketch of the religion and law of Islam shows the reservations which must be borne in mind when we consider the disintegration of the ʿAbbāsid Caliphate into a series of independent states from the mid-10th century to its downfall in 1258. Subsequently, in the case of the Mongol Empire and its collapse in the 14th century and the Tīmūrid campaigns (1370–1405) it makes sense to speak largely in political terms; but previously, despite the usurpation of the ʿAbbāsids' power, first by the Buwayhids (945–1055) and then by the Seljuks (1055–1157), their history is still that of a theocracy. The Buwayhids were satisfied with the title of Chief Emir, though ʿAḍud al-Dawla's coronation in 977 in accordance with revived Persian ceremonial suggests that they wished for the trappings, as well as the realities, of power. The Seljuks, who ousted them in 1055, demanded the full title of Sultan, the secular representative of the caliph, and this was sealed by a marriage between Tughril Beg and a daughter of the Caliph al-Qāʾim (1063).

The Islamic world in the 10th century.

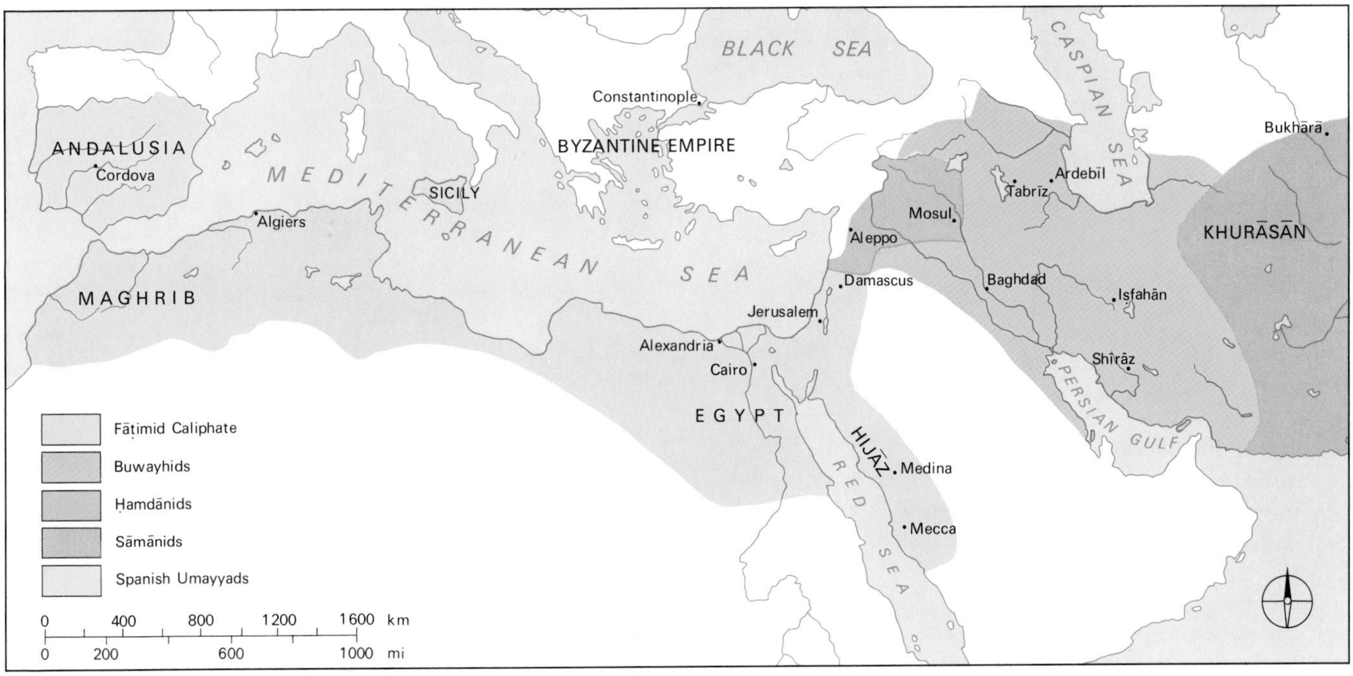

The Seljuks made their appearance first shortly before 1040, when they defeated the Ghaznavids at Dandānaqān, as the chiefs of a confederation of Islamicized Turkish tribes and occupied the whole area from the Oxus to Syria, Palestine and Mesopotamia. One branch settled at Kirmān (1041–1187), and there were later states, both disputed by rival principalities, in Syria (1094–1117) and in Iraq (1117–94). Under Malikshāh (1072–92), who apparently intended to make Baghdad his capital and was probably buried there, a tremendous program of military, civil and institutional works was executed, perhaps at the prompting of his vizier Niẓām al-Mulk who did so much to establish Seljuk power. The Fāṭimids were expelled from Syria and Palestine by his general Atsiz, and even Cairo felt itself menaced (1087–91); officially sponsored *madrasas* were built; and all over his domains, from Nīshāpūr and Iṣfahān to Damascus and Diyarbekir, major buildings were founded or restored.

But the empire of the Great Seljuks was soon eroded. The Ghaznavids, though defeated in 1040, continued to rule in Afghanistan and parts of Khurāsān and at least one of these later rulers, Masʿūd III (1099–1115), rivaled the glories of his much more famous predecessor, Maḥmūd (997–1030); in Transoxania the Qarākhānids lived on; and in the west there was a constant tendency for the *atābegs*, nominally the emirs in charge of the crown prince, to establish themselves as independent dynasties, not only in Iraq but also in western Persia (Fars and Luristan), with similar independent states in northwest Persia/Azerbaidzhan and Upper Mesopotamia (in particular, the Artuqids at Diyarbekir, Mardin and Ḥiṣn Kayfā).

The real cause of the downfall of the Great Seljuks was, however, their relations with the (nomadic) Ghuzz/Oghuz Turks from whom they had originated, and who never entirely accepted the Seljuks as the single ruling family. Their attacks became more and more serious and the last of the Great Seljuks, Sanjar, spent five years a prisoner in their hands before his death in 1157. The Ghuzz created no state of their own. Instead there appeared a dynasty, the Khwārizmshāhs, with a capital at Urgench in Khwārizm, which claimed vast areas of territory from Khurāsān to Afghanistan, where the Ghaznavids had finally been superseded by a further Turkish dynasty, the Ghūrids (1147–1215). In 1218 Muhammad Khwārizmshāh's barbarous treatment of a Mongol delegation provoked retaliation in the shape of the first Mongol invasions. He himself died soon after the destruction of Urgench in 1220–21, but his son, Jalāl al-Dīn, a military genius, escaped and although pursued everywhere by the Mongols from the Caucasus to the Indus, survived for almost ten years, disorganizing and disrupting everything in his path.

On the fall of the Great Seljuks northern Iraq broke into principalities with capitals at Mosul, Aleppo and Sinjār; under Badr al-Dīn Lu'lu' (1233–59) Mosul became a miniature Baghdad, with a palace, the Qarāsaray, a school of manuscript illustration and even a court historian, Ibn al-Athīr, one of the most important Arabic historians of the Crusades.

Baghdad itself had little history after the 9th century, except for the reign of the Caliph al-Nāṣir (1180–1225), a remarkable figure who attempted to revive the power and significance of the early ʿAbbāsid Caliphate. It was too late. In 1258 the Mongols under Hülegü sacked and totally destroyed Baghdad and murdered al-Mustaʿṣim who had no successor; a puppet caliphate was established in Egypt and was paid a show of respect by first the Mamlūks and then the Ottomans, till the death of the last caliph in 1528, when the office was assumed by the Ottoman sultans. Iraq became a Mongol province, and some time after the collapse of the Īl-Khāns in Persia (1336) was occupied by an independent dynasty, the Jalā'irids who, to judge from the splendid manuscripts they commissioned, survived even the sack of Baghdad by Tīmūr. But the history of Iraq after the decline of the Great Seljuks, like that of Arabia after the first conquests of Islam, still remains to be written.

The unity of Persia even under the Great Seljuks was at best questionable, but after their downfall there was no major state till the foundation of the Mongol Īl-Khānate by Hülegü (1256). This almost certainly explains the lack of major buildings in the 12th century. The Īl-Khāns actually claimed sovereignty from the Lebanon to Kashmir, but they were essentially Persian-based and after their official conversion to Islam in 1296 thought of themselves as first and foremost Persians. The death of the last Īl-Khān, Abū Saʿīd (1336), again split Persia into petty dynasties, mostly based upon the towns – Tabrīz; Iṣfahān, Yazd and Kirmān; Shīrāz; and Herāt. The eastern part of Persia regained a semblance of unity under Tīmūr's son, Shāh Rukh (1404–47), but northwest Persia, apart from a short period in the late 14th century when Tabrīz was occupied by the Jalā'irids, was continuously disputed by two Turcoman confederations, the Black Sheep and the White Sheep. There were periods of tranquillity, notably the reign of the White Sheep Uzūn Ḥasan (1453–78), who not only built a palace and splendid mosque, the Blue Mosque, at Tabrīz but also attained fame in Western Europe. However, not till the Ṣafawid conquest in the early 16th century did Persia re-emerge united as a violently Shīʿī nationalist state.

Egypt had been lost to the Caliphate since 868, when Ibn Ṭūlūn, a Turkish military governor sent there from Sāmarrā, proclaimed his independence. The dynasty was short-lived, possibly because his descendants, particularly his son Khumarawayh (884–95), spent more time on

The Great Mosque at Iṣfahān. The first datable remains are late 11th century (dome over the *miḥrāb* pre-1092; north dome 1088), though recent excavations have revealed much of an earlier building. A cruciform courtyard was imposed upon it, probably after 1121. This *īwān*, on the cross-axis, shows some signs of 16th-century work, but much of it, and the arcades on either side, have subsequently been heavily restored.

luxury than administration. After a further brief period of military domination under the Ikhshīdids (935–69) Egypt was invaded by the Ismāʿīlī Fāṭimids (969–1170) from Mahdiyya in Tunisia who established an anti-Caliphate. However, with the exception of the reign of al-Ḥākim (996–1021), who persecuted Christians and largely destroyed the Church of the Holy Sepulcher in Jerusalem (restored 1028), it was a period of tranquil prosperity. Al-Ḥākim may well have been mad: his death was a matter of presumption since he simply disappeared, and he is believed by the Druse to be their Messiah. Relations with both Byzantium and Europe improved and international trade reached a peak. The *dīwāns* were efficient and ordinary life was probably little disrupted by the Fāṭimids' insistence upon their esoteric mission, which was of extraordinary complexity. The succession was normally designated secretly, though by the late 11th century power was in the hands of an Armenian commander in chief, Badr al-Jamālī, and then of his son, al-Afḍal Shāhanshāh. In 1094 a split occurred over the accession of the young Caliph al-Mustaʿlī, and part of the Fāṭimids seceded to Persia to join the Ismāʿīlī sect of the Assassins which had been founded in 1090 by Ḥasan b. Ṣabāḥ. Their heterodoxy shocked the historians less, however, than their cynical use of the Hilālī Bedouin in 1041, called in to punish the Zīrids, whom they had left behind as their governors in Tunisia but who had recognized the authority of the ʿAbbāsid Caliphate. They were only temporarily subdued, but North Africa never recovered from the frightful destruction wrought by the Bedouin, perhaps the worst attack of the Desert upon the Sown in the history of Islam.

Outside Egypt Syria was lost to the Seljuks in 1079. They were later superseded by the Zengids, originally one of the states that had seized power as the Seljuks' authority waned. The principal figure, Nūr al-Dīn (1146–74), devoted himself to establishing Sunnī orthodoxy on two fronts: against the remnants of Ismāʿīlī resistance, both Fāṭimid and Assassin; and against the Crusaders. But it was left to his Kurdish lieutenant, Saladin, to conquer Egypt and restore orthodoxy, while simultaneously fighting brilliant campaigns against the Crusaders. His ideal of Islam reunited against its enemies died with him (1193) and the dynasty he founded, the Ayyūbids, was fragmented into local kingdoms in Syria and Mesopotamia – at Damascus, Ḥomṣ, Ḥamāʾ, Aleppo and Mayyafāriqīn; and in Egypt, where the last Ayyūbid, al-Ṣāliḥ Najm al-Dīn Ayyūb, was killed fighting against the Crusaders at the Battle of Manṣūra (1249).

In the west, the Umayyad state founded by ʿAbd al-Raḥmān (756) with its capital at Cordova gradually increased its power till in the 10th century, under a series of brilliant rulers, ʿAbd al-Raḥmān II (912–61), al-Ḥakam II (961–76) and Hishām II (976–1009), it not only proclaimed itself a Caliphate, in opposition to the anti-Caliphate of the Fāṭimids (929), but became a capital rivaling the splendor of Baghdad. It was strongly Sunnī, only the Mālikī School being officially recognized, and a considerable patron of the arts and literature; it encouraged Christians and Jews, among them Maimonides, as well as Muslims, and through its numerous commercial and intellectual contacts was probably the most important channel to Western Europe for the knowledge of Islam and the Classical tradition. Yet, in spite of its internal unity, it fell into the hands of a series of Andalusian viziers and after 1031 was succeeded by a series of city states (the Reyes Taifas), which one by one fell a prey to the Christian counter-attack (the Reconquista), leaving at last only the small Naṣrid city state of Granada (1238–1492).

All these dynasties, notwithstanding their splendor and achievements, were remarkably ephemeral, rarely surviving more than three or four generations and often dependent totally upon the power of a single individual. An era of rapid expansion was generally succeeded by a period of stabilization in which city life, the arts, literature and trade prospered and a program of administrative and legal reform was inaugurated. Then came disaster and the same sequence began in the hands of a new regime, generally established in a new center. The causes are equally regular: the lack of a principle of succession, which was as marked among the independent, "secular" rulers as in the caliphates; the burden of taxes to support a large standing army, which often interfered disastrously in politics, and the religious or social discontent the fiscal policy evoked; difficulties of communication over the vast and often uninhabited areas within the dynasty's domains; over-centralization and the inevitable secession of provinces which nevertheless did little good to expensive and ponderous bureaucracy. External factors were so rarely the cause of decline that Ibn Khaldūn, the 14th-century historian, was led to suggest that states, like individuals, are born, come to maturity and die. The idea is attractive, and has seduced many historians and Orientalists; but it takes no account of the much greater stability of the regimes which succeeded the fall of the ʿAbbāsid Caliphate in 1258, which has too often been taken to mark the end of the Classical period of Islam. Of these the most important were the Mongols, the Mamlūks in Egypt and Syria, and the Anatolian Seljuks and their successors, the early Ottomans.

The Mongols. The Mongol invasions of 1220–21 were as rapid as the early Muslim conquests, and the actual number of Mongols involved was relatively small, exactly as with the Bedouin in the 7th century or with the Seljuk Turks in the 11th. In all these cases the military superiority of the nomads lay in their tribal unity (the Mongols were even further organized into multiples of ten), reinforced by strict military discipline, and in their mobility which was infinitely better adapted to the conditions in which they fought than the heavy armaments of the disaffected mercenary troops who opposed them. All these nomad armies had some heavy armaments, particularly siege engines, which in the Mongol armies were chiefly the responsibility of Chinese and Muslim engineers. But nomad armies, contrary to what is often said, were no disorderly rabble: provisioning and reinforcements demanded even greater organization because of the enormous distances they traveled; and although they lived by plunder, this was usually strictly controlled. Later nomadic confederations, like the Beluch in east Persia or the Turcoman tribes in 17th-century Turkey, certainly were rapacious, disorderly and disruptive. But their activities were as much provoked by discontent with the central administration as by their own greed.

By 1260 the Mongol Empire had been divided up into various states under the authority of an elected Great Khān at Qarāqorum in Mongolia. After 1264 the eastern empire ceases to interest us, since it became progressively more Chinese and in the 1270s moved to Peking. The other dominions were the Lands of the Golden Horde (south Russia, the northern Caucasus and Khwārizm up to the Oxus), the Īl-Khānate (essentially Persia and Iraq) and the territory (*ulus*) of Chaghatay (Transoxania and much of western Siberia). By 1260 the Golden Horde was at odds with the Īl-Khānate, and by 1270 the Īl-Khānate was at odds with the *ulus* of Chaghatay. The Golden Horde had a Muslim ruler by 1258, Berke, who built a new palace, Saray Berke/Novy Saray near the mouth of the Volga, and Islam was further consolidated by Uzbek Khān (1314–40), by which time the original Mongol element (the Tatar tribe) had become entirely submerged in the native Qipchāq Turk population. Enmity with the Īl-Khāns led to close ties with their bitter enemies, the Mamlūks in Egypt, to whom they were the principal purveyors of slaves (evidently pagans, since Islam forbids the enslavement of a free-born Muslim). The state was well placed to tap both the northern trade with Muscovy and the western trade, through the Genoese colonies established in the Black Sea ports, particularly Kaffa. However, the Black Death was disastrous to the slave trade (1348), and the Golden Horde had then to contend with the Grand-Dukes of Muscovy, who defeated them at the Battle of Kulikovo Pole (1380). Moscow was sacked in retaliation two years later, but there then followed ten years of warfare with Tīmūr who finally crushed the ruler Ṭoqṭamish (1395). By the mid-15th century the Golden Horde was a cluster of small independent states of which only the Crimean Khānate survived for a century and a half as an Ottoman protectorate.

Soviet archaeology has recently done much to increase our knowledge of the Golden Horde in the 13th and 14th centuries.

The Īl-Khānate in Persia was inaugurated with a series of campaigns, first to eradicate the Assassins from Persia, and then to subjugate Syria and Iraq, which resulted in the death of the last ʿAbbāsid caliph in 1258. Expansion into Palestine and Egypt was, however, halted by a defeat at the Battle of ʿAyn Jālūt (1259), not decisive, but a significant indication that the Mongols were not invincible. They withdrew, but for more than 60 years Syria and Palestine were a battleground between Mongols and Mamlūks. The first Īl-Khāns were Buddhists but generally tolerant in matters of religion. If Islam suffered it was by being deposed from its traditionally privileged position. Even this was righted, however, by the official conversion of Ghāzān in 1296 (perhaps to Shīʿism, not Sunnī orthodoxy, since his successor Öljeytü (1304–16) was certainly Shīʿī for a time and Shīʿism gained considerable ground in 14th-century Persia). Under Ghāzān and his vizier, the historian and doctor, Rashīd al-Dīn (died 1318), there was radical agricultural and fiscal reform, revision of the land-registers and a massive program of state caravansarays, post-houses and bridges which transformed Tabrīz and Sulṭānīye into the principal centers of east-west trade, which had been impeded by the Mamlūk destruction of the Latin Kingdom of Jerusalem and disturbances inside the *ulus* of Chaghatay. The period 1296 to 1336 really justifies the commonly applied description of it as the *pax mongolica*. Like all peace it did not last. The Mongols had become too Iranicized to maintain their tradition of succession by election, and on Abū Saʿīd's death in 1336 the Īl-Khānate distintegrated in squabbles among his heirs.

The facade of the Great Mosque at Cordova built by Caliph al-Ḥakam II (961–76). During the 10th century Cordova steadily increased its power and became a capital rivaling the splendor of Baghdad.

The *ulus* of Chaghatay comprised Russian Turkestan (mostly western Siberia) and the domains of the Khwārizmshāhs in Transoxania and Khurāsān. The western frontier south of the Oxus was ill defined, which led to warfare with the Īl-Khānate, but the populations of these very diverse areas did not mix at all. The Mongols' interest was principally in the eastern half, with a largely

The Shahrestān Bridge south of Iṣfahān. The foundations are Sasanian but on the Roman model: note the rounded breakwaters downstream. The superstructure was restored in the 11th and 12th centuries and later. The ruined pavilion was probably a customs post or tollgate to collect dues from caravans leaving or entering Iṣfahān.

nomadic population of Shamanists, Buddhists and Nestorian Christians which combined to overthrow the first Muslim ruler of the area, Tarmashīrīn Khān (1326–34), who had made Bukhārā his capital. Despite the Muslim historians' horrific accounts of the devastation wrought by the Mongol invasions in this area, town life did not apparently suffer excessively, and it would doubtless have returned to something of its former prosperity but for the frontier disputes with the Īl-Khāns which ravaged Samarkand, Bukhārā and the other great cities of Transoxania.

On Tarmashīrīn's deposition chaos again reigned, and Tīmūr (1336–1405), a Turk born near Shahr-i Sabz with a taste for conquest rather than empire, succeeded in proclaiming himself ruler of Transoxania at Samarkand in 1371. In 1380–82 he campaigned in Khurāsān, capturing Herāt and deporting many of its inhabitants, and had captured Iṣfahān and Shīrāz by 1387. Urgench was sacked and its population deported in 1388. In 1398 he sacked Delhi, the climax of a two-year Indian campaign, and on his return set off west sacking Aleppo and Sivas (1400), Damascus and Baghdad (1401). He reached the coast of western Turkey and captured the Ottoman ruler Bayezid I at the Battle of Ankara (1402). Returning to Samarkand in 1404, he immediately made plans to march on China. He set out but died east of Samarkand in 1405.

Tīmūr married a descendant of Chaghatay and thereafter assumed the genealogy of Genghis Khan, to which he had no right; it was later inscribed on the cenotaph of his tomb, the Gūr-i Mīr at Samarkand (see Visual Story). However, unlike Genghis, he failed to provide for the succession, and his son Shāh Rukh only succeeded him after considerable dispute. Nor did he make any provision for the administration of occupied territory, except the threat of further chastizement should tribute not be regularly paid. Shāh Rukh was an active patron of learning and the arts all over Persia. He made Herāt his capital, leaving his son Ūlūgh Beg in charge of Samarkand. The stability was, however, deceptive: Shāh Rukh's death (1447) precipitated Ūlūgh Beg's assassination (1449) and the empire passed into the hands of a series of Tīmūr's minor descendants. Among them Ḥusayn Bāyqarā (1470–1506) at Herāt, with his vizier, the poet and polymath, ʿAlī Shīr Nevā'ī, was outstanding for his patronage of the arts. However, by his death most of the Tīmūrid domains were in the hands of an Uzbek, Muḥammad Shaybanī (c. 1451–1510), who established a new dynasty. After many years of hopeless fighting one of the last, and probably the nicest, of Tīmūr's descendants, Bābur, was forced to found an empire in India (1526), that of the Great Moghuls.

The Mamlūks. The Mamlūks were originally a private army of slave troops bought by the last Ayyūbid ruler of Egypt, al-Ṣāliḥ Najm al-Dīn Ayyūb, after 1227. They were mostly Qipchāq Turks from the south Russian steppes, with a sprinkling of Russians, Mongols and other nationalities. In Cairo they were quartered on the Nile (*baḥr al-Nīl*) from which they gained their name of Baḥrī Mamlūks; they were converted to Islam, were manumitted and took an oath of loyalty to their ruler. After his death in 1249 there ensued a series of intrigues, as a result of which the Mamlūk Baybars finally came to the throne (1259). He gave shelter to a relative of the ʿAbbāsid caliph in Baghdad and used him to claim jurisdiction over the Holy Places, Mecca and Medina, and to expel the Franks from Syria and Palestine. This was a policy in which his successor Qalā'ūn (1279–93) and his son al-Ashraf Khalīl (1293–94) followed him, conquering all Syria and Palestine, Cilicia and even part of the Upper Euphrates. A further son of Qalā'ūn, al-Nāṣir Muḥammad (died 1341), was not only a conspicuously efficient sultan but refortified much of Syria and Palestine, built up the navy and liberally restored buildings all over his domains. His descendants, who, contrary to initial practice, succeeded by virtue of heredity, not election, suffered from being too young; power therefore was for the most part in the hands of emirs or viceroys, and the impossibility of governing in the face of so many factions led to the rise of a new group, the Circassians (probably Ossetes/Ās, who had been renowned among both the Byzantines and the earlier Islamic dynasties for their qualities as mercenaries), of whom Barqūq (1382–99) was the first sultan. In the 15th century they were involved in alliances with or campaigns against the dynasties of Iraq and western Persia and ultimately came into conflict with the Ottomans who were already securely established at Istanbul. Despite the military genius and public beneficence of rulers like Qāyt Bāy (1469–96), amounting to a revival of the triumphs of the early Baḥrī period, the

Ottoman armies and navy were too strong for them and first Syria (1516) and then Egypt (1517) were absorbed into the Ottoman Empire.

Mamlūk society conceals many paradoxes. Though born slaves and nominally pagans, an essential qualification for high office, they became free and often devout Muslims. Though devoted to expelling the Franks from the eastern Mediterranean, they were Ḥanafī, generally agreed to be the broadest minded of the schools of law, and encouraged not only international trade but relations with Europe, and practiced a policy of judicious toleration of Christian pilgrimage to the Holy Land. Though they themselves might reach the highest office, their children, who were not born slaves, were automatically disqualified from it, and only in times of exceptional crisis, for example the aftermath of the Black Death (1350s) or the financial and economic disaster of the early 15th century, was this rule rescinded. Though their historians, including Maqrīzī (died 1427), are rightly famous and their pious foundations are splendid, they appear to have had no interest in any science save geography (al-ʿUmarī died 1345). And though they saw themselves as primarily Turks, there was no period in which an Islamic dynasty can be more properly described as Egyptian.

So numerous are the paradoxes that it might well be wondered how Mamlūk society worked at all. The distinction between enslaved nobles and their free children was perhaps the greatest drawback to continuity, and the growth of disruptive factions probably owes much to it. However, the concern of both Mamlūks and native Egyptian merchants with international trade very probably absorbed most of the active children of emirs into a capacious local middle class. In any case, there were links of loyalty, which must have been usually strong: the newly freed Mamlūk owed his first loyalty to his first owner, and since many Mamlūk emirs held more than one important office successively, a personal relationship might stretch very far. The regime, like any military regime, had its disadvantages. However, in the final analysis, the Mamlūk state was no worse than a system of military apprenticeship or an officer-cadet school turned government.

The Anatolian Seljuks and the early Ottomans. The Seljuks in Anatolia come last, because the Ottoman Empire which they ushered in lasted the longest of the great Muslim states. After Alp Arslān's victory at Manzikert (1071) much of Anatolia was ruled by emirs, whose territories were gradually absorbed (1180 onwards) into a sultanate with a capital at Konya. The greatest ruler of the dynasty,

Map of the world by the 12th-century Sicilian geographer Idrīsī. The Mediterranean is recognizable up to the Straits of Gibraltar, but the Atlantic coasts of Spain and Africa, India and SE Asia show ignorance. By contrast, south Russia, Central Asia and China are shown in some detail. The titling of the map is upside down. Idrīsī traveled widely and plainly knew much more of the Muslim world than appears here. His map shows how dependent Islam still was upon Ptolemy's *Geography*. Bodleian Library, Oxford, MS. Pococke 375 (dated 1403).

The Castle of Rumeli Hisar dominating the Bosphorus, built by Meḥmed II in 1452, a year before the fall of Constantinople.

Kayqubād I (1219–36), extended the Seljuk domains to the Mediterranean coast and to Erzurum in the east (1230). His successor was defeated by the Mongols at Kösedağ, near Erzincan (1243), but Mongol tutelage was exceptionally mild and, except for a disastrous rebellion in 1276–77, would probably have remained so. The Anatolian Seljuks, though aware of their traditional Persian past, were geographically in a special position, having common frontiers with Byzantium and ruling over an extremely mixed population in which Christians were often in the majority. Proximity to Byzantium afforded emirs or even rulers in disgrace a convenient refuge; but the frontiers were also a useful position to station the Turcoman tribes who had been pushed west into Anatolia by the Mongol invasions of 1220–21 and 1258–59, away from the large towns where they might have had a disruptive force. The 15th-century Ottoman historians certainly saw these Turcomans as *ghāzīs*, warriors for the faith. However, it is doubtful that the Seljuks shared their view, since the Turcoman states, of which the Karamanids were one of the earliest to develop, represented a serious threat to their own power. By about 1300 most of Anatolia was Turcoman emirates (Beyliks), living in a state of uneasy equilibrium.

Among these was the small Ottoman state, with a capital at Bursa. In 1342 it annexed the emirate of Karesi on the Dardanelles and under its rulers Orhan (c. 1324–60), Murād I (1360–89) and Bayezid I (1389–1402) began to expand into the Balkan provinces of the Byzantine Empire. Adrianople/Edirne was captured in 1361, Thessalonica in 1387, and Bosnia and Serbia subjugated after the Battle of Kosovo Polje (1389). Simultaneously Albania, Bulgaria and the Dobrudja were reduced to vassalage, providing money and troops on demand. The Ottomans allied themselves even more closely with these areas by taking Balkan princesses as wives. On the home front, using the pretext that disunity among Muslims was equivalent to comforting the enemy, they annexed Sivas and the emirate of Karaman (1398) and were well on the way to Constantinople, when Tīmūr swept across Asia Minor and defeated the Ottoman forces at Ankara (1402), taking Bayezid I prisoner. The Balkan provinces remained in Ottoman hands, but many of the emirates seized the opportunity to make themselves independent again. By 1468 all but the eastern part of Turkey was in Ottoman hands but this was so riven with alliances between Turcoman tribes, Ṣafawid propagandists and Mamlūk intrigue that it was not until the decisive defeat of the Ṣafawids at Çaldiran (1514) and the conquest of Egypt and Syria (1516–17) that all the emirates capitulated. In Europe Hungary remained invincible, was contained by a treaty of 1444 and was to remain outside Ottoman penetration till the 16th century. And though the Crimea was occupied in the period 1475–84, Muscovy was never attacked. So much stress is normally placed by Western historians upon the fall of Constantinople (1453) that it is important to realize that this was only a step in the complete Ottoman conquest of the Near East. It provided Meḥmed II with a new capital and much of the prestige of the vanquished empire; but it was far from conciliating his Muslim rivals.

It has been remarked that, paradoxically, the Ottomans, while again preaching the Holy War, eventually became the protectors of the Orthodox Church. Again, however, the *jihād* was probably less important than political aims; certainly Byzantium, though legally Dār al-Ḥarb and conquered by force, so that the population had no choice but conversion or slavery, was not treated as such. But with the conquest of Constantinople there came the idea that the Ottomans were the defenders of Sunnī orthodoxy. So long as the Mamlūk state existed, with its puppet ʿAbbāsid caliph, this pretense could not be justified, since the link with early Islam, though tenuous, was sufficient to guarantee the prestige of the *ʿulamāʾ* of Damascus and Cairo. This was an important reason for the Ottoman campaigns against the Mamlūks. Once they had been absorbed, the link was broken and the Ottomans were free to develop as they wished. But after 1500 the Ottoman Empire runs a course that is beyond the scope of this book.

The Citadel of Aleppo

VISUAL STORY

The origins of Aleppo are lost in legend. It is mentioned in the Egyptian accounts of the Battle of Qadesh (1268 BC). In the 9th and 8th centuries BC it became a provincial capital of the Assyrian Empire, but the first archaeologically identifiable indications of urban settlement are Hellenistic, when the town was replanned and enlarged by Seleucus Nicator (301–281 BC) under the name Berrhoea. Traces of the rectangular plan and its Roman modifications are clearly apparent in the disposition of its medieval bazaars (*souqs*), the most extensive and best preserved of their kind in the Islamic world. Aleppo owes its commercial importance to its position as a frontier post on the caravan route from Mesopotamia westwards: it is also the last of the stone towns of northern Mesopotamia and beyond lie the hot, dusty plains and the wide valleys of the Euphrates and the Tigris with their essentially brick architecture.

The Citadel rises dramatically 36 meters above the white stone buildings of the town. It is man-made (there are 16 meters or so of debris) but it does not appear to be a tell, the lower levels being solid rock. Fragments of a black basalt Hittite temple were excavated under the French mandate in the 1930s, but no Hellenistic remains have come to light, and although the Citadel became a Roman garrison and was later fortified by Justinian in the course of his campaigns against the Persians on the eastern frontiers of the Byzantine Empire, the only remains of this period are a few bases of Byzantine cisterns. The Citadel fell to Khusraw I Ānūshīrwān in 540, when the walls were apparently restored in brick. However, when Aleppo fell to the Arabs in 636 the walls were again in ruins.

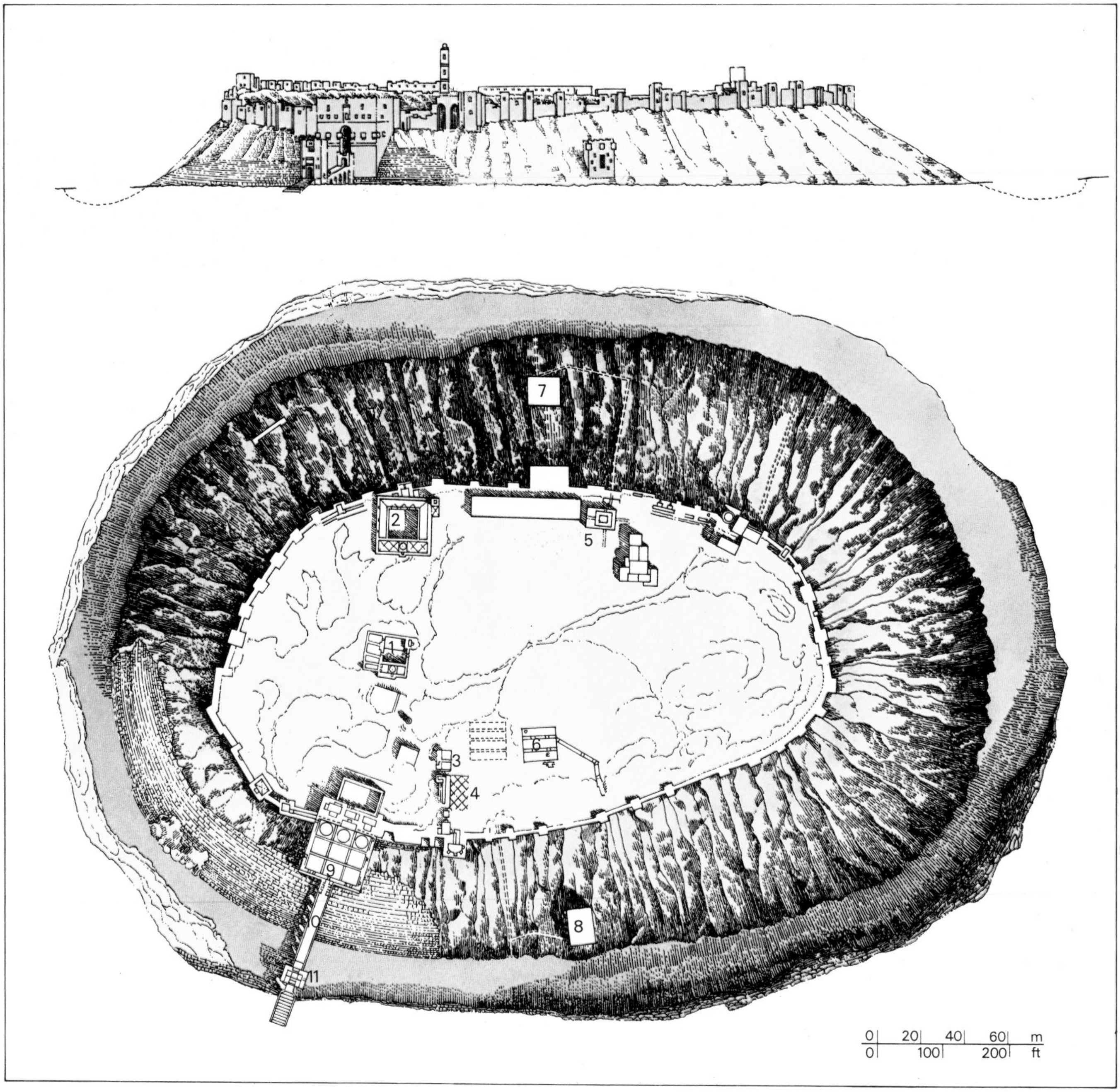

The Hellenistic walled town of Seleucus Nicator was built so that the Citadel lay athwart the east wall. The Citadel may have been refortified by the Umayyads. However, in 962, when the Byzantine Emperor Nicephorus Phocas captured Aleppo, the walls were in no state to withstand a siege. The Ḥamdānids, particularly Saʿd al-Dawla in 977–78, then seriously set about repairing the fortifications though they still followed the Seleucid plan. The extension of the town walls to the east, so that they enclosed the Citadel, dates only from the reigns of the last Mamlūk sultans, Qāyt Bāy and Qānṣūh al-Ghūrī (1472–1509), probably in the face of the threat of Ottoman expansion. Aleppo capitulated peacefully to the Ottomans in 1516 after the defeat of the Mamlūks at the Battle of Marj Dābiq. Although the town retained much of its former importance, the Citadel shows little sign of Ottoman occupation and gradually fell into decay.

The Citadel, enclosed by walls which follow the contours of the steep hill it crowns, is now a mass of ruins which give little idea of its original configuration. The extant remains include two shrines (1 and 2) (*maqāms*) (one of which is a mosque with a prominent minaret), a 13th-century palace (3) and the emplacement of an adjoining arsenal (4); there is also a deep well (*saṭūra*) (5), built in 1209, with 125 steps leading down to water level and originally with some mechanical appliance for raising the water, as well as numerous cisterns (6) for collecting rain water. Plan after Herzfeld.

Under the Mamlūks the Citadel housed the palace of the governor general (*nā'ib*) and the principle offices of state. It was considerably strengthened in the mid-14th century.

The towers on the north (7) and south (8) sides of the Citadel date substantially from the reign of the Mamlūk Sultan Faraj ibn Barqūq (1406). They indicate the original alignment of the Seleucid/early medieval town wall which was finally razed by Barsbāy (1422–35). The south tower is shown *left*.

The Ayyūbid entrance (9) (*right*), perhaps the most imposing of all Muslim fortifications, does not appear to be earlier than al-Ẓāhir Ghāzī (1209–10). Through it a passageway (see plan *below*, after Herzfeld) leads by no fewer than five 90° turns, each of which is dominated by arrow slits and can be shut off in case of emergency, to the main paved road up to the crown of the Citadel. Staircases communicate directly with the upper story, the arrow slits of which, in accordance with the principles of Islamic fortification, are disposed differently from those at bridge level, in order to increase the fire coverage.

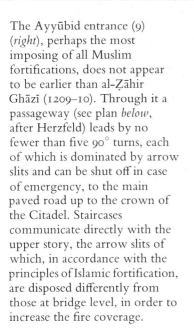

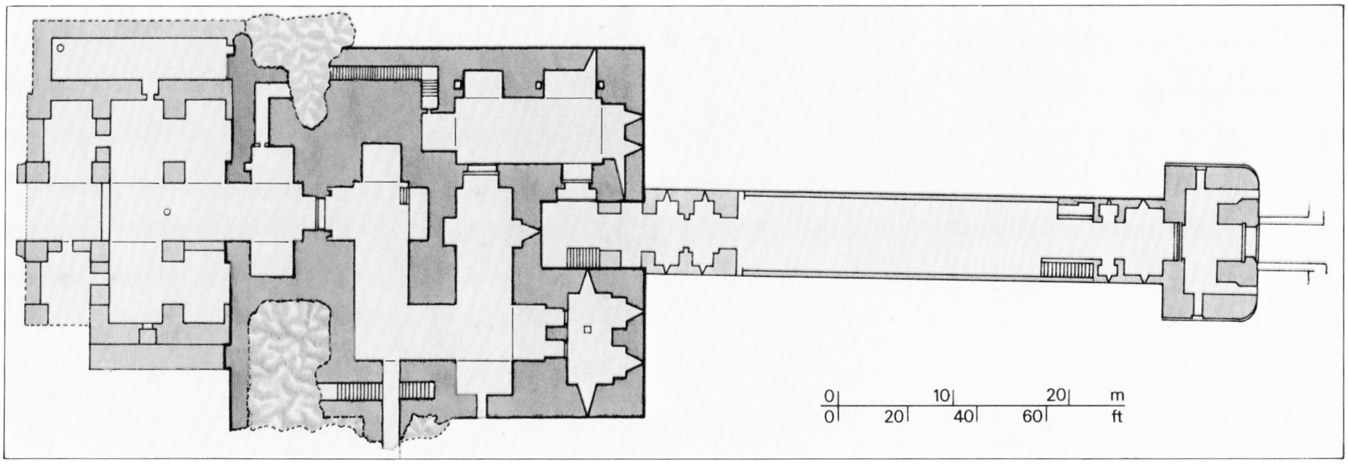

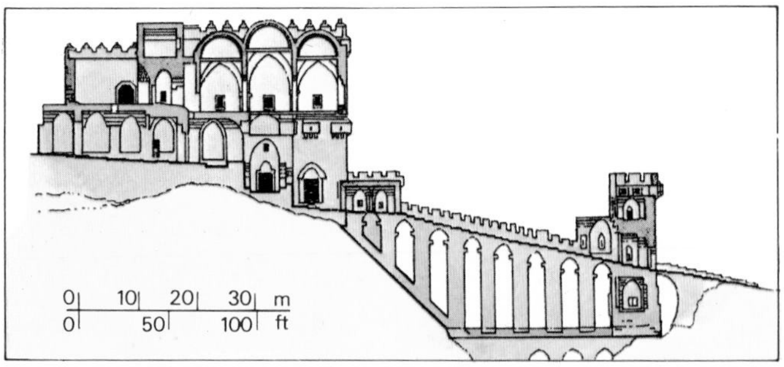

The entrance tower (11) guarding the bridge (10) across the moat leading to the great entrance fortification of the Ayyūbid al-Ẓāhir Ghāzī was entirely rebuilt by the Mamlūk Sultan Qānṣūh al-Ghūrī in 1507. But the steeply rising bridge (*left*; section *above*, after Sauvaget), the paved moat and the talus and glacis built against the Citadel mound where the gradient was not already precipitous are all the work of al-Zāhir Ghāzi (1209–10).

Like the dragons of the Talisman Gate at Baghdad (*below*) (1221, now destroyed), the dragons over the entrance to the Ayyūbid Citadel (*right*) may be reminiscent of Mesopotamian symbols of royalty: the Citadel had become closely associated with the Ayyūbid dynasty in the reign of Saladin, who installed his brother al-Ādil (Saphadin) there, and the dragon theme is frequent on metalwork, stone carving and even glassware ordered by the Ayyūbid court. Lions and other characteristically royal animals appear on the second and third gateways of the entrance fortifications.

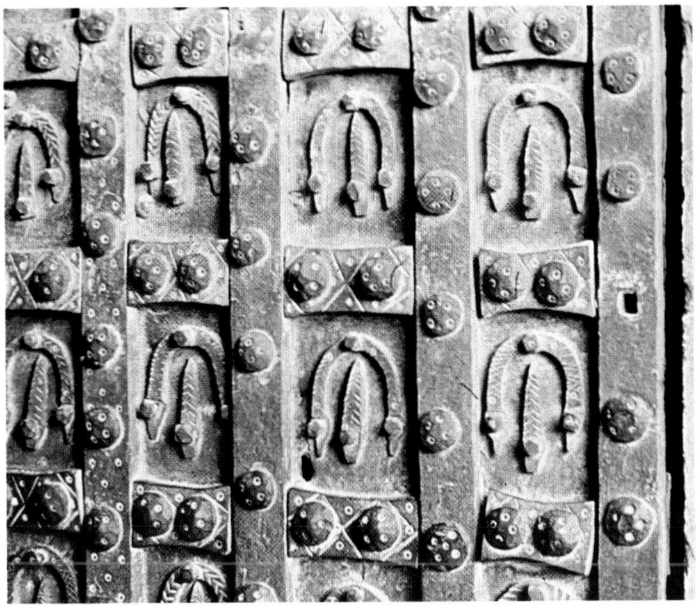

Above: the gates can be closed off by three successive iron-plated doors studded with large nails, each set in a bay with ample room for a portcullis. The nails form a rectangular grid filled with horseshoe- or lance-like motifs and inscriptions in the name of al-Ẓāhir Ghāzī.

Below: the Lower Shrine (*maqām*), here seen from above, which was traditionally believed to contain the stone on which Abraham sat while milking his flocks, was rebuilt in 1168 by Nūr al-Dīn with a dome before the *miḥrāb*, a dado of polychrome marble and wooden frames for the windows.

Above: the Upper Shrine had housed the head of St John the Baptist since 1043–44 and was also believed to house the altar on which Abraham sacrificed Isaac. After the sack of the Citadel by the Mongols in 1259–60 it was removed to the Great Mosque of Aleppo.

In the early 13th century the Ayyūbid ruler al-Ẓāhir Ghāzī added a palace (*above left*) with an inner courtyard and a garden with trees and flowers inside. In 1212, in the course of the wedding celebrations of al-Ẓāhir Ghāzī and Ḍayfa Khātūn, the palace and the arsenal beside it caught fire. In 1228 al-Malik al-ʿAzīz rebuilt the arsenal (which is now ruined) and, three years later, the palace. Its entrance porch (*above right*) is 10 meters high, with inlaid panels in strapwork designs of white marble on black basalt and a fine stalactite canopy. The porch led by a double right-angled bend into a large reception hall (*below left*) with a *salsabīl* and the remains of a central fountain. The only other identifiable remains are of a bath (*below right*, viewed from above). The palace was evidently still inhabited in the 14th century, since the porch bears an inscription dated 1367 recording the repair of the waterworks of the Citadel.

3. Town and Country

Land tenure. By the 9th to 10th centuries most Islamic societies had evolved a fourfold distinction: state property held by the sovereign or his dependants; lands held by soldiers or high administrative officials during their term of office (*iqṭā'* – one might call them fiefs, though they were not hereditary); private property, which was always vulnerable to confiscation; and the endowments of religious foundations, which were non-taxable and, theoretically, immune to confiscation.

The *iqṭā'* lent itself to a dangerous abuse: the holder could mulct the lands granted him, claim that they were insufficiently productive and demand others. This impoverished the land and increased the demand for *iqṭā'*, at the expense of state lands and private property – mostly in the country since there are few urban *iqṭā'*s recorded. The danger to private property and the non-hereditary character of the *iqṭā'* then explain the importance of religious foundations (*waqf* or *ḥabs*), the equivalent of the Byzantine *piae causae* – for the upkeep of hospices, orphanages, schools or hospitals – or of a modern registered charity. It was subject to two requirements, that the property should be the founder's own (hence not *iqṭā'*) and that the founder should be free. But in one form, the *waqf ahlī*, or family trust, the founder or his kin might benefit from the residuary income, which in Mongol Persia or Mamlūk Egypt was often more than half the total income. Pious foundations were guaranteed in perpetuity by legally attested documents (*waqfiyyas*), registered in a special archive and specifying in minute detail the constitution of the foundation, its bounds and the bounds of its endowments and the income they were to provide. This makes the surviving medieval *waqfiyyas* particularly valuable to the historian and the archaeologist.

Waqfs were not restricted to Muslims. Early Muslim practice, summarized in the probably fictitious "Covenant of 'Umar," had assigned the protected minorities some of their places of worship, which they were permitted to maintain in good order, though they could build no new ones. Their upkeep was largely assured by *waqfs* in their favor. The Mongols in Persia even extended *waqf* to Buddhist foundations, though Islam repudiated Buddhism. It is perhaps odd that family trusts, which were set up primarily for investment, should have been legally protected. But they represented almost the only means of furnishing medieval Islamic cities with many of their amenities – mosques, schools, hospitals or foundations – and the means for their upkeep. These were also frequently modernized, since it suited founders better to destroy and rebuild an institution which had fallen into decay, to ensure that the surplus revenue went thereafter to their own families. Only institutions famous throughout Islam, like the hospital in Cairo founded by the Mamlūk Sultan Qalā'ūn (1284–85), were regularly re-endowed.

To the beneficiaries the disadvantage of *waqf* was its vulnerability to inflation. But it also had a social disadvantage: there was no provision made for the upkeep of endowments, and town centers rapidly became choked up with *waqf* property, which could neither be sold nor developed, and which was also untaxable. And despite regular land surveys to control titles to property registered in the archives, *iqṭā'* lands were constantly being made *waqf* illegally. The successive invasions of Persia and Mesopotamia by foreign dynasties tended to regularize the situation; but the only solution in a stable society like Mamlūk Egypt (13th to early 16th centuries) was the further illegality of confiscation of *waqfs*. The illegality, however, was only apparent in such cases since the land should not have been made *waqf* in the first place. The pressure from both holders of *iqṭā'* and founders of *waqf* upon the peasantry is indisputable; but the peasants were not necessarily worse off than in Byzantium or in medieval feudal Europe and at least benefited from the pious foundations.

Epigraphy. The importance of epigraphy, the reading and analysis of inscriptions in "Islamic archaeology,"

Previous page: a landscape in eastern Anatolia.

Below: Bāmyān, Afghanistan. Note the precipitous mudbrick castle of Qal'a-yi Zohhāk/Dhuhhāk which may date from the pre-Islamic period but was evidently inhabited till the destruction of Bāmyān by Genghis Khān in the first Mongol invasions.

Opposite: Khiva in Soviet Uzbekistan. Khiva was almost entirely rebuilt in the 19th century, but this view of a gate, a covered street lit by pierced domes and a domed crossing is characteristic of earlier Central Asian markets.

needs some explanation. *Waqfiyya*s, the legal documents guaranteeing pious foundations, could not be drawn up before the building was completed and were often executed years later. Till then the status of the building remained undefined. However, such was the pressure on space in city centers that any unendowed building ran the risk of confiscation or, in the event of the builder's death, appropriation by someone else, who would then take the credit for the foundation – and the capital invested. Such, moreover, was the contrast between the ordinary, overcrowded housing of any city and the ease in which the Ṣūfīs of a royal *khānqāh* lived that any empty building was liable to be overrun by squatters.

Meanwhile, on the completion of the building, a foundation inscription was customarily erected, though the date it gives is normally that when work was first begun; and only major restorations (presumably involving some re-endowment) might be similarly recorded. Foundation inscriptions did not have the legal force of *waqfiyya*s, but their formal terminology, the elaborate titulature accorded to the reigning monarch, the founder's name or titles and the designation of the building were evidently expedients to give it semi-legal status until the *waqfiyya* was drawn up, specifying its constitution in detail. Some details could be changed, particularly when the foundation was for an eccentric purpose, like feeding stray cats. Sauvaget cites a puzzling decree concerning the Madrasa al-ʿUmariyya at Damascus dated 1422, suppressing some distributions of free food, but at the same time making a new *waqf* to circumcise those of its inmates not already circumcised and distributing grilled chick peas to those who recited the Koran there on Fridays.

However, instances of foundation inscriptions unjustifiably erected by depredators are so rare that foundation inscriptions must have been respected for their quasi-legal force. They are all the more important in that for every contemporary *waqfiyya* extant there are 40 inscriptions.

Foundation inscriptions are most useful for single institutions, since, as complex institutions developed – a hospital, a *madrasa* or a *khānqāh* attached to a mausoleum – they may not mention each of the constituents. For there was a hierarchy, in descending order, of mosques or *masjid*s, then *madrasa*s or hospitals, then *khānqāh*s, but never tombs (*qubba*), which had no standing as pious foundations. There are also foundation inscriptions on secular buildings, for example on the palaces of Qūṣūn (c. 1337) or Beshtāk (1337 or 1339), perhaps because they were official residences not private houses, or in a palace of Masʿūd III (1099–1115) at Ghazna in Afghanistan, where two marble screens dated 1112 have recently been discovered. They are also frequent on fortifications, dockyards (*tersāne*s), arsenals (*zardkhāne*s) and royal baths. though not, I think, on prisons. This suggests that the idea of a "pious" foundation was rather loose.

With very few exceptions foundation inscriptions up to 1400 are in Arabic, although, as on some Christian monuments in Armenia or Mesopotamia, they may be accompanied by a text in the vernacular for the benefit of the local population. After 1400 Persian becomes commoner in Persia and Central Asia, though it never entirely displaces Arabic; while there are virtually no foundation inscriptions in Turkish before the 17th century.

Islamic architecture is also frequently covered with finely written religious inscriptions – verses, or whole chapters, from the Koran or Tradition (*ḥadīth*), pious ejaculations, prayers (*duʿā*) or even sententious proverbs. Few of these last have yet been analyzed since they are difficult to read and their conceits are bombastic and wearisome; however, they may contain chronograms, dates composed by adding up the numerical values of letters of the alphabet, and hence may be a valuable adjunct to the precise dating of much still unascribed material. There is sometimes an obvious reason for their choice: the Koranic inscriptions relating to ritual purification inside the domed fountain (*fawwāra*) built in the courtyard of the mosque of Ibn Ṭūlūn in Cairo by the Mamlūk Sultan Lājīn in 1296 suggest that, contrary to the general Cairene practice, it was an ablution fountain. However, these inscriptions are often pure convention and the use of them to interpret a building is inevitably conjectural.

Attention should also be drawn to the Arabic inscriptions of palaces like the Alhambra (14th century) or the Norman palaces at Palermo of Roger II (1105–54), William I (1154–66) and William II (1166–89) and to the long Persian inscription recently brought to light by Italian excavations in the palace of Masʿūd III at Ghazna (1112) celebrating the glories of the ruler and his race or describing the splendor of the palaces in high-flown terms. Like the 13th-century walls of Konya, the remaining fragments of which bear out the contemporary panegyrist, these may not be sheer invention.

Epigraphy rightly claims prime importance in Classical archaeology. However, the peculiarly Islamic practice of building and then endowing an institution, as it were imposing an institution upon a pre-existing architectural form, gives Islamic epigraphy a unique status in the recreation of the Islamic past.

Towns in medieval Islam. The dramatic incursions of nomads into the Middle East between 600 and 1400 AD – Bedouin, Berbers, Turks and Mongols – make it important to stress the fact that Islam is, nevertheless, an urban civilization. The Umayyad rulers of 7th- to 8th-century Egypt and Syria and, later, Spain, the ʿAbbāsids in 8th- to 10th-century Iraq and Persia, the 9th- to 11th-century dynasties of the North African littoral, and even the Mongols in 13th-century Persia, all founded numerous towns, often named after their founders, much as Alexander and his Hellenistic successors founded Alexandrias, Antiochs and Seleucias all over their dominions. However, this may give a misleading impression, since in the Middle East certain constants – climate, topography and water supply – determine settlement. This is obviously true of harbor sites (the harbor of Fāṭimid Mahdiyya in Tunisia was probably Carthaginian, then Roman, and later occupied by Catalans, Portuguese and Turks); but it applies equally to inland sites, which require space to accommodate new concentrations of population and accessible building materials, an adequate water supply and a hinterland of cultivation to provide the town with staple goods and raw materials.

Judged by these requirements many Islamic foundations are simply earlier sites recolonized. Baghdad (762–67 AD) depended upon a network of canals and irrigation tunnels originally serving a suburb of the Hellenistic-Sasanian city of Seleucia on the Tigris. Fusṭāṭ to the south of Cairo, founded by ʿAmr in 641 AD, probably occupied a northern suburb of Memphis, and Scanlon's excavations there have recently brought to light Byzantine coins and pottery. Its siting was also determined by its proximity to a Trajanic-Byzantine fortress, now Old Cairo, and the Amnis Trajanus, a canal linking the Nile with the Red Sea near Suez, which guaranteed communication with the Ḥijāz (northern Arabia) throughout the year. Sometimes new dynasties appear to have chosen ancient sites deliberately to establish their claims to power, as did the Mongol Īl-Khān of Persia, Ābāqā, who in 1271 AD built a palace at Takht-i Sulaymān in northwest Persia, an excellently conserved Sasanian shrine with Parthian and Achaemenid levels. At Qayrawān in Tunisia (654 AD), which was founded for purely strategic reasons, there ensued a period of more than 50 years' migration to other sites in the area in search of an adequate water supply, which was only obtained when aqueducts similar to the Roman aqueducts in North Africa were built to provide for Qayrawān.

These recolonizations, however, frequently show a marked shift from earlier town centers. Many conquering dynasties found it prudent to build palaces or palace-cities to keep their new subjects at a distance. Such were the strongly Shīʿī Fāṭimids who conquered Egypt in 969 AD and built a walled enceinte, al-Qāhira (Cairo), from which the Sunnī Egyptian population was excluded, containing their palace, the principal offices of state and the Mosque of al-Azhar. This remained apart from the residential areas for almost a century.

Urban life in Islam was subject to other disruptive changes. The larger industrial towns, including the potteries and glassworks of north Syria and Persia, which were suprisingly localized, were stable. However, rulers often failed to take economic factors into account in choosing a capital, and when they moved there was little in the way of a middle class to maintain city life once the court and its attendants had moved elsewhere. The transfer of the Caliphate to Iraq in the 8th century under the ʿAbbāsids diminished even Damascus, but was catastrophic for other towns of the Syrian plateau, of which there are no remains earlier than the Zengid-Ayyūbid revival of the 12th century. And the shifts of the Great

The Bāb Zuwayla, one of three Fāṭimid gates to the city of Cairo built in 1087–91. The gate was later used as the base for the two minarets of the Mosque of al-Mu'ayyad which appear in the background.

Seljuks' capital between Nīshāpūr, Iṣfahān, Baghdad and Merv (1050–1157) were a strain on the resources of these cities, which were insufficient to cope with the ensuing recession when the capital moved elsewhere.

A striking instance is Sāmarrā, founded on the Tigris by the Caliph al-Muʿtaṣim in 836 AD, 48 miles (three days' journey in medieval terms) above Baghdad, primarily to house his Turkish troops, whose insurgency in Baghdad had made life there impossible. For them he built barracks, well away from the *souqs* (which have not so far been identified), provided with mosques and schools and a regular supply of Turkish wives so that they should not intermarry with the population of Baghdad. He himself built a palace, the Jawsaq al-Khāqānī, with terraced gardens, fountains, a clover-leaf race track, a game preserve and port installations, as well as a Great Mosque. In 892 AD, following the recurrence of political trouble in Baghdad, the caliphs returned there. Sāmarrā did not collapse immediately, as used to be supposed. However the city, which at its peak had been almost 22 miles long and up to 3 miles broad, soon shrank to a small pilgrimage town clustering round various Shīʿī shrines.

This dramatic expansion and contraction can be ascribed to a variety of factors, but scarcely to nomadism. With Sāmarrā natural conditions, demography and pre-existing settlement determined its fate. This was equally the case with Shahr-i Sabz in Transoxiana which, Bābur

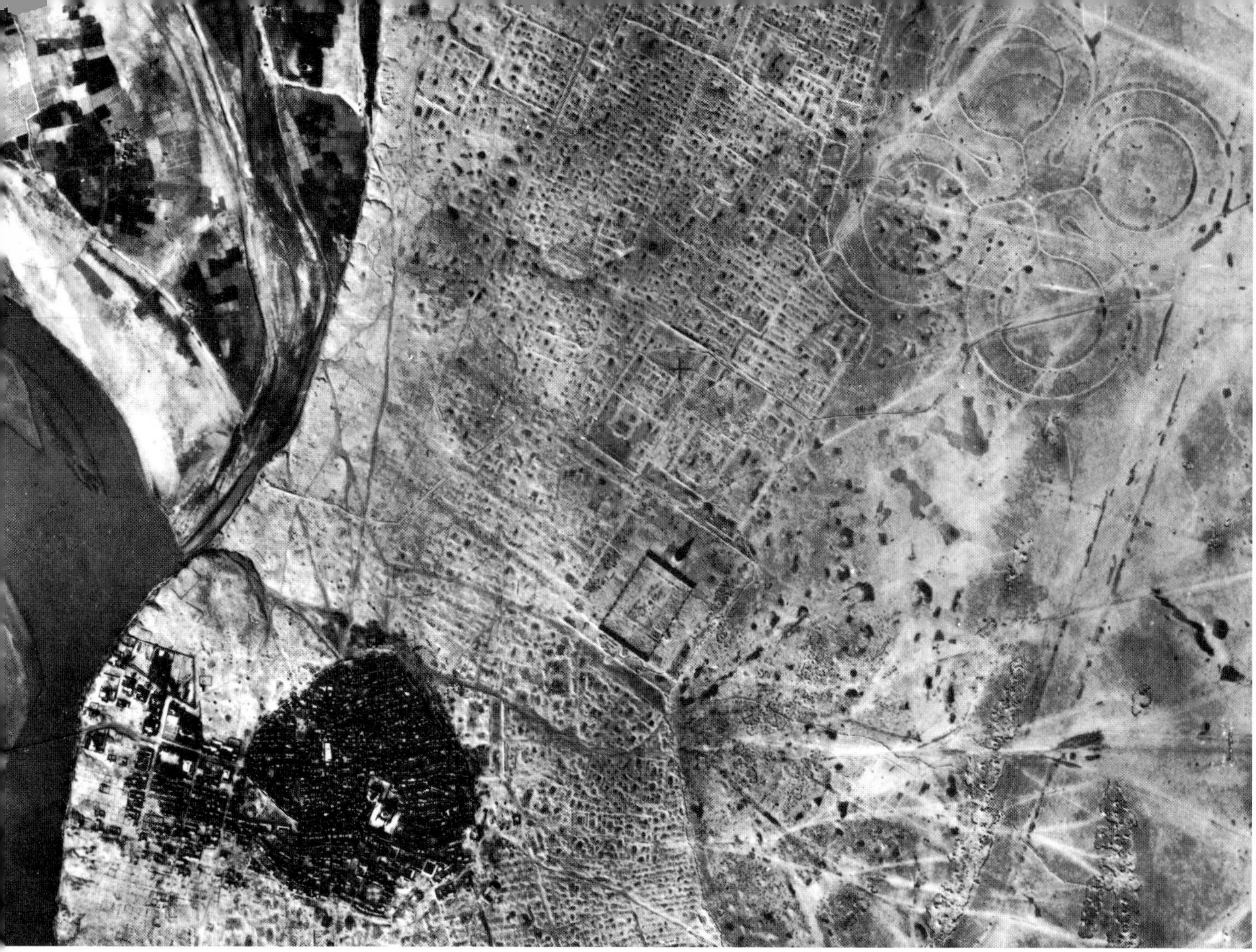

An aerial view of part of the city of Sāmarrā. In the top right corner note the clover-leaf race track, and in the center the Great Mosque of al-Mutawakkil (begun 847) and its minaret casting a strong shadow.

says, Tīmūr failed (evidently in the 1370s) to make his capital, and with Samarkand, where he only succeeded by the mass deportations from Herāt and Khwārizm of peasants, craftsmen and notables. The same must have been true in North Africa where, in the 9th to 13th centuries, as one center took pre-eminence, its predecessors fell into decay. Only one instance of a permanent city foundation in a hitherto uninhabited area off the main trade routes is known to me, Sulṭānīye, founded by the Īl-Khān Arghūn (1284–91) in a high valley, south of Tabrīz. It was perhaps conceived as no more than a summer resort, but under Ghāzān (1295–1304) and Öljeytü (1304–16), who built his own mausoleum there, it became the capital of Mongol Persia and even a Latin archbishopric (1318). Although the town plan can no longer be made out, the main functionaries naturally followed the ruler and by long-established tradition built palaces and barracks near him.

Nomads. The vicissitudes of Islamic cities were, perhaps, no greater than in medieval Europe, but their Islamic populations do appear to have been more mobile. The towns to which they moved, while gaining from their influx or the arrival of the court, were partially self-sufficient, with a resident population of merchants, lawyers and craftsmen and a solidly established hinterland of cultivation. But in this story it is striking how small a part nomadism has to play. Nomad society is often presented as disorderly when it has merely been rapacious. On the contrary, it had a strongly cohesive internal social structure, and there was often a symbiosis between nomads and the towns; for towns were necessary as an outlet for the products of their economy (wool, furs, carpets and some dairy products), and nomads were valuable customers for staple urban manufactures, raw materials or arms for life on the steppes. Nomad encroachment following the Mongol invasions certainly led to the decrease of cultivated land at the expense of pasture; but the towns benefited from the increase in the labor force which flocked in from the country.

"Nomads," moreover, have consistently shown a tendency to settle. There were Arab settlements in Egypt and Iraq by 641 AD; the Touareg Almoravids who first appear as North African nomads c. 1045 were ensconced in Spain as the partisans of settled Andalusia by 1086; the Seljuks, after defeating the Ghaznavids at the Battle of Dandānaqān in 1040, were at Baghdad by 1055 and anxious to stay there; while 14 years after the great Mongol invasions of 1220–21, the Great Khān Ögedei had already restored Herāt and was building himself a capital at Qarāqorum in Turkestan. There are two main reasons for this. First there is no precise distinction between settled and nomadic life. Barbaro's memoirs of Tana (1436–52) describe the nomads (mostly Qipchāqs and Tatars) of the Volga-Don steppe, the Lands of the Golden Horde, who sowed corn, continued on to other pastures and returned in time to reap. Secondly, even the most notorious incursions have been relatively few in numbers. The Seljuks, if they were still nomads by 1040, have been numbered in tens of thousands, and the Mongols were probably 160,000 in all. They needed the local Muslim bureaucracy, which was centered in the towns, to carry on government, and, whatever their origins, they all had some notion of power centralized in a ruler, khan, sultan or caliph. Despite the Mongols' or Tīmūr's depredations (which were often much exaggerated by contemporaries) nomadic invasions made relatively little difference to Islamic town life.

The great Islamic cities were not officially self-governing: the notables often influenced rulers but in the last instance they were at their command, and there is nothing in Islam equivalent to the free towns or republics of medieval and Renaissance Europe, governed by an executive council and sponsoring public works. This lack of autonomy is reflected in the creation of new palace quarters which the city was obliged to follow. In Egypt, the first Islamic settlement, al-Fusṭāṭ (641 AD), was soon augmented by a northern suburb, al-ʿAskar (7th to 8th century). There then ensued a steady progression northwards, first to al-Qaṭāʾiʿ founded by Ibn Ṭūlūn (860 onwards), then to al-Qāhira (founded in 969 AD), then to the Citadel (1170 onwards), which comprised palaces as well as a fortress, and even later to the grand Mamlūk suburb of the 14th to 15th century, al-Ḥusayniyya, beyond the Fāṭimid north wall of Cairo, of which little now remains. The industrial quarters at Fusṭāṭ mostly stayed put, but at each move north the notables and the *ʿulamāʾ* were obliged to follow, sometimes leaving whole areas abandoned, with the earlier grand houses colonized by craftsmen or slums.

Town planning. There are signs in the layout of most Western cities of some controlling imagination, prospects, public gardens or grand public architecture. The casual observer of Islamic cities from Tangier to Delhi will be struck by the evident contrast: narrow, winding streets where one's sense of direction is soon lost, enclosed by walls in which the entrances to private houses are hidden, no public gardens and very few open spaces. There may also be, even in towns as modern as Kuwait, whole streets in disrepair, houses crumbling into ruin or colonized by squatters until new palaces are built in their place. It is tempting to ascribe this confusion to over-population in recent times, but Maqrīzī's description of 15th-century Cairo demonstrates that even then decay and splendor were inextricably mixed. It has with some justice been ascribed to the absence of town planning in medieval Islamic cities. However the *muḥtasib*, preeminently the regulator of public morals and the markets, had discretionary powers to order the widening of streets or the destruction of buildings which were a public danger, though he neither planned the city as a whole nor had the means to keep public utilities in working order.

The absence of town planning very often poses a historical problem. When an Islamic capital occupies the site of a Hellenistic/Roman city how does the typical rectangular grid with its island blocks (*insulae*) and colonnaded main streets with a monumental intersection (the *tetrapylon*) "degenerate" into the formlessness of the medieval city? Sauvaget proposed a brilliant explanation, by reference to the Hellenistic/Roman plan of Berrhoea which became the *souqs* of medieval Aleppo: the walls of the Hellenistic shops along the colonnades gradually extended forwards to block it, even encroaching upon the public way, so that the original *insulae* on either side of it sometimes met, thus causing a diversion. Other Syrian cities appear to have developed in similar ways. Town planning, it has often been said, was ultimately less important than the strict social organization of Islamic cities in which the markets were rigidly organized by trade,

The transformation of a main street in Hellenistic Berrhoea into the *souq* of Aleppo. After Sauvaget. One sees the successive stages: (1) Hellenistic paved way with colonnades and large shops behind them; (2) the shops occupy the colonnade, becoming smaller in the process, and even encroach upon the paved way; (3) the paving stones are taken up and used for building, the public way is occupied by dwellings or shops, and the road diverges along the original colonnades.

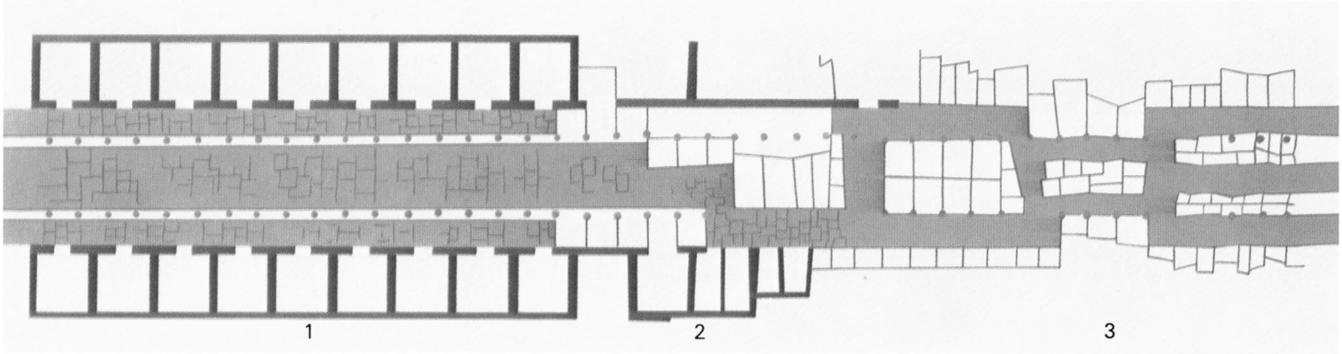

The Roman city of Timgad, Algeria, seen from the air. The nucleus is a rectangular grid (100 AD) but late 2nd-century additions are as irregular as any Islamic town plan.

though this structure is also basically Hellenistic/Roman. Islamic cities which colonized such sites very probably perpetuated the same distinctions.

However, recent archaeological discoveries suggest that the contrast between the regularity of the Classical city and the irregularity of the Islamic city has been overstated. A rectangular grid is most appropriate for a fortress (*castrum*) in flat terrain and can only easily be imposed upon a previously uncolonized site, like Philippolis (now al-Shahba) in the Syrian Hauran, founded by Philippus Arabus in 244–49 AD. But Rome itself can never have been so regular, and the impossibility of imposing an overall rectangular grid is very clear in large Roman provincial cities like Cuicul/Djemila (96–97 AD) and Thamagudi/Timgad (100 AD) in Algeria, where the nucleus is a rectangular grid but where late 2nd-century additions are as irregular as any Islamic town plan. The terrain was rarely suitable, moreover, and the grid an artificial ideal to which even the most devoted Hellenistic town planners could only approximate. At Palmyra, for example, the principal colonnades met at so sharp an angle that an irregular *tetrapylon* had to be built to disguise it. Once strict control was relaxed, therefore, the grid was abandoned.

Comparison of the *souqs* of Aleppo on their Hellenistic foundations and the (later) industrial quarters outside shows, moreover, that only the latter are "characteristically" irregular. There is a striking similarity to Sīrāf on the Persian Gulf, where the medieval houses recently excavated are aligned at right angles, but the potteries are irregularly planned.

There is one famous Islamic round city, that built by the ʿAbbāsid Caliph al-Manṣūr at Baghdad in 762–67, which has been convincingly reconstructed by Herzfeld and Creswell from contemporary descriptions. The Round City, basically a series of outer zones surrounding the caliphal palace and mosque, was enclosed by an outer wall more than 2,500 meters in diameter pierced by monumental gates with bent entrances on the NW, SW, SE and NE axes. These led to further monumental gates on the same axes giving on to a ring-road from which the residential quarters, arranged like the spokes of a wheel, could be reached. This second intervallum was flanked by deep arcades, evidently barracks for the guard of a thousand men assigned, we are told, to each gate. Finally came gateways into the vast central esplanade with the royal palace and its mosque. There was no direct connection between this and the residential quarters, which could be sealed off in case of riots.

The round plan is less of an innovation than might appear. At least two Sasanian towns in southwest Persia, Darabgird and Gur/Fīrūzābād (the latter built by Ardashīr in 224 AD), are almost perfect circles. However, if the Round City was a *city* it did not remain separate for long. For as the walls of Baghdad were built, the city gradually

A plan of the round city built by the ʿAbbāsid Caliph al-Manṣūr at Baghdad in 762–67. After Creswell. Note the mosque (1), palace (2) and gateways (3).

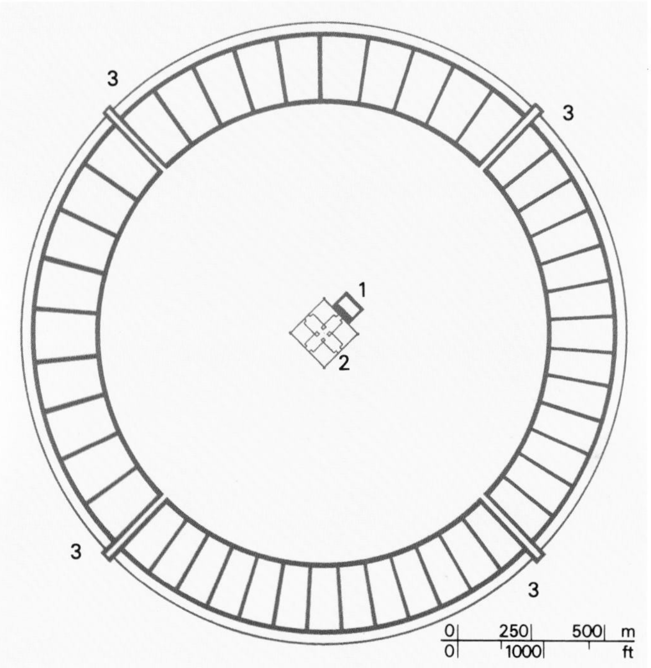

A colonnaded street in the city of ʿAnjar, Lebanon (probably 714–15). The columns and the shops behind are clearly visible in the foreground. The plan is so similar to that of a Roman fort that archaeologists formerly argued that it was a pre-Islamic foundation.

split into autonomous quarters with some common unifying feature – Sunnī, Shīʿi or Nestorian – each with its own *souq* and Friday Mosque.

Generally speaking, the Classical tradition of town planning in Syria and North Africa persisted under early Muslim rule; in ʿAbbāsid Persia and Iraq Sasanian town plans were revived; and in Central Asia Islam evidently drew upon the eclectic Soghdian tradition of the 4th to 7th centuries. In many cases, therefore, the characteristically "Oriental" features of Islamic cities may be comparatively recent, and it is dangerous to assume that all Islamic cities share them.

The generally accepted assumptions of medieval Islamic town planning are compatible with considerable architectural variation. Many royal palaces, for example, had a grand approach leading to an esplanade. At Sāmarrā al-Mutawakkil built the Shāriʿ al-Aʿẓam as an approach to his new palace-city, the Jaʿfariyya (861 AD), and the mosque of Ibn Ṭūlūn in Cairo (876–79) was similarly connected by a broad way leading to an esplanade, the Qarāmaydān, below the modern Citadel of Cairo, on which his palace stood. Ibn Ṭūlūn's Sāmarrā origins doubtless account for the similarity; but the Ghaznavid palace complex at Lashkarī Bazar (11th to 12th century) in southwestern Afghanistan was similarly connected to the town of Bust; at Merv the palace, mosque and mausoleum of the last Great Seljuk Sultan, Sanjar (who died in captivity in 1157), were joined by paved pathways inside the citadel; and even as late as 1400 Tīmūr's palace, the Āqsarāī, at Shahr-i Sabz, his first capital, gave on to a

The inner courtyard (*ṣaḥn*) of the mosque of Ibn Ṭūlūn, Cairo (876–79). A rocky eminence was leveled to accommodate it, and the hillside below was terraced to provide a dignified forecourt.

vast esplanade which was perhaps used for military reviews.

Otherwise open spaces were few. It was so uncommon for the Great Mosque of a city to stand by itself that Western historians have sometimes assumed a direct connection between the principal mosque and the bazaars which surrounded it. The Great Mosque at Iṣfahān, for example, is so deep in the bazaars that it even serves as a thoroughfare for them; but there is no evidence to show that the association was deliberate. Public squares of any sort are rare, and it is, therefore, very striking when an early writer on Samarkand describes a square (*maydān*) in which there were statues of animals in cypress wood. The 14th-century geographer al-ʿUmarī reinterprets this to mean that in a palace garden *outside* Samarkand there were cypresses trimmed like elephants, camels, oxen and beasts of prey, and even if cypresses do not lend themselves to topiary this is perhaps more plausible.

Islamic urban social organization also had architectural consequences. The palace and chief offices of state were mostly isolated inside a walled citadel. Inside or nearby were the guards' barracks with the trades dependent upon them clustered around – military contractors, farriers, armorers, bars and brothels. The great mosque was either near the palace or the bazaars, where each trade had its own quarter, the location of which rarely changed. This division now strikes any traveler in Islam, but it was already implicit in the organization of Roman markets (the Shippers' Forum at Roman Ostia or the Via Biberatica, the Spice Market, outside Trajan's Market Hall (c. 100 AD) in the center of Rome), and left many reminiscences in European cities. It was, anyway, only true of the central markets of a city: small markets catering for purely local needs were as diversified as any cluster of shops in a modern European suburb.

Between the bustling social life of the markets and the residential quarters with their life behind enclosed walls, however geometrically planned, there was a sharp contrast. Quarters, Monneret suggests, were well understood by the Venetians who in 1123 offered to aid the Franks in Palestine in the attack on Ashkelon and Tyre in return for a street, a piazza, a church, a bakery and a bath in every town the Crusaders captured. These quarters were often inhabited by a single social group, for example shaykhs, but they were particularly important for foreign communities, both Muslim and non-Muslim – North Africans and Palestinians or Greeks and Franks in Cairo – or the protected non-Muslim minorities, with a church or temple as their focus and the palace of their religious head.

Although the boundaries of such quarters were not necessarily rigid, they often had mud walls and gates with a porter which were locked at night, partly for self-protection, but also to ensure that any disorder within the quarter did not spread. These cellular units first appear in the plan of al-Manṣūr's Round City at Baghdad, but 10th-century descriptions of Bukhārā mention quarters outside the walled citadel, both trading and residential, with iron gates to shut off one from the other. These early walls have mostly disappeared and quarters can now only be reconstructed from street names.

In the *souqs* the main commodity markets, together with the money changers and the luxury trades, were at the center, while cemeteries and dirty, smelly or dangerous trades, like tanning, lime kilns and vinegar factories, were well outside the walls, if possible to leeward. The markets were remarkably stable. Raymond has recently shown, for example, that a 17th-century association of tanners just outside the southern Fāṭimid gate of Cairo is a survival of the main Fāṭimid tanneries, which by 1600 had moved far to the south; in the 10th to 12th centuries, therefore, the area can only have been sparsely populated.

No quarter was completely outside the control of the *muḥtasib*. However, only in North Africa was there a legal obligation to keep the streets clear; elsewhere street maintenance, refuse disposal and other public amenities were often neglected, and the cellular divisions by trade or community must have made a general order difficult to implement. The main streets of even the greatest cities were constantly clogged by street markets, first of all on wheelbarrows, but then in booths which gradually became mean houses, and it was rarely possible to keep a street wider than the minimum in which two loaded pack animals could pass. So narrow were the streets of Fusṭāṭ, says the Persian traveler Nāṣir-i Khusraw (1047), that even at noon they had to be lit – incidentally, one of the few references to street lighting in medieval Islam. The 10th-century geographer Ibn Ḥawqal states that, exceptionally, Samarkand and Bukhārā had paved streets. But Scanlon's excavations at Fusṭāṭ (principally 9th to 12th centuries) show a great concern for drainage, with sunken sewers covered by stone slabs, to facilitate clearance of blockages, running along the streets and redug as new building demanded changes in their course. The streets themselves were regularly resurfaced with crushed limestone to give purchase to wheeled traffic. The resurfacing, in spite of constant sweeping, and the accumulation of rubbish, led the street level, even in central Cairo, to rise by at least a foot a century. This must have been the same virtually everywhere in Islam.

Public works. For certain public works Islamic rulers accepted some responsibility. These included fortifications, harbors or dockyards, cisterns or large aqueducts and bridges, built usually at royal expense and often executed by the army, though for skilled work masons or other craftsmen would be conscripted.

Fortresses garrisoned at strategic points – even those as grand as the Syrian castles built against the Crusaders in the 12th and 13th centuries – are essentially adaptations of the general principles of military architecture to a particular site. Although the Crusaders themselves learned much from Muslim fortification, it had little effect upon

Right: the mudbrick walls of Yazd, central Persia. These have been almost entirely demolished in the past decade. The pronounced batter of the buttresses is to allow the winter rains to run off without deeply penetrating the brick.

Below: the Yedi Kardeş (seven brothers) at Diyarbekir, SE Turkey, one of two massive 12th-century towers added to the mainly 11th-century black basalt walls of the city by its Artuqid rulers. The upper floors and terrace are ruined; the projections at the top of the photograph are the remains of a machicoulis.

the development of Islamic architecture as a whole and will therefore play a comparatively small part in the present discussion of Islamic town life.

In many Islamic cities the citadel was a Byzantine or a Sasanian fortress. Alternatively, as at Baghdad and Cairo, fortified enceintes might be built to protect the palaces of new dynasties, ʿAbbāsid, Fāṭimid or Ayyūbid, but not as urban defenses. Fortified cities, in fact, are relatively uncommon in Islam and their walls, if defensive, are generally a response to a sudden military threat. Tavernier, who traveled in Persia in the late 17th century, was struck by the mud walls of Iṣfahān (most probably post-1500), since most of the towns he visited were unwalled, and Yazd is now one of the few Persian cities with remains of medieval mud walls. Qayrawān was never walled. In Syria the Roman walls of Damascus were allowed to fall into ruin and were only restored in the 12th century as part of the Zengid-Ayyūbid program of fortification against the Crusaders. The stone walls of Cairo were built, more than a century after its foundation in 969 AD, between 1087 and 1091, to stave off a Seljuk attack which never materialized. Saladin partially rebuilt them a century later and also planned a fortified enceinte for himself which now occupies the northern half of the citadel. He also started to enclose part of the ruins of Fusṭāṭ and a few traces of this have been discovered; however, he did not live to see it completed and his successors merely completed the walled enceinte.

Invasions have played such a large part in the history of Islam that the infrequency and lateness of urban fortifica-

The walls of the Rab'-i Rashīdī outside Tabrīz, a suburb built by the Persian vizier and historian, Rashīd al-Dīn, with *madrasas*, hospitals, mills and shops. It was sacked at his death in 1318 and again in 1336 but was inhabited for some time afterwards.

tion must appear surprising. But fortifications are often a mixed blessing: while defending a provincial town they also create an impregnable barrier when the garrison mutinies or the townspeople riot. They were, therefore, particularly associated with cities that became capitals: hence the late 11th-century walls of Baghdad when the Seljuk Sultan Malikshāh was attempting to make it the Seljuk capital. Tīmūr, significantly, fortified Samarkand (1370) and Shahr-i Sabz (1379–80) before building a royal palace there. And 'Alā' al-Dīn Kayqubād fortified Konya in 1220–21 in great style, at a time when it stood in no danger of attack. To judge from the 13th-century chronicler, Ibn Bībī, the plates in Léon de Laborde's *Voyage de l'Asie Mineure* (1838) and the extant fragments in the museums of Konya, its walls were decorated with figural sculpture, including a Hercules and late Roman sarcophagi, relief sculptures of genii and animal friezes newly carved, and proverbs, citations from Firdawsī's *Book of Kings* and other inscriptions glorifying the sultan, all gilt.

The gilt has worn off and the walls of Konya were destroyed 50 years ago, but the walls and gates of Diyarbekir, Aleppo, Cairo and Damascus, with their imposingly named gates of Victory, Rejoicing, Felicity and Paradise, built principally to impress the peaceful visitor with the ruler's magnificence, survive. The Bāb al-Naṣr on the north side of Cairo (1087 AD) was decorated with carved trophies of shields and swords, to discourage any evil-intentioned visitors. And the Bāb Zuwayla on the south, which was originally approached by a granite glacis, destroyed in the 13th century as too dangerous for horsemen, had two massive hemicylindrical towers with a recessed balcony where at sunrise and sunset an orchestra of pipes and drums would play for the sovereign's pleasure.

The common association of fortified cities and capitals explains the importance of gates and their inscriptions in the eyes of Muslim historians. Ibn Shaddād (13th century) cites a Greek inscription which, he claims, was affixed to an arch near the Bāb Antākiya at Aleppo:

"This town was built when Scorpio was in the ascendant and Jupiter was in this sign in conjunction with Mercury. Praise be to God. The Prince of Mosul [whom Ibn Shaddād, quite implausibly, identifies with the Hellenistic ruler, Seleucus Nicator] built it."

Ibn Shaddād's interest reflects the already widespread Islamic belief that astrology was relevant to the fortification of a city. Al-Manṣūr had consulted his court astrologers before work was begun on his Round City. And the Fāṭimids were so obsessed with astrology that they named the city they founded on the conquest of Egypt al-Qāhira (from which Cairo takes its name), to avert the evil influence of Mars, the bringer of war and ruin, which was in the ascendant when, by mistake, work on it was begun in 969 AD.

The walls and gates of Aleppo, built first in the 10th century and substantially rebuilt in the 12th and 13th centuries, may actually have been defensive in purpose. But although, as at Diyarbekir, they were proof against all medieval siege artillery, their elaborately planned defenses were subordinate to the impressiveness of their facade. Walls soon came to be seen as a convenient means of containing urban populations, while the main gates served as customs barriers where taxes could be levied on goods passing through. After 1200 urban fortifications are rare: some of the last are the walls and gates of Rabāṭ in Morocco (c. 1195–99). But the walls of Tabrīz, built under Ghāzān Khān (1295–1304), were deliberately combined, at the vizier Rashīd al-Dīn's suggestion, with customs posts and caravansarays just within the city gates where the rich east-west trade could be taxed, and from the 13th century onwards the walls of Cairo served a very similar purpose.

Harbors and naval arsenals. The distinction between urban fortifications and strategic fortresses on the main military routes is perhaps somewhat artificial, as is that between harbors and naval arsenals. But so little remains of either. The harbor installations at both Sāmarrā and Fusṭāṭ have disappeared with changes in the courses of the Tigris and the Nile. The Syrian-Crusader port of Antioch, Port St Siméon, which was a main outlet in the 12th and 13th centuries for pottery and enameled glass from the Syrian factories, has silted up so that it is now several miles inland; and its contemporary rivals, Tyre, Acre and Cilician Ayās/Lajazzo, were destroyed in a series of Mamlūk attacks in the 13th and 14th centuries, the last being now an insignificant village, Yumurtalik, on the Turkish coast east of Tarsus.

The Mamlūk ports have fared little better. In 1477–79 the Mamlūk Sultan Qāyt Bāy built a fortress at Alexandria, said by contemporaries to be on the site of the ancient

Pharos and almost certainly at the tip of the mole, to serve as an arsenal. It was apparently built by one of his Mamlūks, a German from Oppenheim on the Rhine, though it is closest in appearance to the 13th-century Hohenstaufen castles of Apulia. Plans by Gravier d'Ortières (17th century), Cassas (1772) and in the *Description de l'Égypte* corroborate Ibn Iyās' statement that the topmost tower served as a lighthouse and an observation post, and remains of long barrel vaults on the seaward side suggest that it included a naval arsenal or dockyard. The fortress was captured in 1517 by the Ottoman Sultan Selim I and its rich armory carried off to Istanbul where it is now to be seen in the Topkapi Saray; but the Ottomans continued to occupy it. However, the site of the earlier arsenal, from which the Mamlūk fleet regularly engaged in battle against the Venetians and the Genoese in the 14th and 15th centuries, is now unknown.

At Sīrāf on the Persian Gulf and ʿAydhāb on the Red Sea, after Basra the two most important Islamic ports concerned with the China and India trades in the 9th to 14th centuries, excavation has not yet shown whether their harbors were artificially reinforced, and elsewhere there are so far only traces of two naval arsenals. The first, at Mahdiyya on the Tunisian coast, most probably dates from the reign of the Fāṭimid Caliph ʿUbayd Allāh (910–34). It consists of a rectangular harbor, with a narrow medieval entrance guarded by towers from which a chain could be lowered to block access, and the remains of medieval walls inside, probably to prevent unauthorized landings. The arsenal was a separate construction with submarine foundations and quays on artificial terracing which ran into the Fāṭimid sea walls. It was originally an enclosed basin, protected from both land and sea, covered, to judge from the scanty remains extant, with longitudinal barrel vaults. Contemporaries state that it was large enough to hold 200 ships at a time; the Fāṭimid navy must certainly have been large since a fleet of 80 was reported destroyed off Rosetta in 920 AD.

Underwater surveys in the 1960s near the palace of Kubādābād, built by the Seljuk Sultan Kayqubād I (pre-1236) on Lake Beyşehir in Anatolian Pisidia, showed traces of submarine foundations on the lake side which may have been a miniature arsenal. However, there is a well-preserved Seljuk arsenal on the Mediterranean coast of Turkey which was built in 1226–31 for Kayqubād I as part of his extensive refortification of Hellenistic Korakesium (Byzantine Kalonoros, Frankish Scandelore) which was then renamed ʿAlāʾiyya/Alanya, by Abūʿ Alī b. Abiʾl-Rakhāʾ al-Ḥalabī. To judge from his name he was born in Aleppo, and he was evidently their principal naval contractor.

The arsenal was a dry dock in which ships could be built in safety and secrecy. It consists of a series of intercommunicating pointed barrel-vaulted galleries 40 meters deep, lit by holes in the roof, two or four to a bay. The

The Kizil Kule (red tower) at Alanya, S Turkey. The site was an ancient stronghold refortified by the Seljuks (1226–31) to include a naval arsenal – a dry dock and a harbor with a stone quay and magazines. The Kizil Kule was its principal landward defense.

facade was stone with rectangular crenellations. On the landward side are the remains of a stone quay with magazines carved out of the rock, evidently the Seljuk anchorage, and a massive five-storied octagonal tower with a slight batter surrounded by outworks, the Kizil Kule, its upper part brick with carefully staggered openings on the exterior and an enormous cistern inside built into the pier supporting the upper floors. On the seaward side the arsenal was protected by the Tophane, a tower built at sea level. Above, the fortifications were basically a main wall surrounded by an apron wall preceded by a dry ditch almost entirely carved out of the rock. The whole fortress is covered with cisterns, built of baked brick in concrete and mostly vaulted, since the only spring is near the Kizil Kule, almost at sea level.

Why an arsenal was built at Alanya is unclear. It was probably not much used. The main Seljuk Mediterranean port was just across the bay at Antalya, which was captured in 1207. The fortress of Kalonoros was already impregnable without Kayqubād's additions and only came into Seljuk hands because its Armenian seigneur surrendered it in exchange for lands elsewhere. By 1230 the main impetus of Seljuk expansion had slackened, and there is no epigraphic evidence for additions to the fortifications after Kayqubād's death in 1236. After 1300 it was controlled by various Turcoman emirates, none of whom had navies. Its preservation is probably to be attributed, therefore, to the fact that it was scarcely ever used.

Waterworks. From the beginning Muslim rulers made the provision and maintenance of a water supply one of their prime concerns. In the reign of the Umayyad Caliph Sulaymān (715–17) the Barada river, which supplied Damascus with water, seemed on the point of drying up. He therefore ordered works at the spring, actually at the cave of ʿAyn Fīja below the watershed, to be redug. An iron grille came to light, Ibn al-ʿAsākir relates (pre-1176), through which water gushed with the noise of fish in turmoil inside. Elsewhere state support might be indirect. The principal watercourse in medieval Samarkand, which supplied every house with piped water and which was carried across the markets in a leaden channel on wooden supports, was maintained at the expense of the Zoroastrian community who in return were exempted from the land tax. With the exception of public fountains erected by later rulers as an act of private piety, royal waterworks comprise cisterns, aqueducts and dams.

In Cairo there were two great open cisterns, the Birkat al-Fīl and the Birkat al-Ḥabash (the Elephants' Pool and the Abyssinians' Pool), natural hollows which would fill with water during the Nile flood where it then stood for several months. The 17th-century Armenian traveler from Lvov, Simeon Lekhatsi, describes with horror how people would wash clothes, bathe naked in cisterns and then take the water home to drink, though the Nile can have been scarcely less unhygienic. The convenience of these cisterns was that virtually all well water in Cairo is brackish; when they were exhausted the population went back to using water brought in skins from the Nile.

Open cisterns depend upon an abundant water supply, since the loss from evaporation is enormous. In Persia the general practice is for the drinking water to be collected from the winter rains in a vaulted reservoir normally well below ground level, with a built-up porch and a steep flight of stairs leading down to the water, which is kept clear by periodically throwing potsherds into it which precipitate the dust in suspension – so that eventually the whole cistern has to be cleaned out. Most sherds are difficult to date but the custom is evidently deeply rooted.

There is also a great open cistern at Boṣrā in the Syrian Hauran to catch the relatively abundant winter rains, with walls of basalt set in waterproof concrete. It is apparently Ayyūbid in date (12th to 13th century) but there are no traces of vaults, and conservation of the water must therefore have been impossible. Perhaps, however, it had a double function, like the cisterns built in 860–63 by the Aghlabids for their capital at Qayrawān; but the Islamic type working on the decantation principle, of which several examples are known in Tunisia, is apparently an Islamic invention and is not directly based on Roman prototypes. In the center of each polygonal cistern is a square pier which was originally topped by a pavilion with four doors and on 11 columns; at high water the Aghlabid ruler would sail in a boat on the larger cistern which was elaborately buttressed inside and out.

The state also financed elaborate waterworks. Near Merv in the early Middle Ages the waters of the River Murghāb were dammed back into a large circular pool with four major canals radiating from it to the city and the suburbs where it was stored in cisterns. The height was regulated by sluices and by dams which were breached in the rainy season. Upstream, at Marv al-Rūd, the river bed was artificially deepened and had embankments faced with wooden planks to prevent subsidence; these works were under the supervision of a water bailiff, who was an emir, with a staff of 10,000, including horse guards, to see to its maintenance.

Surviving waterworks are more stoutly built and are chiefly dams, aqueducts and mechanisms for raising water to a certain height. Islamic irrigation greatly extended the area of land under cultivation, since the Greeks and Romans had chiefly practiced dry farming. The least complicated form of waterworks was the *qānāt* system, known in Achaemenid Persia but perhaps an Armenian invention – underground channels working on the gravity principle, carefully calculated to raise a stream of water over low natural obstacles without causing too large a head of pressure. In North Africa, up to its drastic depopulation in the 11th and 12th centuries, in Spain and in Ottoman Istanbul the Roman systems of dams and aqueducts were adopted without change. But in Syria, for example, at Ḥamāʾ on the Orontes there is a great undershot Vitruvian waterwheel which is fed by a chute and which raises water into an aqueduct which originally spanned the valley. Such wheels were well known in the Roman world, but the one at Ḥamā' may have been part of the works of Saladin who restored the town in 1178 after it had been razed by an earthquake in 1157. Smaller wheels were used to work oil mills on the Guadalquivir at Cordova, and there were evidently large wheels in the Maghrib, since one of the miniatures in the 13th-century romance *Bayād and Riyaḍ* – one of the few illustrated North African manuscripts known – shows the hero lying senseless by a waterwheel quite as large as that at Ḥamā'.

In Iran the monumental dams which are known (many popularly ascribed to the 10th-century dynasty, the Buwayhids, but most actually 16th century or even later) are mostly associated with irrigation systems, not aqueducts; and some, like the Band-i Amīr (conceivably 10th century) in the mountains near Shīrāz, simultaneously served as bridges. There are medieval brick or rubble dams in Khurāsān. They mostly contain a well in the body of the dam with an interior staircase to clear the channels at various levels, thus permitting surface water to flow from the reservoir into the well where it was gradually released by sluices. Channels right at the base of these constructions show that in summer the reservoir would become dry. The disadvantage of this type of dam was that it tended to silt up. However, some of the east Persian dams have sluices, the position of which has been altered to compensate for this. These are probably Tīmūrid restorations (late 14th to 15th century).

Curiously, neither these Persian dams, nor the regulator built by Baybars at Illāhūn in the 1260s with a system of sluices to control the flow of the Nile into the irrigation canals of the Fayoum oasis, attempts to exploit the reserves of power offered by dams. There was an unsuccessful 14th-century effort to dam the Nile to divert a greater flow into a canal built by al-Nāṣir Muḥammad, the Khalīj al-Nāṣirī, but in Egypt the most commonly used mechanism for raising water was the buffalo-driven *sāqiya*, the horizontal waterwheel which has probably been in use since the first centuries BC. The best-preserved aqueduct of several mentioned by the medieval historians is that built by al-Nāṣir Muḥammad which was probably completed just before his death in 1340. It consisted of one or more large intake towers, like the Sab'a Sawāqī now by the Nile, with six buffalo-driven wheels, which raised the water to a height from which it flowed gently downwards towards the citadel, eventually running along the city wall begun by Saladin, to fill deep cisterns at the base of the citadel. From here it was raised to ground level by a series of buffalo wheels. Since the population of the citadel in the 14th and 15th centuries ran to several thousands the intake must have been very considerable.

It remains to mention one invention associated with state waterworks: a device for measuring the quantity of water provided. The most famous of all was the Nilometer on the southern tip of the island of Rawḍa at Cairo. In

Undershot Vitruvian waterwheels on the Orontes at Ḥamā', N. Syria. The wheels raised water to an aqueduct which spanned the valley (part of it can be seen in the foreground) and which may well have been built by Saladin in 1178.

Egypt the land tax was traditionally assessed according to the height of the Nile flood which governed the harvest. Graduated columns were therefore erected to measure the rise (one appears on a 6th-century Byzantine silver plate in the Hermitage). The present Nilometer, though more than once broken and repaired, is that erected in 861–62 under the 'Abbāsid Caliph al-Mutawakkil by a mathematician, known to the 13th-century biographer Ibn Khallikān as Aḥmad b. Muḥammad al-Ḥāsib al-Qarasānī – perhaps a corruption of al-*Farghānī*, the celebrated 9th-century astronomer known to the West as Alfraganus.

This Nilometer is a graduated octagonal column on a pedestal set on a millstone to distribute its weight over a wooden floor in a square stone shaft, cylindrical at the base, with a staircase running all the way down. There are intake tunnels at three levels, the topmost originally being surmounted by a lion's head through which the water evidently spouted when the Nile flood reached 16 cubits. The column was kept vertical by a wooden beam bearing the date 861–62, still legible in the 18th century, though the rest of the inscription was defaced, possibly by Ibn Ṭūlūn who carried out works at the Nilometer in 872–73 and who may have wished to assert his independence of the 'Abbāsid Caliphate. On the walls of the shaft were Koranic rogations for rain and an abundant harvest, carved in gold on a blue ground. When the shaft was restored it was discovered that much of the stone was reused architectural elements from Coptic churches.

Industry. Apart from state waterworks there was some state industry. The *ṭirāz* factories of medieval Egypt (Alexandria and Tinnis in the Delta) and Baghdad produced luxurious silks and linens woven with the rulers' titles and often enhanced with gold or silver thread, invariably strictly supervised by state officials. This was not so much because the state claimed a monopoly of fine textiles as because the *ṭirāz* factories produced the material for robes of honor (*khilʿas*) which were distributed on grand occasions to high officials and which were in fact uniforms. Hence the unfortunate misunderstanding between Hārūn al-Rashīd and Charlemagne which arose over two *khilʿas* bearing the ʿAbbāsid *ṭirāz* sent as presents for his coronation in 800 AD. Charlemagne graciously accepted them, but without responding as expected, by recognizing Hārūn al-Rashīd as his suzerain. There were almost certainly paper mills to produce high-quality paper for chancery documents, and as cotton papers became more important it is possible that the state controlled part of the cotton crop in important producing areas like Central Asia and east Persia. Otherwise, the most important state industry was gold- or silver-mining, about which little is known in detail until the 16th century when there is much Ottoman evidence of mining in the Balkans. Earlier mines were often worked by prisoners and technology was primitive. The silver mines at Banjahīr/Panj-hīr, which was a mint city under the Ṣaffārids (868–908) in the Hindu Kūsh at one of the sources of the Kabul River, were worked by 10,000 men, by torchlight, in caverns hollowed out of the mountainside. By the 14th century the workings were disused but Yāqūt (pre-1220) gives a long description of the riotous life the miners lived, recklessly spending vast sums on sinking new shafts and gambling wildly, fortunes changing hands overnight.

The Nilometer at the southern tip of the island of Rawḍa, Cairo, built by command of the ʿAbbāsid Caliph al-Mutawakkil (861–62) to measure the height of the annual Nile flood. The photograph shows one of the intake shafts.

Islamic rulers have a reputation for bridge-building. But the Qanṭarat Hurzādh/Khurdād, near Idāj in the Iṣfahān area, a single arch with its stones cramped with iron, was, according to Yāqūt, built by the mother of Ardashīr (207–c. 239 AD). It was restored by a Buwayhid emir in the 10th century, partly at state expense. Up until 1500 most Persian bridges are on Sasanian, or possibly Roman, foundations. The bridges at Shushtar, most probably built by Roman engineers after the defeat of the Emperor Valerian by Shāpūr I in 260 AD, and at Shahrestān near Iṣfahān still show the characteristic Roman profiling of their piers, rounded downstream but with pointed breakwaters upstream, though the arches, dating from the Seljuk period onwards, are of brick and are pointed to give greater elevation.

In Turkey and Upper Mesopotamia (the Jazīra) there are, however, many original Islamic bridges. The earliest of them appears to be the flat bridge over the Tigris at Diyarbekir, built by the Marwānid emirs of the city in 1065–84, evidently to replace an old bridge built in 742 by the Umayyad Caliph Hishām and destroyed by the Byzantine forces under John Tzimisces in 973 AD. There is a steeply pitched single-span bridge, 7 meters wide and 150 meters long, on the Batman Su, on the Silvan-Bitlis road, with a foundation inscription of the Artuqid ruler Timurtāsh b. Īl-Ghāzī dated 1147, and a bridge of the same period at Jazīrat ibn ʿUmar on the Tigris, the ruined piers of which were faced with carved marble plaques showing signs of the zodiac (some now in the Diyarbekir Museum). A third Artuqid bridge in the same area, at Ḥiṣn Kayfā, was probably built in 1116. Only the piers were to be seen when Gabriel surveyed it in the 1930s, but the faces of the pointed breakwaters were likewise faced with reliefs, much abraded but probably Parthian. The 13th-century historian Ibn Shaddād states that the central part of the bridge was wood and could be removed in case of attack.

In Seljuk Anatolia bridges were built on the principal caravan routes, for example a double bridge, the Kesik Köprü, with a caravansaray near it, one stage west of Sivas on the Kayseri road. At Tokat there is also one of the

The Çoban Köprü over the Araxes River (probably 1316–36 but restored in the Ottoman period) at an important crossroads on the route east from Erzurum to Tabrīz. Such bridges were a convenience to merchants but also useful points for collecting tolls.

few remaining medieval bridges inside a town, built in 1249 by a local notable for the reigning triumvirate of Seljuk sultans. And east of Erzurum at the junction of the road east to Kars and Tabrīz with the road south to Lake Van, there is a stone bridge, 220 meters long, perhaps built on wooden piles, across the River Araxes. This is the Çoban Köprü, undated but perhaps the work of the Emir Chobān, the vizier of Abu Saʿīd, the last of the Īl-Khāns of Persia (1316–36). Curiously, one of the piers of this bridge has become a cult spot and the crevices between the stone are stuffed with votive rags.

At Baghdad, Cairo and most of the towns beside the Oxus bridges were replaced by pontoons or bridges of boats, even though Muslim engineers were evidently perfectly competent to bridge wide rivers. But bridges were expensive, and where military or economic factors did not make them essential, pontoons were favored as being cheaper, equally practical and necessary when the flow varies greatly. Bridges made excellent customs posts. This explains the pavilions still to be seen at the entrances to bridges at Shahrestān or on the Batman Su.

In 1443 the Ottoman ruler Murād II built a bridge of 174 arches, 392 meters long, across the River Ergene near Edirne, with a hostel, a mosque and a *madrasa* at its head financed by a bath, a *buza* (a fermented liquor which the Ottomans regarded as licit) shop and a small market nearby as well as by property inside Edirne. On the Edirne side he settled Turcoman nomads as guards; on the other old soldiers were allotted farming land, which became the town of Uzunköprü, the modern frontier post on the Turkish-Bulgarian border. In 1443 Edirne was still the Ottoman capital, so Murād was able to control both trade inside the European provinces of the Empire and the land trade between Byantium and the West. Inalcik supposes that the famous Ottoman bridges of Bosnia (Sarajevo and Kozja, both c. 1550) and at Mostar (1556) were founded for similar reasons and that they played an equally important part in the development of settlement around them.

Markets and their buildings. There is a basic architectural distinction between central markets and local markets which served a residential quarter. These latter, except in

A plan of the market at Sīrāf, SW Persia. After Whitehouse. The bazaar (9th to 12th century) is typical of Islamic markets in having booths on both sides of the street.

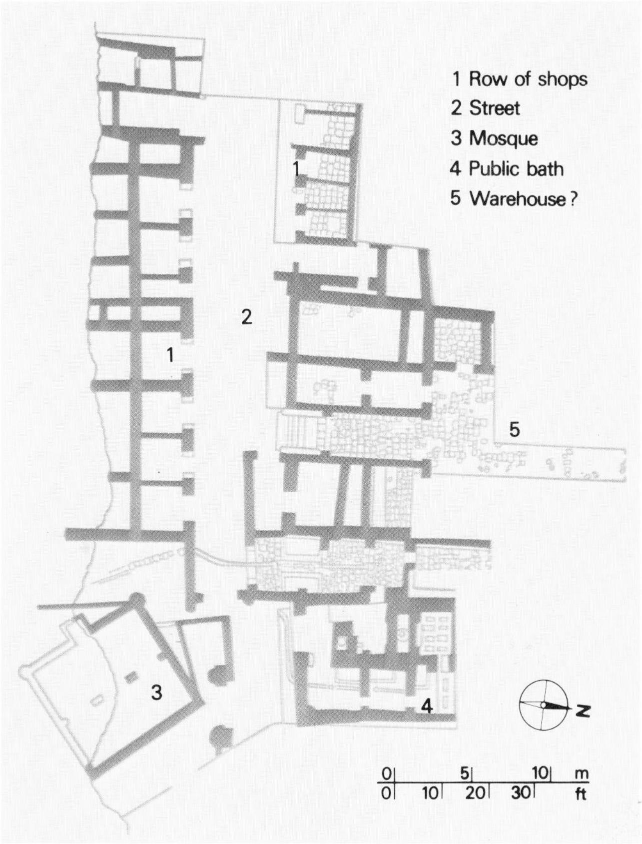

Istanbul, where they were part of the deliberate transformation of the city under Ottoman rule in the 15th and 16th centuries, were simply agglomerations of shops of all sorts to suit local needs, though both in Aleppo and at Istanbul this did not prevent their being regularly planned. The central markets, divided up by trades, are architecturally much more important. To some extent they consisted, as at Sīrāf (9th to 12th century), of rows of booths along the street with no nucleus. This perhaps explains why, in 9th- to 11th-century Baghdad and again in 13th-century Damascus, markets could be displaced surprisingly quickly. But for the most part the trades remained stable over many centuries, and even towns like Iṣfahān and Bukhārā, which never had a vestige of the Hellenistic gridiron plan, very often mark the crossing of two main streets in the markets by domes or vaults with an oculus.

The principal market building was the *khān*, sometimes with a row of shops on the exterior, a grand entrance and a central courtyard with a pool or fountain, with latrines, a *masjid* (oratory) or even a bath. Round this the craftsmen had their shops. It is very probable that such buildings go back to the closed markets of towns like Hellenistic Miletus; at Dura-Europos in the 3rd century there are Hellenistic agoras which already look like Islamic *khāns*. Probably the earliest Islamic *khān*, however, is an 8th- or 9th-century courtyard building recently excavated at Apamaea in Syria evidently used by ironmongers or bronze-casters. As the large pieces of clinker found demonstrate, there was little difference between factories and shops; or between wholesale and retail trade, though the *khāns* dealing in raw materials – soap, honey, spices or, in Cairo, even garlic – benefited from the obvious economies of scale.

Division of the markets by trades was an administrative convenience, since through the heads of the trade associations urban discontent could be controlled and taxes imposed upon the tradesmen as a group collected. It is often asserted that these trade associations were guilds, and were characteristic of medieval Islam by the 13th century. However, there is little evidence for their functioning before the Ottoman period, and, unlike medieval European guilds, they neither controlled the quality of production nor had funds to help their members in need. They frequented particular mosques or shrines; but they did not build corporately or endow corporate *waqfs*. The only supervision of the markets was by the *muḥtasib*, who inspected weights and measures, arbitrated in disputes between craftsmen and their clients (occasionally "strikes" are recorded in which all tradesmen shut up their shops for a day or two), and controlled prices, though somewhat inefficiently, since in times of scarcity or gross inflation the *muḥtasib* could promulgate little but draconian, and usually unenforceable, measures against speculators.

Khāns were owned either by emirs or merchants or by the trustees of *waqfs*. The tradespeople rented their shops, sometimes on leases of as little as a month. The staff was minimal, with only a porter, sometimes installed in a monumental portico like that of the "Khān al-Khalīlī" in Cairo, rebuilt by the Mamlūk Sultan al-Ghūrī (1501–16), and an intendant to let shops, collect rents and see that the *khān* was kept in good order. The shops, where the craftsmen worked or displayed their wares, were booths with a raised platform, sometimes, as in the *khāns* of Aleppo, with an ingenious awning which could be lowered to close the shop; the booths sometimes had storerooms attached or a safe in the floor, though in the larger *khāns* visiting merchants deposited the considerable amounts of cash they carried, in default of an organized banking system, in a sort of communal treasury.

Visiting traders rented shops in these *khāns* and very probably lived above them. However, both Maqrīzī (15th century) and the relevant Cairene *waqfiyyas* (deeds of endowment) always describe the upper floors as if they were separate buildings (tenement houses). *Khāns* were naturally not always residential, but the import or export trades (cloth, paper, spices or soap) could not have existed without living quarters; indeed, they formed national enclaves, since these trades tended to be in the hands of foreigners, much like the *fondachi* of the Italian trading republics – the Germans at Venice, the Pisans or Amalfitans in Cairo under the Fāṭimids, or the Genoese in Sivas and Tabrīz in the late 13th and 14th centuries – which also included a church. There is an odd parallel with 1st- and 2nd-century Roman markets, like that of Pozzuoli/Puteoli, where the building includes an apse fronted by a colonnade which housed a statue of the local divinity, probably Serapis, as well as public latrines in each corner. However, medieval *khāns* occasionally catered for more worldly diversions. The biography of the famous 13th-century mystic Jalāl al-Dīn Rūmī, the founder of the order of the Whirling Dervishes, recounts one of his more spectacular conversions: that of a prostitute, Ṭāūs, who inhabited one of the *khāns* of Konya.

There were also *qaysāriyyas*, which perhaps derive from Roman or Byzantine imperial markets, built partly as a public service and partly to enable the ruler to gain directly from the luxury trades. In Islam they are generally considered to have been lockup markets, particularly for valuables, patrolled by night-watchmen and hence with no living quarters. A typical *qaysāriyya* is al-Ghūrī's misleadingly named "Khān al-Khalīlī" in Cairo (1501–16), rebuilt on the site of a late 13th-century *khān*, with an entrance block giving on to a street with monumental gates at each end and a three-story *qaysāriyya* inside. It remained the center of the luxury cloth trade up to the 18th century. Similar constructions were a central feature of Ottoman markets. And as late as the 1600s Shāh ʿAbbās dignified Iṣfahān with a *qaysāriyya*, of which the facade, on his main square, is the most conspicuous element: from its porch, at dawn and sunset, strange music of pipes and drums is still played. But Cairene Mamlūk usage was different: *qaysāriyyas* were evidently small specialized markets, often for the sale of local produce, with several entrances, so that they served as thoroughfares.

For ordinary travelers there were hostelries (*funduqs*), descendants of Byzantine hostelries like those at the shrine of St Simeon Stylites/Qal'at Sim'ān in northern Syria; but, apart from a pair of buildings round central courtyards in the Armenian town of Ānī, built probably between 1200 and 1236 in evident imitation of Islamic hostelries, none remain in Islam. Few of them were free: in Cairo and Jerusalem such free lodgings were generally termed *ribāṭs* (here, hospices), but they evidently had no particular plan. *Funduqs* tended to cluster round the gates of a city for travelers while they paid their customs dues or satisfied other formalities. For the levying of taxes on local produce entering the city there were most probably small posts at each gate; but for international trade further regulation was necessary. Rashīd al-Dīn has described how the gates of Tabrīz built under Ghāzān (1295–1304) had customs houses nearby. None of these survive, but in Cairo there are 14th- and 15th-century *wikālas* (literally, intendancies), mostly located near the northern gates of the walled city where the rich Syrian trade arrived. Of the earliest known, that erected by the Emir Qūṣūn (between 1321 and 1342), nothing remains but the entrance with a foundation inscription and a pharaonic granite threshold with a cartouche; but a late 14th-century *wikāla* (1481), built by the Mamlūk Sultan Qāyt Bāy at one of these gates as *waqf* for Medina-bound pilgrims, was strategically placed for customs and excise and was almost certainly built to replace a *wikāla* built by Barqūq (1382–99). These *wikālas* are so similar to *khāns* in plan that they have often been considered local variants, all the more so since some of them are described as *khāns* in their foundation inscriptions; but this is only to be expected. The clearance of large caravans of diverse merchandise could well have taken weeks and made lodgings and storerooms essential; while much trade could have been carried on there while the goods were still in bond.

The *wikālas* known are Cairene but there were certainly equivalents elsewhere. One of the earliest known was perhaps a large rectangular building, 50 meters by nearly 38, near the harbor at Sīrāf, evidently abandoned in the 13th century. It consists of an outer arcaded courtyard, behind which are ranges of cells or storerooms and an equivalent area, probably covered, with massive piers marking off the central aisle, though since only the foundations survive it is impossible to deduce whether it was multi-storied. At Aleppo the largest *khāns* are grouped at the center of the *souqs*, but they now include the Ottoman customs house which very probably was built on the site of the Mamlūk customs. There are no *khāns* at the gates of Aleppo, possibly because, unlike Cairo, it was a producing not a consuming center, and taxes, generally speaking, were on imports and consumption, not on production.

At Baghdad also there is an extant medieval *khān*, the Khān Ortma, built by the Emir Amīn al-Dīn Mīrjān in 1359, which was used as a customs house by the Ottomans

A lockup market, the Bazar-i Vakīl, at Shīrāz. It dates from the 18th century, but its lighting, ventilation and open shops are typical of earlier Islamic markets. After Dieulafoy.

and which almost certainly served as the customs in the 14th and 15th centuries. However, its inscription declares it to be a *yām*, that is, a post house, with lodging, horses and spare messengers, described in detail by Marco Polo, who states that they were founded all over the Mongol dominions and that news could be transmitted ten times faster by them than by single riders riding daily stages.

Mills. Mills of all types were used in Islamic towns and the countryside, not only the Vitruvian waterwheels, like the one at Ḥamā' in northern Syria, which were evidently part of a state-financed aqueduct, but private mills for cloth fulling, felt making and, above all, paper making, which is believed to have been introduced into Islam by Chinese craftsmen captured at the Battle of Samarkand in 750 AD. Watermills almost everywhere were less frequent than animal-driven cornmills or oil-presses. But Islamic windmills also appear to have been important in any area with a strong prevailing wind. Those characteristic of Seistān (east Persia – Afghanistan), where during the summer a gale-force wind blows daily, are driven not by sails but by air vents in vertical towers which lead the wind to a

A widespread means of ventilation in Islam was the wind tower, a shaft positioned to trap the cool wind and direct it downwards into the building. The towers are particularly characteristic of the 18th- and 19th-century houses of Yazd (shown here), but many medieval buildings in Egypt, Syria and Iraq had them.

"screw," the rotation of which works the millstones. The towers have louvers to close down the mill when the wind becomes too strong. These mills are recorded as early as 1340 by the geographer Qazwīnī in the Herāt area, but their origins are obscure. In the Herāt area they are mostly cornmills, but in medieval Egypt, Morocco and Andalusia they were also used in sugar factories to crush the sugar cane. Windmills with sails are uncommon: the earliest extant windmills in Egypt appear to be those built by Napoleon to the south of Fusṭāṭ; and although they are now used in the Lebanon and at Aden to raise seawater into salt pans, this may well be a recent innovation.

Air power was so well understood in medieval Islam that it is suprising to note that windmills were not used to work irrigation pumps. But air was used to disperse encroaching sand dunes, which in many desert areas are a dangerous threat to cultivation. An enclosure of matting higher than the dune with an opening at the base is built on the side facing the prevailing wind. If a low wall is built on the other side of the dune the wind enters and disperses the dune in a whirlwind. The practice was first described in Seistān by the 10th-century historian al-Masʿūdī, and the 13th-century geographer al-Dimashqī also refers to it. Since strong winds are characteristic of desert climates the practice was doubtless widespread, though it was somewhat hazardous: it was impossible to control the direction of the whirlwind and the dune might therefore land on some other cultivated area.

Caravansarays. Although caravansarays were primarily intended to lodge travelers between towns and not as market buildings or customs houses, they are rather confusingly known as *khāns* in most of Islam, except in Persia, where the word *ribāṭ* (in the sense of "hospice") is used. Since they were often frequented by merchants they must also have been trading centers; and Balduccio Pegolotti's description of the route from the Mediterranean to Tabrīz in his *Pratica della mercatura* (1340) chiefly mentions caravansarays as posts where dues were exacted by the local authorities. However, caravansarays also served as lodgings for rulers touring their dominions; barracks or winter quarters for their troops; post houses; and, on certain routes, free accommodation for pilgrims to Mecca. The same building may often have served all these purposes.

There were certainly Byzantine and Sasanian caravansarays on the main trade routes, since the Muslim conquest moderated neither the climate nor the hazards of travel. Moreover, trade routes changed little between the reign of Justinian in the 6th century and the coming of the railway, and the assumption that on the main routes there was a *khān* at least every 15 to 20 miles, a standard day's journey over not too difficult terrain, has enabled Soviet archaeologists to plot a series of medieval caravansarays, which they date to the 10th to 12th centuries, mostly so ruined that their plans are conjectural, on the routes from Merv to Khwārizm, Bukhārā, Shāsh/Tashkent and Samarkand. Other routes could certainly be determined by plotting ruins and water holes in the deserts of Afghanistan.

The earliest dated *khān* appears to be that at Qaṣr al-Ḥayr al-Gharbī, a long stage, 37 miles, west of Palmyra. It was a mudbrick building on stone foundations, almost square, with a central colonnaded courtyard and three ranges consisting of single, long, vaulted galleries, each with two entrances. The entrance range had six rooms of varying sizes and a staircase beyond giving on to what was evidently a flat roof. The facade, which runs north-south, had two long projecting wings, the southern with a *miḥrāb*, so that it evidently served as an oratory, and the northern with a drinking trough perhaps sheltered by a wooden portico. The lintel was dated in the Roman fashion with bronze letters pegged into the stone. These have disappeared, but from the peg-holes and the grooves cut for the letters it can be read that it was erected under the Caliph Hishām in 727. There is perhaps a second Umayyad *khān* extant, at Qaṣr al-Ḥayr al-Sharqī, 40 miles, two stages, east of Palmyra. The smaller of two enclosures, its stone exterior is heavily buttressed with rounded towers, and the entrance, surmounted by a pair of turrets with elaborate decoration in brick and stucco, has a machicoulis. It has not been completely excavated, but it evidently consisted of vaulted rooms, 12 meters deep, with larger, darker rooms, perhaps magazines, at the corners, disposed round a central colonnaded courtyard, though the colonnade had evidently only a sloping wooden roof. There was a staircase in the gateway to an upper room, but the upper floor of the rest of the building, which may have been added in the ʿAbbāsid period, was never completed. It may appear odd for the gate of a *khān* to have a machicoulis, but the distinction between forts and *khān*s was never entirely clarified. And the situation of Qaṣr al-Ḥayr al-Sharqī on the eastern frontiers of the Umayyad Caliphate may have made fortification desirable.

There are also few identifiable ʿAbbāsid *khān*s, though the desert castle of Ukhayḍir in Iraq (evidently post-775) has a curious annexe in the northwestern corner of the main enclosure. It consists of a courtyard with a portico on the west side, where the entrance probably was, and a tower with a spiral staircase at the northwest corner. The east side of the courtyard is occupied by a range of rooms with pointed transverse arches. This extends northwards beyond the courtyard with eight larger vaulted rooms, one of which is a broad passageway, only half-vaulted, so that it has a forecourt. There is also a staircase leading upwards to a flat roof, and possibly also downwards to a blocked-up *sardāb* (literally, "cold water"), an underground chamber common in many Iraqi and Persian houses to which the family retreats in the hottest weather. Since this annexe is inside the palace enclosure it is not exactly a *khān*; but its plan suggests a guest-house, with stabling and accommodation for servants.

Halfway between Ukhayḍir and Kūfa, a distance of 50 miles, there is a small, very stoutly built, fortified brick *khān*, Khān ʿAtshān. Its internal plan is a rough square surrounded by rooms of various sizes, one of which Gertrude Bell identified as a kitchen. But its principal feature is a large barrel-vaulted hall, nearly 12 meters long, with a semi-domed alcove at one end which suggests a reception room. Its projecting entrance porch with grooves for a portcullis, and its rounded buttresses, suggest that it is contemporary with Ukhayḍir, and Creswell has plausibly suggested that it was a staging post for important visitors to Ukhayḍir.

In Persia there are no indisputably early caravansarays. But Niẓām al-Mulk who was assassinated in 1092, many of whose precepts in his *Siyāset-nāme* or *Book of Counsel for Kings* are clearly based upon Sasanian practice, urged the just ruler to build roads, bridges and caravansarays all over his kingdom. Even if his precepts were mainly theory, there are a number of grand caravansarays extant dating from the Great Seljuk period.

Probably the best preserved of these is Ribāṭ-i Sharaf, restored in 1154 by the wife of Sanjar, the last of the Great Seljuks, but built, perhaps in the 1120s, by one of his viziers. It consists of two courtyards, each with a grand entrance with a guardroom or pavilion above it, a *masjid* with stucco decoration and four cruciform *īwān*s (portals) fronting domed chambers. The outer courtyard is smaller and is surrounded by a continuous barrel-vaulted passage, evidently stables; its water supply was from a large vaulted brick cistern built outside the main entrance to trap the winter rains. The inner courtyard forms a self-contained unit with a central cistern and ranges of apartments including a two-bay mosque with carved and painted stucco decoration. A magnificently decorated axial *īwān*, probably approached by a flight of stairs, bears the royal restoration inscription of 1154 and suggests that it served as the royal audience chamber. The Merv-Nīshāpūr road joined the two principal cities of Sanjar's empire, and Ribāṭ-i Sharaf was almost certainly a stage on the royal road, though in the absence of the sovereign the outer courtyard doubtless accommodated government officials or prominent merchants. It does not appear to have been frequented much after the 12th century, since after the Mongol invasion this route lost its importance.

In Seljuk Anatolia there are two royal caravansarays, the Sultan Hans between Konya and Aksaray and between Kayseri and Sivas, both built about 1230 AD by the Sultan ʿAlāʾ al-Dīn Kayqubād I, which, the contemporary historians imply, served a similar purpose. But royal caravansarays in Seljuk Anatolia are in the minority (between five and seven out of a recorded total of nearly 60), and most

were built between 1200 and 1250 by emirs. One of the most splendid of these is the Karatay Han on the Kayseri-Malatya route. Like most Anatolian caravansarays it consists of a basilical hall, roofed with barrel vaulting against the winter and lit by a domed lantern over the crossing, as well as an outer rectangular courtyard surrounded by various appurtenances, which was completed in 1240 AD, perhaps ten years after the hall. Each has an elaborately decorated entrance porch. The stone walls, which are nearly five feet thick, are buttressed at the corners and along their length with three-quarter towers which give the *khān* the appearance of a fortress. However, neither the Karatay Han nor the Seljuk royal caravansarays nor Ribāṭ-i Sharaf were designed as fortresses. Unlike Khān ʿAtshān, they are not well enough equipped for defense and although both Ribāṭ-i Sharaf and the caravansarays of central Anatolia had to contend with nomad raids less than 20 years after they were built, this could not have been foreseen at the time.

The Karatay Han is particularly well documented. It was first described by a Mamlūk in the entourage of Bāybars during his Anatolian campaign of 1276–77, and

Above: the caravansaray of Ribāṭ-i Sharaf in E Persia. It probably served as a palace and staging post for Sanjar, the last of the Great Seljuks. *Below:* the main entrance to Ribāt-i Sharaf.

Above: a detail of the carved stucco decoration on the arch of the inner courtyard at Ribāṭ-i Sharaf. This courtyard was a self-contained unit with its own cistern.

Below: entrance to the covered hall of the Sultan Han near Aksaray (c. 1230). Caravansarays like this one and the Sultan Han near Kayseri served as occasional royal palaces.

the description is preserved by the 14th-century geographer al-ʿUmarī; to Pegolotti (1340) it was known as the "Gavvazera dell'Ammiraglio" (the emir's caravansaray). Its original *waqfiyya*, dated 1247, the existence of which proves that it was a charitable foundation, has also been published. Among the appurtenances of the caravansaray it specifies a paved courtyard with shops (possibly in the village nearby), stables, a bath, a *masjid*, an infirmary with an attendant doctor and a blacksmith's. Food, including a special issue of sweetmeats during the month of Ramadān, was free to all comers, though when the sultan was in residence only he was to be fed, since otherwise too much of a strain would be placed on the resources. The staff included a general supervisor, an *imām* and a muezzin whose job it was to call the faithful to prayer. There was also, exceptionally, a mausoleum attached, though this is not mentioned in the *waqfiyya*. Such was the importance of the *khān* and its situation that it almost certainly served as an entrepot in the east-west trade.

The Karatay Han is exceptional in so many ways that it is difficult to generalize from its *waqfiyya*. Other 13th-century *waqfiyya*s of Anatolian caravansarays are known, but we cannot tell whether either of the Sultan Hans was similarly endowed or exactly how they were run. Some Anatolian *khān*s, like the Hekim Han (1218) near Malatya, as their inscriptions attest, were similar to town *khān*s in that they were intended to bring in revenue. Such must also have been the case with a chain of caravansarays, one of which at Iğdir behind Mount Ararat still exists, built down the Araxes by the Mkhargrdzelis, a minor Georgian dynasty of Christianized Kurds who controlled most of Armenia (1200–36), their purpose being to tap the riches of the trade between Tabrīz and the west and to finance the Mkhargrdzelis' many rich architectural foundations. On the other hand, there is a series of 12th- to 14th-century caravansarays, identified by Sauvaget on the Aleppo-Damascus road, which appear to have been free. One of the earliest, Khān al-ʿArūs, was founded by Saladin in 1181–82 and its massive iron doors and the fountain in the center of its courtyard were described by the traveler Ibn Jubayr in 1184.

Few of the great caravansarays founded by royal command in Īl-Khānid Persia survive today. Rashīd al-Dīn (died 1318) prescribed that there should be *khāns* along all the main routes of the Mongol dominions and Qazwīnī (1340) describes many of them, though he does not always distinguish between Mongol and pre-Mongol foundations. One of the few remaining is at Sarcham (1333), near Iṣfahān. However, its inscription states merely that it was built partly at the expense of the ruler Abū Saʿīd (1316–36); we do not know whether it, or any of the others, was free. It may be that the caravansarays of central Syria were free because they were founded primarily for pilgrims on their way to Mecca; alternatively it may have been left to the discretion of the intendant: if many of the richest lodgers were Frankish or Christian merchants why should they not pay for the privilege?

What the Turks and the Mongols needed in the country was winter quarters: Siroux has demonstrated that these existed, though their plan is quite different. Two such buildings, both about 44 meters square, at Chahārābād and Dombī, one stage (20 miles) apart on the Naṭanz-Iṣfahān road, may be instanced. They consist basically of a recessed entrance giving on to a square courtyard and two ranges composed of a single long tunnel vault with numerous transverse arches on brick piers, with a fireplace in one corner so that, in principle, they could be heated in winter. The other two sides of the courtyard housed separate buildings, each with its own entrance, one of which may have been a kitchen. Both are jerry-built, though that at Dombī has traces of stucco decoration characteristic of the period 1315–25. Siroux's discoveries will doubtless lead to others. They are demonstrably not caravansarays; however, they are not large enough to house a considerable body of men in winter quarters, and may therefore have been intended as post houses.

Except for Mamlūk Syria (14th and 15th centuries) there is a dearth of caravansarays after the Mongol period. In Persia none are known till the Ṣafawid period (16th or 17th century), while in Turkey there are few pre-15th-century Ottoman foundations. However, one further building, apparently never finished, which has been described as a caravansaray, deserves mention, at Yarbekir Kale in Khwārizm west of the Oxus. The building is a square divided into four by two main passageways which intersect at right angles, each quadrant consisting of a square courtyard surrounded by rooms. But it can hardly have been a caravansaray, since these rooms open on to the main passageway also and surround the building opening outwards; and there is neither enclosure wall nor main entrance, so that it can hardly have been a barracks housing a garrison. It most resembles one of the markets built in 15th-century Ottoman Istanbul, but a building of its size (200 meters square) would scarcely have been appropriate even to the capital of Khwārizm, Urgench, the market building of which excited the admiration of Yāqūt in the 13th century. The effects of the Mongol invasion on the population of Khwārizm are described in horrific detail by 13th-century historians, but however much they exaggerate, Yarbekir Kale appears to have been away from any large town. What, then, can the building have been?

The ʿAbbāsid caliphs had Turkish slave (*mamlūk*) armies as early as the 9th century, and their successors continued the practice. It reached its most highly organized form in the Mamlūk states of Egypt and Syria (13th to 16th centuries), in which the military commanders, the highest court officials and many of the sultans were manumitted slaves. No Muslim can be enslaved and Mamlūks were therefore imported from areas sufficiently far away for the fiction that they were pagan to be plausibly maintained, mostly in this later period from the Lands of the Golden Horde, which stretched from the Crimea to the Oxus. This area was Muslim by 1260, but much of the nomadic Turkish population must still have remained pagan. In any case, parents, seeing enslavement as the path to advancement, willingly sold their children to the official slave merchants of the Mamlūk state. The demand was always considerable, for the Turkish element in the ʿAbbāsid armies numbered tens of thousands, while the Mamlūk sultans of Egypt purchased a new lot of Mamlūks of their own when they succeeded to the throne. Little is known of the demography of Khwārizm between the 10th and the 15th centuries, but the "pagans" would have to be collected together from a very wide area, and the enormous building at Yarbekir Kale may have been intended as a mustering center.

The Art of Islamic Calligraphy

VISUAL STORY

The importance accorded Islamic calligraphy, even by those who cannot read it, is baffling. Calligraphers were rightly esteemed, but for a sound practical reason: there was no printing in Islam till the 18th century, and without constant encouragement fine hands would have died out. But the inflated claims of Muslim calligraphers, like the Qāḍī Aḥmad in his treatise of 1606, concerned to demonstrate the distinction of their profession, have frequently been taken literally by Western writers, particularly regarding its decorative value to which they sometimes attach a mystical significance. Islamic calligraphy is indeed decorative, but no more so than Western calligraphy, and often adopts similar means such as animated scripts or plaiting, used both in Kufic and in broken Gothic capitals.

The Arabic alphabet (used also for Persian, Urdu and Ottoman Turkish) developed, it is now thought, from Syriac: it is essentially a cursive script, reading from right to left, without a majuscule. A handful of letter types, generally distinguished by dots above or below, make up the consonants and long vowels; the short vowels are indicated by pointing (*ḥaraka*) but are often omitted. Most of the letters have three forms – initial, medial and final – but the initial forms are only emphasized in *thuluth*. In illuminated manuscripts, therefore, whole-page illuminations take the place of the illuminated initials of contemporary Western manuscripts.

Scripts are square ("Kufic") or rounded (*naskhī*, *thuluth; nastaʿliq*, a Persian hand, is not known before 1388 and is not used on architecture before the 16th century). These terms apply partly to the forms of the letters and partly to the line: Kufic is steadily horizontal, often with a weighted base; the round scripts form lines composed of a series of loops. Kufic is more illegible than the rounded scripts and had plainly become archaic as a current hand over most of Islam by the 12th century, except in the West where it survived as *Maghribī*. But, with the exception of foundation inscriptions or decrees carved on mosques, legibility was rarely a prime requirement in Islamic inscriptions. The Koran was usually known by heart; chancery scribes prided themselves upon their ability to read undotted Arabic; royal decrees, like those of many Western chanceries, often appear all the grander for being not wholly legible; and they are correspondingly more difficult to forge.

Above: ivory box (*pyxis*) bearing an inscription in the name of a son of the Caliph ʿAbd-al Raḥmān III (Cordova, dated 968 AD). Musée du Louvre, Paris. The severe Kufic inscription is not decoration but a title of ownership.
Below: leaf from a Koran (Sūra XXVI): characteristic oblong format with Kufic typical of 10th-century Iraq (British Library MS. Or. 1397).

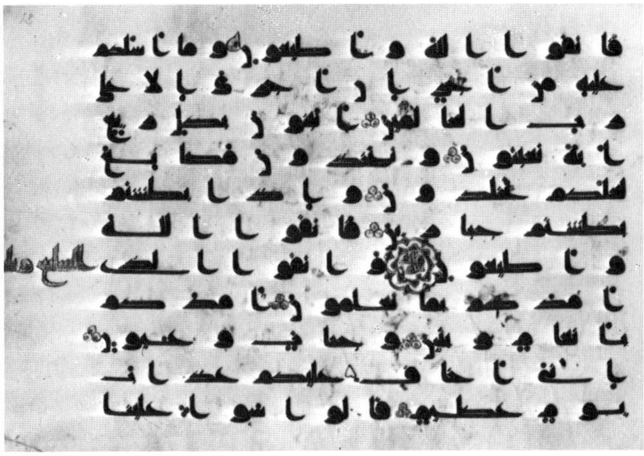

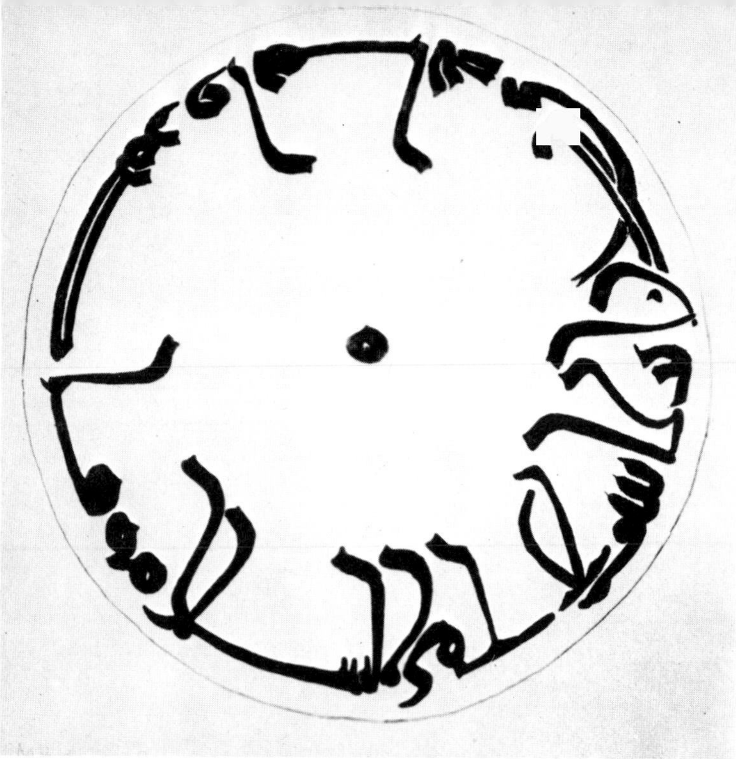

Above: page of a Koran, possibly Persian, 11th or 12th century. Two dated Korans (1073 at Mashhad, and 1171, National Library, Cairo) give plausible termini for this elegant, stylized, rather illegible script. The Koran was so often learned by heart that legibility was not a prime requirement. Such virtuoso Korans are the pious work of eminent calligraphers and they cannot therefore be used as a norm for the development of Islamic scripts.

Above left: inscription from a flat "Sāmānid" dish in a Japanese collection, painted in black slip on a plain white ground. The type was made in Afrāsiyāb and Nīshāpūr (and perhaps elsewhere) in the 10th and 11th centuries (and perhaps later). Although in thick black slip, not ink, these inscriptions often imitate book hands and must have been written with an instrument cut like a pen. They are mostly stilted Arabic proverbs, apparently chosen so that the ascenders form fairly regular radii. This preference for appearance over sense is exceptional, as is the genuinely calligraphic character.

Left: Mesopotamian tin-glazed bowl, 9th to 11th centuries, Damascus Museum. Slip-painting or carving were the ideal methods of inscribing medieval Islamic pottery since the inscriptions and their decoration kept their sharpness.

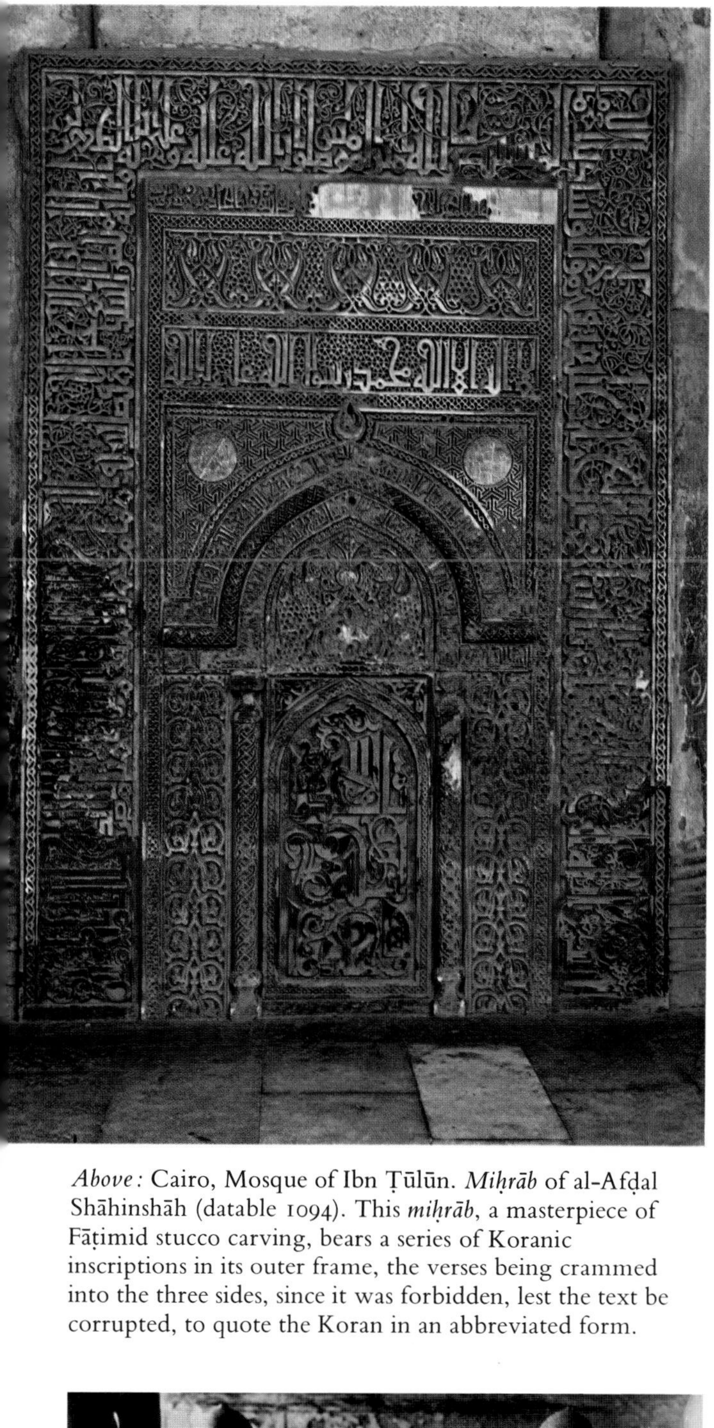

Above: Cairo, Mosque of Ibn Ṭūlūn. *Miḥrāb* of al-Afḍal Shāhinshāh (datable 1094). This *miḥrāb*, a masterpiece of Fāṭimid stucco carving, bears a series of Koranic inscriptions in its outer frame, the verses being crammed into the three sides, since it was forbidden, lest the text be corrupted, to quote the Koran in an abbreviated form.

Above: part of a terracotta inscription frieze from a foundation near Khwāf, Khurāsān, of the Seljuk vizier, Niẓām al-Mulk (assassinated 1092), not from a Niẓāmiyya *madrasa* as was formerly thought. The base line is probably weighted for better legibility from the ground. The heavily foliated serifs of the ascenders are characteristic of east Persian 12th-century inscriptions. Teheran Museum.

Above: the foundation inscription of glazed turquoise on a terracotta ground from the recently discovered Ghūrid *īwān* (c. 1200) of the Great Mosque at Herāt. Foundation inscriptions on the front arches of major Islamic monuments are a common way of drawing attention to the founder.

Left: carved marble Koranic inscription. Cenotaph of the Mamlūk Sultan al-Mu'ayyad in his mosque (1415–21) at the Bāb Zuwayla in Cairo. Al-Mu'ayyad acquired marble from many sources: the present inscription is the kerb of a tomb datable c. 950. This exaggeratedly stylized Kufic was much admired in Mamlūk Cairo.

Above: Dāmghān, Pīri-i ʿAlamdār mausoleum (1027). Painted inscription from the interior. After Pope. An example of calligraphy in which the actual inscription is of less importance than its ascenders which are plaited or broken and have decorative finials with pendant ornaments as if they were miniature lamp-posts. For the sake of regularity, false ascenders have been added to terminal letters or as finials to the letters in the middle of words.

Right: Ribāṭ-i Sharaf, Khurāsān. *Masjid* of inner courtyard (c. 1125). Stucco *miḥrāb* with a double Koranic inscription frame. The shafts of the letters of the inner inscriptions are elaborately plaited, yet the decoration is not allowed to obscure the content of the inscription. Whereas it is usual to dot and point Kufic Korans completely, there are few Kufic inscriptions with dots and points.

Below: a *Maghribī* Koran made in 1568 for ʿAbd Allāh, second Sharīfī sultan of Morocco (British Library MS. Or. 1405). *Maghribī* remained the principal manuscript hand in the West from the 12th to the 18th century. It keeps the uninterrupted horizontal line of Kufic while rounding many of the letters and adding particularly recognizable swirling terminations to many final letters.

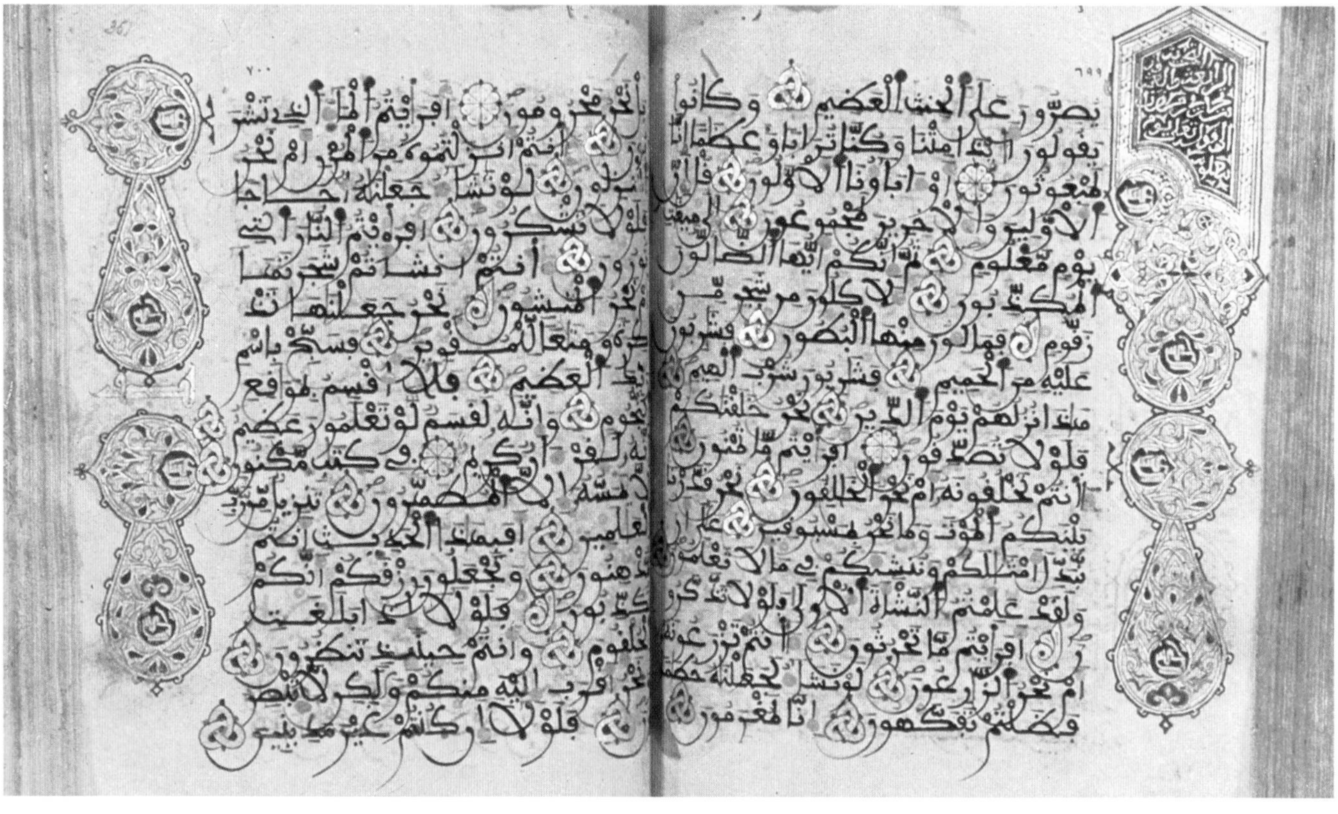

One common, though remote, derivative of Kufic is "square Kufic" (mostly 13th century and later). In Persia it was probably inspired by earlier uses of Kufic to form stars as in the mausoleum of Öljeytü at Sulṭānīye (*above left*) (1310–16). The square variety is so illegible that only the most stereotyped formulas could be used, for example in the Great Mosque of Yazd (*above right*) (decoration of 1375).

Below left: initial illuminated page of a Koran written in 1304 (British Library MS. Add. 22406).

Below: great stucco Koranic frieze from the *qibla īwān* of the Mosque of Sultan Ḥasan, Cairo (1356–62). The script is the stylized Kufic of contemporary illuminated Korans.

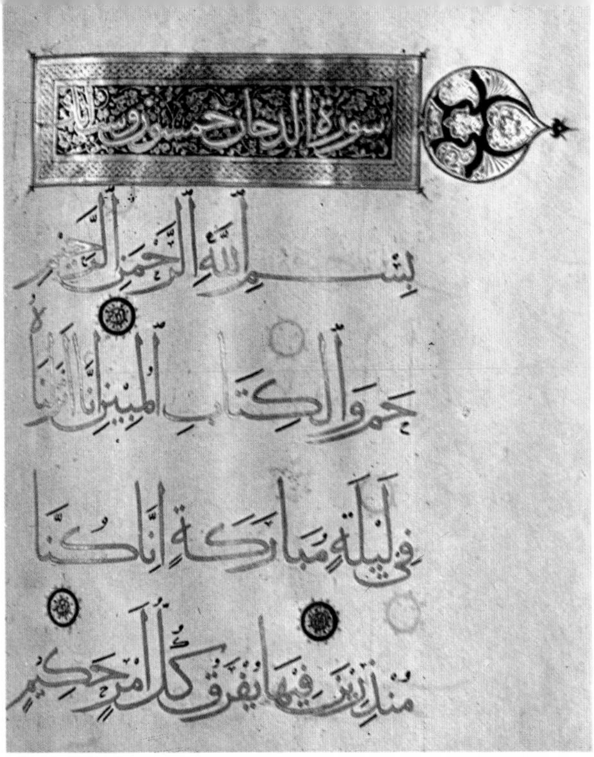

A *thuluth* Koran written and illuminated at Mosul in 1310 for the Īl-Khān Öljeytü (British Library MS. Or. 4945). Mamlūk represents in many respects the ideal of Islamic calligraphy – free, elegant, easily written and legible and equally suitable for manuscript, movable objects and architecture.

Above: inscription in turquoise on a luxuriantly carved terracotta ground from the Great Mosque at Ashtarjān, Persia (1315). This is midway between the terracotta inscriptions (mausolea at Uzgend 1152, 1186) of the pre-Mongol period and the glazed carved terracotta inscriptions of the Shāh-i Zinde. These all employ square as well as rounded scripts, though they are kept separate, and the more important inscriptions are invariably rounded.

Koranic scripts sometimes play such a large part in the decoration of mosques or other pious foundations that it is tempting to use them to interpret buildings. For the most part, however, the texts are too stereotyped to allow this, compare the *thuluth* relief inscriptions, probably gilt, of the Blue Mosque at Tabrīz (*left*) (1465), now ruined but the only building of its period in western Persia. Note the extension of some letters to form long horizontal lines, a characteristic of Persian and Turkish monumental inscriptions from the later 15th century onwards.

Right: the Bobrinsky "Kettle" from Herāt, 1163 (Hermitage Museum, Leningrad). Cast bronze inlaid with silver and copper. This small cauldron is noteworthy both for the scenes of court life it depicts including a game of chess and for its inscription bands in a variety of scripts. Those in *naskhī* (top and bottom) are squat and of unvarying thickness, but have shafts in the form of human heads. In the later 12th and 13th centuries these animated scripts developed till the animation took over entirely, and even the most banal *naskhī* inscriptions are barely legible ("Everlasting Glory"). Both Kufic and *naskhī* were animated, though the latter persisted longer.

Left: iron key inlaid with gold presented to the Kaʿba by Faraj ibn Barqūq, Mamlūk sultan of Egypt, probably to commemorate restoration works there completed in 1405 (Musée du Louvre, Paris, No. 6738). The inscriptions comprise a commemorative text in the name of Faraj and appropriate Koranic verses.

Below: block printed linen from Mamlūk Egypt (14th century) with a bold *naskhī* inscription on a ground of scrolls bearing animals' heads (Islamic Museum, Cairo, No. 14472). Although it is common for Kufic inscriptions to be decorated with plaiting or foliated terminals, manuscript hands in rounded script are never decorated.

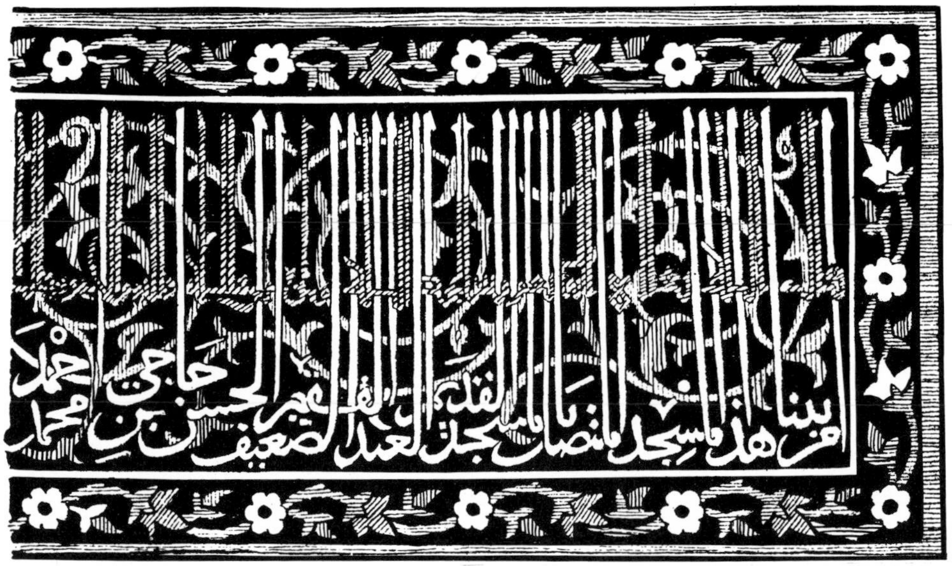

The *ṭughrā*, the ornamental "monogram" of the Ottoman sultans authenticating imperial decrees, deliberately formal and illegible, is a compound of the sultan's name and genealogy, highly compressed like that of Murad III (*right*) (1590) (Museum für Islamische Kunst, East Berlin). The Seljuk *ṭughrā*, known only from 11th-century coins, was in the form of a bow and arrow, but a type of *thuluth* with enormously elongated shafts became known as *ṭughrāī* in the Mamlūk chancery where it did duty for the sultan's signature (*below*). Exceptionally, this script was used in architecture, for example in the Great Mosque at Abarqūh, central Persia, for the foundation inscription of a 15th-century *miḥrāb* (*above*). Here, across the *ṭughrāī* inscription, runs a Koranic inscription in stylized Kufic. This combination was frequent in Mongol stucco inscriptions in Persia but is rare in Egypt and unknown on documents. After Pope.

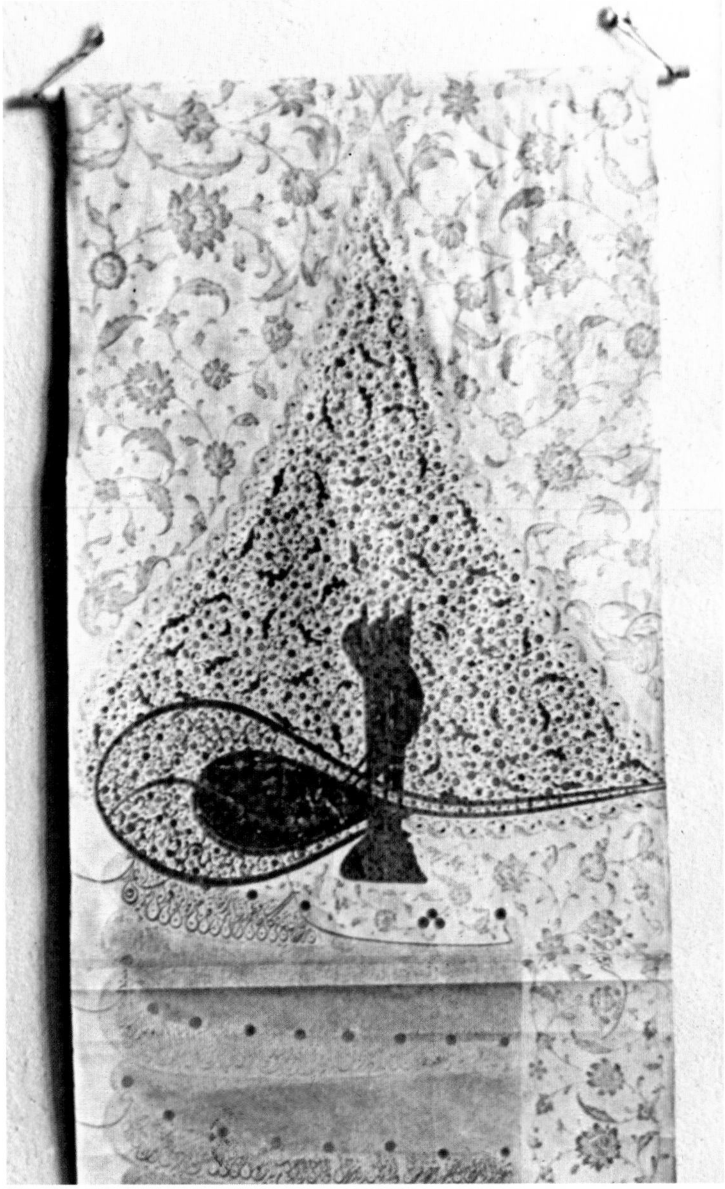

4. Religion, Education and Mysticism

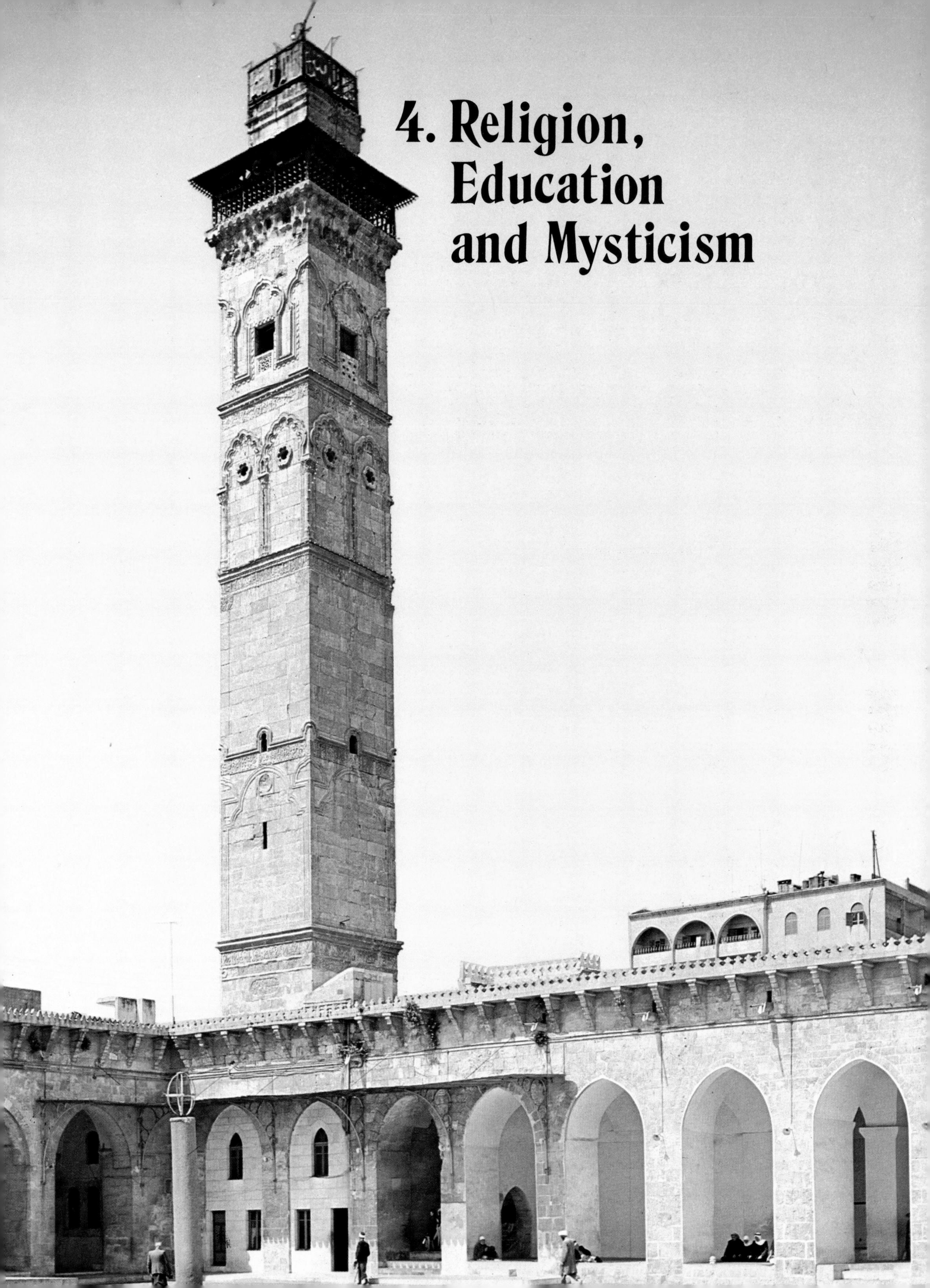

Mosques

A European medieval archaeologist, accustomed to every theological nuance, might well interpret church architecture in liturgical terms; but Islam is devoid of liturgy, which cannot, therefore, be used to explain radical innovations. On the contrary, Islamic theology is so conservative ("innovation" (*bidʿa*) is a common term for heresy) that important developments were probably too gradual to attract the theologians' notice, or else have been very carefully justified by reference to the rich and often spurious body of Islamic Tradition. Individual mosques, therefore, often diverge considerably from the norm.

The five daily prayers may be said anywhere facing the *qibla* (the direction of Mecca), or in special oratories (*masjids*) erected as pious works. Only on Friday was attendance at the great mosque compulsory for every adult free man. Early mosques therefore were buildings capable of accommodating the greater part of a town's population, with the whole *qibla* wall facing Mecca, normally with a niche in the center of it (the *miḥrāb*) at which stood the Imām, leading the prayers. To the right of the *miḥrāb* is the *minbar*, a pulpit from which a Friday sermon in the ruler's name, the *khuṭba*, is preached. The area adjoining the *qibla* is normally covered and the floor strewn with carpets or mats on which the faithful pray barefoot after ritual ablution outside the mosque. From a minaret the call to prayer is given five times daily by a muezzin. Larger mosques also employed *muwaqqitīn* (timekeepers) to undertake the calculation of the times for prayer, since in medieval Islam the day and night were customarily divided into 12 hours each. Yet this deceptively simple description glides over some formidable difficulties. Mosques naturally vary in plan with climate and period; nevertheless, the variation is less than in, for example, domestic architecture, and their component parts – *qibla* arcades for prayers, a *miḥrāb*, a *minbar* and a minaret – are standard.

Mosques do not give sanctuary, nor are they legally holy ground. All *waqf* constructions, despite their endowment in perpetuity, tend to be short-lived because the endowments are not immune to inflation. Nevertheless, there is something paradoxical in the fact that mosques, particularly royal foundations, built for the purpose of proclaiming the ruler's or the caliph's authority, should not be considered as state works. This is all the more striking, since the privilege of housing the Friday prayer, the *khuṭba*, was severely controlled, and the installation of a *minbar* was a matter of political concern. Initially only the major capitals of the Umayyad state were allowed them, and only granted them in 749–50: subsequently it was rare to find more than one Friday mosque in a city.

Previous page: the minaret of the Great Mosque at Aleppo built in 1089 by the Seljuk governor for the Sultan Malikshāh. Square minarets are typically Syrian but the carved stone decoration is exceptionally rich.

The first mosques. Cairo and Baghdad were exceptional because of their size. In Cairo the Mosque of ʿAmr at Fusṭāṭ (founded in 640–41; rebuilt in 698–99, 750, 827, between 1260 and 1277, in 1401–02, 1798 and, most recently, with cast concrete columns, in 1973) was supplemented by the Mosque of Ibn Ṭūlūn (completed in 879), then by the Mosque of al-Azhar (970–72), the Mosque of al-Ḥākim (990–1013) and the Mosque of Baybars (1266–69). Only one of these, al-Azhar, lost the *khuṭba*, when the mosque of al-Ḥākim was inaugurated, and did not receive it back till Baybars' restoration of 1266–67. These five *khuṭba* mosques were evidently justified by the pressure of population, as well as their considerable distance from Fusṭāṭ. Subsequently, the *khuṭba* was very much extended, possibly because, as Yāqūt observed in 13th-century Merv, certain mosques were attended only by one rite, and in the 14th century the Citadel of Cairo was ringed by splendid mosques built by Mamlūk emirs, of which that of al-Māridānī (1339–40) is probably the best preserved. With a diversity of Friday mosques it is perhaps less surprising that some fall into disuse; but in Aleppo, according to Sibṭ ibn al-ʿAjamī, the Great Mosque was only restored after the Mongol invasions of 1258–59 because people voluntarily annexed their own *waqfs* to it.

On the Islamic conquests many standing buildings were appropriated as mosques, including the tomb of Cyrus at Pasargadae, and basilical halls at Iṣṭakhr and Qazwīn, the latter with bull-headed capitals attributed to Muḥammad ibn al-Ḥajjāj who died in 710, like those of the more famous *apadana* of the Achaemenid palace at Persepolis, which attracted the attention of the early Muslim geographers. The great *īwān* at Ctesiphon was first used as a prayer place, and explicit instructions were given that its wall paintings were not to be damaged. And at Jerusalem, before the construction of the first Aqṣā Mosque on the Temple Mount, the steps and narthex of the basilica of Constantine were used. The appropriation of local palaces or shrines as mosques emphasized the triumph of Islam, and the transformation of the church of Haghia Sophia into a mosque immediately upon the Turkish conquest of Constantinople in 1453 is typical of Muslim practice in 7th-century Syria and Iraq. Even in the 12th century an acknowledged pagan monument, the Temple of Bel at Palmyra, was turned into a mosque (1132–33) and two fine *miḥrābs*, now in the Damascus Museum, were added.

Few existing buildings, however, were suitable to accommodate the mass of people required to hear the *khuṭba* which was initially a political allocution and not the theological or moral discourse it became under the ʿAbbāsids. At Ḥamā' in Syria a Christian basilica was turned 90 degrees on its axis to face Mecca, so that the congregation faced its length, which certainly helped acoustics. However, in the new cities founded at Fusṭāṭ or at Baṣra, Kūfa and Wāsiṭ in Mesopotamia new solutions had to be evolved. Much attention has been given to these early mosques, which were mostly stockaded or sur-

Above: the Umayyad Great Mosque at Damascus (714–15), a view from the SW showing the Bayt al-Māl (treasury) and the arcades surrounding the courtyard. The NE minaret (shown) is built on one of the four corner towers of the enceinte of the Temple of Jupiter.

Right: mosaic of a tree in the courtyard of the mosque at Damascus. The mosque was formerly covered with similar mosaics but almost all perished in the disastrous fire of 1893.

rounded by a ditch, but the most interesting early *building* is the Umayyad mosque of al-Walīd at Damascus (714–15) which, despite substantial restoration by the Seljuk Sultan Malikshāh (1082–83) and rebuilding after a serious fire in 1893, is typical of a series of Umayyad mosques. It replaced a prayer place within the rectangular enceinte of the Roman temple of Jupiter Damascenus where a Byzantine basilica had been built. This was razed and an oblong three-aisled basilica built on its *qibla* side with a raised crossing fronted by a gabled pediment leading to the *miḥrāb* niche which was very probably preceded by a dome. The remaining area became an arcaded courtyard, with a fountain and a domed treasury, and the four corner towers of the temple enceinte evidently served as minarets. The decoration of split-marble paneling and mosaics on a gold ground did not survive the fire of 1893, except for part of the courtyard arcades, where the elegance of the imaginary palaces and villages set among trees gives some idea of the magnificence of the mosaics in the *qibla* part.

Sauvaget has pointed out the importance of al-Walīd's restoration, or rather rebuilding, of the mosque at Medina, which was Muhammad's own house (707–09), in the planning of the mosque at Damascus. The Prophet's house was never intended as a place of prayer, but rapidly became sacred in Muslim eyes, and respect for its original plan led to some irregularities. The prayer hall was equally richly decorated with marble and mosaics, but, as Sauvaget has brilliantly shown, it also incorporated a raised crossing, a *miḥrāb* niche and four minarets. In all this, liturgy was far less important than secular ceremonial. Umayyad mosques were tribunals, where even the heads of criminals might be exposed; treasuries, though these became redundant when the ʿAbbāsids discontinued their subventions to the Bedouin; armories; and above all public audience halls, where the ruler sat enthroned in state holding a stave or a weapon in his right hand, wearing the secular headdress, the *qalansuwa*, not a turban, and surrounded by his ministers and his personal bodyguard. The *miḥrāb* represents an original niche for the throne (*minbar*), and only when the *minbar* increased in size and was placed within a wooden enclosure (the *maqṣūra*) to the side did it become independent. The central aisle approaching the *miḥrāb* would then have remained empty, but lined for reasons of security by the bodyguard.

It might be objected that this made mosques indistinguishable from palaces. Architecturally, however, these early elements of mosque architecture are very different from throne rooms (see chapter 5); and no Muslim would have been confused because only the mosque was a place of general assembly (*jāmiʿ* – though the term is not regularly used for mosques before the 10th century and does not become frequent in inscriptions till the 12th). The domed pavilions on baroque profiled arches of Mamlūk *minbars* suggest the crowns and veils of Islamic palace ceremonial, and Ibn Jubayr's description of Mecca in the late 12th century (see chapter 6) shows that the tradition was not forgotten. Equally, the severe restriction of the *khuṭba* to certain mosques up to the 14th century emphasizes the prime association of mosques with the sovereign.

The miḥrāb. Nevertheless, the *miḥrāb* came to have an importance which cannot be attributed to a forgotten tradition of early Islamic ceremonial. It was never an apse, since the whole *qibla* wall was oriented towards Mecca; it was too small to decorate the mosque; and it was often invisible, blocked from view by piers, as in Ibn Ṭūlūn's mosque. Yet a small marble *miḥrāb* was placed underneath the Dome of the Rock, very probably when it was built (691–92). That of al-Walīd at Medina, though small, had gold mosaics, marble paneling, a Sasanian trophy known as "the Mirror of Chosroes" and the only lamp in the building hanging before it, an association which was to become important, since *miḥrābs* are often decorated with carved images of a mosque-lamp. Thereafter, *miḥrābs* are often highly decorated.

The mosaics of the *miḥrāb* of al-Ḥakam II added in 965 to the Great Mosque at Cordova suggest the effect intended by the almost contemporary *miḥrāb* (now restored conjecturally) of al-Mutawakkil's mosque at Sāmarrā (848–52). There is a long series of stucco *miḥrābs*, like that added by the vizier al-Afḍal to the mosque of Ibn Ṭūlūn (1094), continuing into the 14th century, with terracotta and stucco confections like that in the mosque at Ashtarjān (1315) near Iṣfahān. Wood paneling was also used, both at Aleppo and also in Persia, at Ābyāne in the mountains near Naṭanz (1103) and in Afghanistan, for example that at Charkh-i Logar near Ghazna recently discovered by an Italian mission. In 13th-century Anatolia ceramic mosaic is used, perhaps the finest being that of the Arslanhane Mosque (1289) at Ankara, while in Persia there are luster-painted tile *miḥrābs* manufactured in 13th-century Kāshān, and later also tile mosaic. In general, *miḥrāb* decoration becomes more splendid as the memory of the original Umayyad court ceremonial fades.

Miḥrābs also became popular as memorials: that under the Dome of the Rock was very probably of this type. *Miḥrāb*-like tombstones in wood or marble are reasonable enough, since the body must be oriented in the tomb and many vaults contain *miḥrābs* in their *qibla* walls. But al-

The Mosque of Ṣāḥib Ātā/Laranda Mosque at Konya (1258). The entrance originally had two minarets. The interior, which contains a fine ceramic *miḥrāb*, backs on to the mausoleum and *khānqāh* of the founder.

A luster-painted *miḥrāb* dated 1226 and signed by the craftsman Ḥasan b. ʿArabshāh al-naqqāsh from the Masjid-i Maydān, Kāshān (Persia). Islamisches Museum, East Berlin.

A limestone *minbar* in the Khānqāh of Faraj ibn Barqūq (1401–11) in the Eastern Cemetery, Cairo, presented by the Mamlūk Sultan Qāyt Bāy in 1483. Stone *minbars* first occur in mid-14th-century Cairo when they are mostly inlaid with marble or porphyry.

Afḍal commemorated his father's restoration of Ibn Ṭūlūn by erecting a *miḥrāb*, as did Lājīn in 1296, who not only redecorated the original one, but added two of his own, one in the *qibla* wall known now as the "*Miḥrāb* of Sayyida Nafīsa," and one on the pier opposite al-Afḍal's, which was an exact copy of it in all but the Shīʿī profession of faith. The Fāṭimid Caliph al-Āmir presented a portable wooden *miḥrāb* to the mosque of al-Azhar (1126). The Mongol Öljeytü made the *miḥrāb* of the winter mosque he built on to the Great Mosque at Isfahān the focal point of his building; and the Ḥaram al-Sharīf at Jerusalem is dotted with Mamlūk and Ottoman open-air *miḥrābs* erected by the pious. In later Mamlūk Egypt and Syria, moreover, there is an evident concern for the *exact* orientation of mosques towards Mecca. The requirement had not always been strictly observed, and in Fāṭimid and Ayyūbid Cairo there are often errors of between 30 and 45 degrees. The obvious conclusion, that *miḥrābs* were holy in themselves and that the *miḥrāb* was therefore the most sacred spot in a mosque, is borne out neither by the jurists nor by modern experience: *miḥrābs* are in no sense Islamic altars.

The minbar. *Miḥrābs* were inessential, liturgically redundant and mostly invisible, yet attracted Muslim pietism. *Minbars*, on the contrary, were essential to mosques, since they were the pulpits from which the essential *khuṭba* was given; yet their much less marked evolution from the 9th to the 15th century suggests that they were often ignored. They are high thrones, either with a back, like that from the Mosque of the Andalusians at Fez/Fās, or with a domed canopy, like that of Lājīn (1296) in the mosque of Ibn Ṭūlūn, approached by a steep staircase with

Above: the minaret of Masʿūd III at Ghazna, Afghanistan (c. 1100). Remains of a second story were still visible a century ago.

Left: the minaret of the Great Mosque of al-Mutawakkil at Sāmarrā (848–52) perhaps inspired by ancient Mesopotamian ziggurats. The spiral ramp steepens in pitch towards the top to allow for stories of equal size.

balustrades set on a triangular base usually through an entrance set in a decorated frame. Even the earliest were wood and were hollow, often with a hinged door in the base, very probably repositories for manuscripts of the Koran.

Although the jurists constantly reiterated the tradition that the Prophet's throne at Medina had six steps, very few craftsmen appear to have cared, since most *minbars* have many more. From the late 11th century onwards they were regularly constructed in Egypt of *mashrabiyya*, turned wooden screenwork, and carved panels inset into a wooden skeleton. The earliest of this type is at Hebron (1091: see chapter 6), but there are equally fine *minbars* in the Great Mosque at Marrakesh, the Kutubiyya (1125–30), which was only brought out on Fridays, several from 12th- and 13th-century Turkey and a long series of 14th- and 15th-century *minbars* still in place in the mosques of Cairo. Stone *minbars* also appear in 14th-century Cairo, notably in the mosque of Āqsunqur (1346–47), with balusters of carved marble and polychrome veneer in hard stone on the sides, and in the mosque of Sultan Ḥasan (see Visual Story). Although they are, naturally, no longer hollow, they almost all have the space at the rear closed by a hinged wooden door. Wooden *minbars* were so liable to destruc-

The Quṭb Minār (begun 1191–92) attached to the Quwwat al-Islām Mosque, Delhi. The upper stories are later additions. Exceptionally it bears Sanskrit as well as Arabic inscriptions.

The minaret at Jām, central Afghanistan (c. 1200). The photograph shows the lowest of its three tiers, a tapering brick shaft faced with panels of terracotta in inscription borders.

tion by fire that it is dangerous to generalize from the areas where they are still most abundant. Nevertheless, they are rarely recorded in Persia.

The minaret. Another feature which rapidly came to be associated with mosque architecture was the minaret. There were towers to call the faithful to prayer possibly as early as 665 or 673, when the mosques at Kūfa and Fusṭāṭ respectively were rebuilt, but there was nothing sacred about them and in the reign of Hishām (724–43) a *qāḍī* ordered their destruction at Kūfa. The Syrian type from the Umayyad period up to the 12th century, widespread both in Persia and in the Maghrib, at Cordova (951–52) or Seville (1172–98), was directly inspired by the square Roman towers of the enceinte of the Umayyad mosque at Damascus and elsewhere. The widespread custom of small pavilions on the mosque roof from which the call to prayer is given – in Aden, the Yemen, parts of southwest Persia, including Sīrāf, and Anatolia – is both closer to original Islamic practice and more practical. At the mosque of Sultan Ḥasan in Cairo, where the twin minarets above the entrance were never completed, a chorus of muezzins gave the call to prayer from the steps in front.

But the history of mosques can be taken as the history of enormous impractical minarets. The minarets of the mosque of al-Mutawakkil (848–52) and Abū Dulāf (860–61) at Sāmarrā with exterior spiral ramps tapering up stories of equal height, the latter reached by a covered passage from the mosque, are structually so extraordinary that they require no decoration. But from the time of the minaret of Qayrawān (perhaps 724–27 if not rebuilt in 836) onwards there is a constant tendency in minarets to exaggerate height, materials and decoration, at the expense of practical utility. Besides the square Syrian type, of which the minaret of the Great Mosque at Aleppo (1089) is both the tallest and the finest, there are cylindrical or octagonal minarets, like those of al-Ḥākim in Cairo. The most remarkable early eastern minarets are those in brick at Ghazna, especially that of Masʿūd III (c. 1100), a high flanged base with the remains of a tapering cylinder above still visible a century ago, and the minaret at Jām in central Afghanistan (c. 1200) roughly 180 feet high with three tapering tiers. They are outdone by the Quṭb Minār at Delhi (begun in 1191–92), five tapering tiers in stone.

Another innovation was multiple minarets, particularly in pairs over an entrance. The two-minaret porch of the mosque of Sultan Ḥasan (see Visual Story) could not be completed, and the twin minarets of the mosque of al-Mu'ayyad (1415–20) on the Fāṭimid Bāb Zuwayla gave endless trouble before they were finally stabilized. In 14th-century Persia minarets also frequently collapsed because they were too high, and only in contemporary Cairo, where minarets were of sharply differentiated stories – square base, octagonal shaft and cylindrical pavilion, crowned from 1340 onwards by a bulbous finial remarkably similar to the bulbous domes of contemporary *minbars* – was a successful tradition of minaret construction maintained. The concern for height and decoration is comprehensible enough as a way of emphasizing the importance of the mosque from a distance, even if it makes the duties of the muezzin impossible.

The facade and porch. Minarets attract attention from outside, *miḥrābs* from inside, yet neither were essential to any mosque. Mosque entrances have a similarly paradoxical history. Although early mosque facades are often crenellated, or even, in the case of the mosque of al-Mutawakkil at Sāmarrā, have glass windows, entrances are often inconspicuous. Facades in Andalusia, for example the mosque at Toledo, now the Cristo de la Luz (999–1000), owe as much to Visigothic as to Islamic art. But a few earlier entrances, in particular that of the Great Mosque at Mahdiyya (c. 916), show striking similarities to Roman triumphal arches.

In Syria it is more difficult to say. The Umayyad mosque was left untouched by the Zengids, who built so much in 12th-century Damascus, and the Great Mosque at Aleppo has no grand entrance. Elsewhere, however, stalactite porches of steadily increasing grandeur, which they attached to their *madrasas*, hospitals and *khānqāhs*, were finally adopted for mosques and in this form penetrated into Seljuk Anatolia, for example in the mosque of Ṣāḥib Ātā at Konya (1258), with pre-Islamic marble sarcophagi at its base and a pair of brick minarets above. The most bizarre of these porches are those of the mosque at Divriği (1228) and the east porch of the mosque of Sunqur Āghā at Niğde (1334–35), a combination of early 13th-century Crusader Gothic and a flattened version of 13th-century Seljuk.

In Cairo, mosque porches of the 14th century adapted the Syrian innovation, and in contemporary Persia, where they were adapted from Anatolia, they rapidly became the most conspicuous part of the mosque, increasingly brilliantly decorated with a ceramic mosaic revetment. The porch of the Great Mosque at Yazd is so much higher than the rest of the mosque that it has complicated masonry buttresses behind it to hold it up. Probably begun in 1329–40, its tile decoration continued till 1375–76, though the pair of spindly minarets which pile Pelion upon Ossa are probably later (1435–52). Monumental porches were, if anything, monuments to founders, for it was here that the foundation inscription, legibly written and situated so as to be read by all, was fixed. They were, therefore, a more or less blatant form of display.

Fountains and timepieces. There are certain inessential features of mosques which nevertheless constantly recur, in particular, fountains or pools under domed canopies. That in the mosque of Ibn Ṭūlūn was evidently originally a gilt domed pentagon with windows in the drum surrounded by an octagonal arcade covering a marble pool with a fountain (burned down in 986). The roof had a teak parapet and bore a sundial. It was eventually replaced in 1296 by a monumental construction with a brick dome with a staircase up to a sundial on the roof. To judge from the Koranic inscriptions in the interior which relate to purification, the fountain was used for minor ablutions, which should normally have been made before entering the mosque. Such fountains occur all over Islam, usually under light domes, and to judge from contemporary reports that they were used for serving sherbet on the inauguration of a mosque, were not generally used for ablutions before the Ottoman conquests.

Mosques also contained elaborate timepieces, more than toys, since the determination of prayer times was a serious business, but nevertheless automata designed to delight as well as work. The most elaborate were perhaps those in the Masjid-i Waqt-u Sāʿat at Yazd (c. 1325), but that at Damascus in the late 12th century has been most illuminatingly described by Ibn Jubayr, who visited it in 1184. It consisted of an arched gallery with 12 inset brass arcades for each hour of the day and night. On the hour a ball fell from two falcons' beaks into a cup, with a sound like a bell, and doors in the appropriate arcade closed to mark the hour. For the night hours there were tympana above each door with a lamp floating on water set to drip for an hour, so that when the level fell the flame showed and every hour another window was lit up. Eleven men were required to regulate the mechanism.

Mosque plans. Consideration of mosque plans has been deliberately left to the last. Western Orientalists, convinced that Christian architecture closely reflects each liturgical change, have been far too inclined to interpret later mosque plans in terms of changes of ritual, for which Islam makes no provision. As Sauvaget has pointed out, and as the preceding remarks on *miḥrābs*, *minbars* and minarets have shown, liturgy in Islam is less important than aesthetics or

Opposite: the Great Mosque at Yazd. The dome over the *miḥrāb* (left) was probably built by 1316 and the *īwān* fronting it (center) by 1330. The colossal entrance (right) followed but its decoration was not complete till the mid-15th century.

The dome before the *miḥrāb* of the Great Mosque of al-Hakam II at Cordova (c. 965).

the mysterious ways of craftsmen. This misleading concentration on liturgy has led many scholars to speak of an "Arab" plan, typified by that of the mosque of al-Walīd at Damascus (completed 714–15), which was later superseded by other national plans.

There is, however, very little evidence anywhere that the sense of the Umayyad plan was retained. At Cordova (785–86) and Qayrawān (rebuilt 836) the basic elements were retained – raised crossing, domed *miḥrāb* and oblong arcades, but the subsequent 10th-century alterations completely swamped them in forests of columns. The fine wooden *maqṣūra* which enclosed the ruler at prayers was augmented at Qayrawān by a superb ribbed dome. These domes rapidly supplanted the *maqṣūra* which then took an architectural form, for example the exquisite domes before the *miḥrāb*s of al-Ḥakam II at Cordova (c. 965) or the Great Mosque at Tlemcen in Algeria (c. 1136); and in particular the dome built by Niẓām al-Mulk (assassinated 1092) in the Great Mosque at Iṣfahān. Moreover, the 10th-century additions to the Cordova mosque left even the domes of al-Ḥakam before and over the *miḥrāb* and the two-tier arcades of the "Capilla de Villaviciosa," the original entrance to his extension, with only the faintest resemblance to the Umayyad mosque at Damascus.

If the plan of the Umayyad mosque at Damascus bears only a faint resemblance to mosques as they developed in the Maghrib, the ʿAbbāsids in the Mashriq were no more faithful. Take the introduction of outer enclosures (*ziyāda*s).

The entrance to the *miḥrāb* at Cordova with mosaic revetment set in a carved marble frame. Exceptionally the *miḥrāb* is so deeply recessed as to make a small chamber, suggesting that it was intended to serve as a caliphal *maqṣūra*.

The mosque of al-Mutawakkil at Sāmarrā was preceded by forecourts on the north, east and west, that on the north containing the spiral minaret, the Malwiyya, and then surrounded by a much larger enclosure, clearly visible on air photographs, 376 by 44 meters in area. A similar development was the multiplication in these mosques of the arcades surrounding the courtyard: the *qibla* arcades grew in size and number; we cannot conclude, however, that only prayers said in the *qibla* arcades were considered valid, since the heavy piers of Ibn Ṭūlūn which made not only the *miḥrāb* invisible but the *khuṭba* inaudible must have forced people attending the Friday prayer right into the courtyard. This implies that whole mosques were regarded as fit only for the ritually pure, which was probably not the case in the courtyards of Umayyad mosques and is still not generalized to the whole building in the Great Mosque at Iṣfahān, where the courtyard serves as a thoroughfare for the bazaars, and only the axial *īwān*s are for the ritually pure.

About 1100, Persian Friday mosques begin to adopt a cruciform plan, with the axial *īwān* fulfilling the role of a crossing to the dome over the *miḥrāb*. But the change is more apparent than real. To judge from the Great Mosque at Iṣfahān, the four *īwān*s were added very probably after a fire in 1121, but well after the dome erected by Niẓām al-Mulk, and never supplanted the arcades. The 14th-century Great Mosque at Yazd shows a similar temporal gap between the dome over the *miḥrāb* (perhaps completed by 1316) and the axial *īwān* approaching it (possibly 15 years later). The origins of the four-*īwān* plan are obscure, since the only frequently cited predecessor of Iṣfahān, Nayrīz, with a *miḥrāb* dated 973, was rebuilt in the 14th century; but the fashion spread rapidly in the Iṣfahān area between 1110 and 1150 and was adopted by the Mongols as a standard plan in the 14th century, for example at Varāmīn (Great Mosque 1322–26) and at Tabrīz in the mosque built by the vizier ʿAlī Shāh (completed by 1322).

Madrasas

As in medieval Europe the value Islam has always placed upon education has been chiefly religious: study and commentary of the Koran and the pronouncements traditionally attributed to Muhammad (*ḥadīth*), canon law and necessary prerequisites like grammar. Primary education was a family responsibility. Though Koran schools were later founded to teach orphans or the children of the poor, there was no direct state control over teaching, even in the imperial Ottoman *maktab*s founded by Meḥmed II in 15th-century Istanbul. Higher education was also informal, despite the continuous demand for qualified administrators or judges in the Muslim bureaucracy, for clerks in the chancery, where Arabic remained the principal language all over Islam up to the 12th century, and for apologists like those needed by the ʿAbbāsids in the 9th century for their cause.

In the later Middle Ages mosques were still the principal centers of higher education. Distinguished scholars were normally appointed to teaching chairs for life, and their classes were open to all. There was no syllabus, and students rarely gained a diploma permitting them to teach without a long personal association; similarly, a teacher's assistants would follow him if he moved to another mosque. The teaching chairs originally carried no remuneration, and scholars had therefore to earn a living by copying manuscripts or else by giving legal opinions, though since law lectures were public, these opinions could often be obtained free. On the other hand, they usually had accommodation provided for themselves and their families, sometimes even inside the mosque.

Early educational institutions and libraries. The earliest educational institutions were in 9th-century Baghdad, among them the Bayt al-Ḥikma, the Dār al-ʿIlm and the Dār al-Kutub. The Bayt al-Ḥikma was primarily a translation bureau, staffed by scholars from the Sasanian academy at Jundīshāpūr founded by Khusraw Ānūshīrwān I (531–79) for the Seven Sages of the Neoplatonic academy at Athens who had been exiled by

The facade of the *madrasa*-mausoleum of the Mamlūk Sultan Qalāʾūn, Cairo (1284–85). The *madrasa* is to the left of the picture. The mausoleum (dome recently restored) occupies the center of the picture. The minaret was completed in 1302–03. Behind the buildings was a hospital.

Justinian in 529 AD. The Bayt al-Ḥikma was founded by the ʿAbbāsid Caliph al-Manṣūr (754–75); it produced Arabic translations, sometimes via Syriac, from Persian (Pehlevi), Sanskrit and Greek: Galen, Hippocrates, Dioscorides, Ptolemy, some of Euclid and Archimedes and many other Classical works of astronomy and mechanics, a version of the Alexander Romance (the legendary exploits of Alexander the Great) and a pseudo-Aristotelian text, the *Theologia*, which, *inter alia*, asserted the eternity of the world. This made the Bayt al-Ḥikma notorious. The translators, who included Muslims as well as Greeks or Oriental Christians, began to speculate upon the consequences of the *Theologia*, just as the scholars of 13th-century Paris were to do when the text reached Western Europe, and particularly upon its denial of God as Creator, in which it flatly contradicted the Koran. The resulting interdict gave Greek philosophy and speculative theology a bad name and led to their explicit exclusion from the curriculum of *madrasa*s from the 11th century onwards, with serious results for the sciences in later Islam. The Dār al-ʿIlm was a small teaching library with a strong legal bias founded in 993 by a Buwayhid vizier. Its influence is difficult to estimate: however, when it was destroyed by fire in 1059, it was promptly rebuilt as the Dār al-Kutub and endowed with a new library. Here, contemporaries report, legal disputations were held.

There is no early library in existence, partly because libraries were at first considered too impermanent to be made *waqf*. The accusation that the Arabs burned the famous Hellenistic library at Alexandria in 641 AD is baseless. But books are inflammable and lighting was so primitive throughout the Middle Ages that fire was a constant risk. By the late 11th century, however, it was generally accepted that libraries and books could be made *waqf*, and, with their scriptoria, corresponding to the monastic scriptoria of medieval Europe, they henceforth played a conspicuous part in Islamic intellectual life, either as independent institutions or attached to funerary foundations. Yāqūt writes nostalgically of the libraries in which he had worked while writing his geography, the *Muʿjam al-Buldān*, which were destroyed in the Mongol invasion of 1221. But the many 12th-century manuscripts still extant or cited by later authors show that even political catastrophe had little permanent effect upon the development of Islamic scriptoria.

The situation changed with the Fāṭimid invasion of Egypt in 969 AD and the foundation of the mosque of al-Azhar (970–72) as a center of Ismāʿīlī propaganda, and an annexe, the Dār al-ʿIlm, with quarters and allowances for students, to teach the higher doctrine to missionaries who were then sent abroad to spread it. They reached Syria, the Yemen and Multan in India, and had connections with the Assassins in Persia. The Seljuks, who from 1055 onwards were the champions of the ʿAbbāsid Caliphate in Baghdad, were sufficiently alarmed by this combination of heterodoxy and imperialism to create rival teaching institutions, modeled upon the Fāṭimid Dār al-ʿIlm, to reinforce orthodoxy. What developed was the *madrasa*, which rapidly became an essential part of Islamic intellectual life, though mosques retained their primacy as teaching institutions right up to the 15th century.

The observatory of Murād III at Istanbul (1579) from the *Shāhanshāhnāme*, Istanbul University Library MS. F1404. See Samarkand for the importance of astronomy.

There are records of 9th-century *madrasa*s which were possibly an Islamic adaptation of Buddhist *vihāra*s, monasteries including both libraries and scriptoria, though their subsequent development owes much to Christian, or even Manichaean, monasteries. The earliest royal foundation, no traces of which have yet come to light on the ground, appears to be a *madrasa* built simultaneously with the Great Mosque of Ghazna by Maḥmūd of Ghazna (died 1030). *Madrasa*s were probably first founded to teach canon law, though, except for the stipulation that speculative theology was not to be taught, they must have covered the whole theological curriculum. Institutions like Dār al-Ḥadīth (literally for Tradition) and Dār al-Ḥuffāẓ (for learning the Koran by heart) were probably equally comprehensive and differed little from *madrasa*s.

Curriculum and organization. The importance of science in *madrasa*s is difficult to estimate. An engaging letter from the astronomer, Ghiyāth al-Dīn Kāshī, to his father boasting of his prowess shows that astronomy was taught in the *madrasa* of Ūlūgh Beg at Samarkand (1420), but when his Observatory was completed the classes may all have been transferred there. Significantly, when the Observatory disbanded after Ūlūgh Beg's assassination (1449), the Astronomer Royal, ʿAlāʾ al-Dīn b. Muḥammad Qushjī, was eventually appointed to a chair in the Mosque of Haghia Sophia in Istanbul by Meḥmed II. This suggests that the curriculum in mosques was sometimes wider. Mathematics and some astronomy were needed to determine the correct orientation of the *qibla* and the proper times for prayer, and in the Umayyad mosque at Damascus, which contained the spectacular astronomical clock described by Ibn Jubayr in the 1180s, official timekeepers apparently kept astronomy alive in the 13th and 14th centuries. Little is known of the other sciences.

The emphasis upon Islamic law is significant. Ideally it was a matter of consensus with various schools of interpretation, or rites (*madhhabs*), sharing a common dogma. In 12th-century Sunnī Islam these were four – the Shāfiʿī, Ḥanafī, Mālikī and Ḥanbalī. The schools also became factions, like the rival faculties of the 13th-century Sorbonne, and their riots often caused serious damage; and in 11th- and 12th-century Baghdad even mosques tended to be associated with particular schools. This rivalry explains why early *madrasas* were private, not public, foundations, restricted to one legal school. They also had no provision for the Friday prayer: if they contained a pulpit this was for sermons. This rule was strictly enforced, even in the 14th century, when attempts to install the Friday prayer in the *madrasa* of Qalāʾūn in Cairo (1284–85) were frustrated on the grounds that this was against the founder's intention.

In the late 11th century an important series of *madrasas* was founded by the Seljuk vizier Niẓām al-Mulk (assassinated in 1092), who established Niẓāmiyya *madrasas* at Baghdad, Nīshāpūr, Merv and other cities, not all of them Seljuk capitals, as institutions for the official propagation of Sunnī orthodoxy. They were residential, with stipends for both students and staff, both something of a novelty. However, this was a mixed blessing since it tempted students to frequent not the best teachers but the richest *madrasas*; and the professors, instead of being appointed for life, were constantly replaced by Niẓām al-Mulk, with consequent harm to the teaching.

Nothing is known of the number of students these *madrasas* housed. Nor is anything known of their appearance. The Niẓāmiyyas may not in fact have been separate buildings. Ettinghausen has plausibly argued, for example, that parts of the Great Mosque at Iṣfahān served as *madrasas* in the Seljuk period and this is equally probable in other large mosques of the period.

Although little is known of the workings of Persian Imāmī *madrasas*, they shared one important principle with those of 12th- and 13th-century Syria: they were essentially for one rite. Early two-rite *madrasas* are not unknown and there was often pressure to found them. The son of the Fāṭimid vizier al-Afḍal, for example, appointed *qāḍīs* for the Ismāʿīlīs, the Imāmīs, the Shāfiʿīs and the Mālikīs in early 12th-century Cairo, the latter two to apply the law for the majority of the Egyptian population who had evidently not become converts to Shīʿism. The four-rite Mustanṣiriyya *madrasa* in Baghdad, one of the largest of Islam (106 by 48 meters), suggests surprising, and certainly misplaced, confidence in the ability of its intendant to subdue the mutual antipathy of the legal schools.

Better documented is the *madrasa* of al-Nāṣir Muḥammad in Cairo (1295–1304), which, though its condition is now poor, represents an earlier building beside the mausoleum of his father Qalāʾūn (see chapter 6) which he bought unfinished and completed himself. The entrance is Gothic, the marble porch of the church of St Andrew at Acre, which had reached Cairo soon after the expulsion of the Crusaders from Palestine and which passed through the hands of several owners before al-Nāṣir bought it for his *madrasa*. Above it is a brick minaret richly decorated with carved stucco. To the right of the entrance was a wooden-domed mausoleum preceded by a small forecourt. The courtyard was large, with four *īwāns*, those on the axis being considerably deeper: the *qibla īwān* was Mālikī with a superb, almost Mongol, stucco *miḥrāb* flanked by a pair of green breccia columns from the Fāṭimid palace, and a large wind shaft. The Shāfiʿīs were allotted the *īwān*

A brass astrolabe made in Toledo and dated 1068. Astrolabes were widely used in navigation and for determining the time or the length of the hours by which prayers were fixed. Museum of the History of Science, Oxford.

opposite. Niches here and in the shallow *īwān*s allotted to the Ḥanafīs and the Ḥānbalīs are probably where the library endowed by al-Nāṣir was stored. Three of the Chief Qāḍīs of Cairo were appointed professors there; the Shāfiʿī professor, a mere shaykh, must nevertheless have been distinguished.

This *madrasa* again raises the problems of housing all four rites simultaneously. The *īwān*s are high enough for there to have been three stories of cells for the students, though these no longer exist; the *qāḍī*s doubtless had residences elsewhere in Cairo. The installation of the Mālikīs in the *qibla īwān* is noteworthy, since Egypt was mostly Shāfiʿī and the Mamlūks themselves very probably Ḥanafī, and some injustice, therefore, must have been done to one or more of the rites. The plan is a nice illustration of the unfairness of symmetry.

The large number of *madrasa*s founded in 14th- and 15th-century Cairo reflects a fairly high turnover of professors. This favored the preeminence of the mosque of al-Azhar, which after 50 years of neglect under the Ayyūbids regained its former importance with the early Mamlūks and was constantly restored or added to throughout the 14th and 15th centuries; two of the most important additions were *madrasas*, that of Ṭaybars (1315), which was evidently not residential at all, and that of Āqbughā (1339). The excessively informal arrangements regarding the admission or graduation of students prevailing in other Cairene *madrasa*s could here have been palliated by some form of meritocratic competition.

Much less is known of *madrasa*s elsewhere. One of the most spectacular discoveries of recent years has been a *madrasa* in northern Afghanistan at a site known as Shāh-i Mashhad, dated 1165–66 and perhaps a commemoration of the Ghūrid ruler Ghiyāth al-Dīn's reconquest of the province of Gharjistān from the Ghuzz Turks. It is a baked brick building, roughly square, with a grand entrance on to a courtyard with an axial *īwān* facing north and the remains of a domed chamber, doubtless a classroom, on the entrance side. Its decoration is remarkably rich, particularly in Koranic inscriptions, in cut brick, terracotta plaques and, to a lesser extent, stucco.

The Seljuk *madrasa*s of Anatolia are also disconcertingly undocumented, though they are architecturally impressive: for we do not know for which school of law they were intended. The Çifte Minare Medrese at Erzurum (now to be dated 1242, although perhaps founded by Kayqubād I before his death in 1236 to commemorate his annexation of the city in 1230); the Çifte Minare and the Gök Medrese at Sivas (both 1271–72); the Ak Medrese at Niğde (1409); and large *madrasa*s at Sinope, Antalya and Konya all testify to their founders' zeal and taste. They have beautifully decorated facades and often splendid interior ceramic decoration. But not one of them had ablutions, fireplaces, kitchens or quarters for the staff, and the students must have learned as much asceticism as theology.

Hospitals. The Mīrjāniyya Madrasa at Baghdad (1357), a royal foundation completed by the Emir Mīrjān, governor of Baghdad, bears part of a *waqfiyya* inscription (not infrequent in the 14th and 15th centuries), one reading of which is that it was also a hospital, though this may possibly have been nearby. This raises the topic of Islamic hospitals, the plans of which, to judge from the surviving buildings, are mostly indistinguishable from *madrasa*s. Hospitals in Islam first appeared at Baghdad, under the influence of the Sasanian medical school of Jundīshāpūr, and were then founded in many large cities in the ʿAbbāsid dominions. They were teaching institutions as well as clinics. Later Rashīd al-Dīn prescribed in his Letters that the hospital at the Rabʿ-i Rashīdī should have eminent surgeons, opticians and bonesetters appointed to it. Medical treatises were also written there.

It is hardly necessary to emphasize how unsuitable the open courtyard "*madrasa*" plan was for hospitals, where segregation of the sexes, of the mad and of the feverish (Islamic medicine included a theory of contagion) was essential. The hospitals at Sivas and Divriği are beautifully built, but there is no protection from the climate and there is not a single chimneypiece identifiable in their buildings.

The hospital built by Qalā'ūn in Cairo (1284–85), in fulfillment of a vow he had made nine years previously when he was treated at the hospital of Nūr al-Dīn in Damascus, again follows a cruciform plan, an apparent incongruity which has led many scholars to suppose that it was determined by the plan of the Fāṭimid palace upon which Qalā'ūn built. However, much of it was away from the central courtyard with its four *īwān*s. Al-Nuwayrī, who was director of the hospital from 1304 to 1308, states that, apart from the *īwān*s with fountains flowing into pools, there were separate wards for surgery, gynecology, dysentery, jaundice and ophthalmia. In addition there were kitchens, dispensaries and depots enough to cope with an overall total of 200 patients. Bedsteads with mattresses, mats, pillows, blankets and wraps were provided free, and Napoleon's Surgeon General, Desgenettes, who inspected the building in 1798, noted that there were also stone beds with a hole in the center for those incapable of walking to the latrine.

Many of the famous doctors of early Islam were Christians or Jews, and they remained important in the medical professions up to the fall of the Ottoman Empire. Where were they trained? The Rabbi Benjamin of Tudela (late 12th century) describes a seminary at Baghdad for the education of rabbis which was evidently run on the lines of a *madrasa*, and there were many Syriac monasteries, particularly in northern Iraq, where famous doctors could have studied. In Mamlūk Egypt or in Ottoman Turkey there were, however, no such opportunities, and, in default of any better explanation, it seems that non-Muslim doctors studied at Muslim hospitals, though the *waqfiyya* of the *madrasa* of Sultan Ḥasan specifies that the doctors attached to the foundation should be Muslim. If so, it raises the

The facade of the Çifte Minare Medrese at Sivas, central Anatolia. The *madrasa* was founded in 1271–72 but only its highly decorated facade now exists.

question whether non-Muslims studied at *madrasas*. It seems eminently likely: the chancery needed educated scribes and there was rarely a religious bar to the employment of non-Muslims. But nothing is known.

It has often been said that *madrasas* were the equivalent of the early European universities. The great difference was that they lacked corporate status, but otherwise the parallel is illuminating. The present account of Muslim educational institutions is necessarily tentative, and it shows the limits of the archaeological evidence.

Khānqāhs

Institutional Ṣūfism is now a spare-time occupation with communal activities restricted to practices including regular Koran readings, sermons, communal prayers and processions. This was not always so. In early Islam Ṣūfism developed from a combination of two separate tendencies – mysticism and asceticism (hence the coarse woollen garment from which Ṣūfis take their name). The principal concern of early Ṣūfis was that people should lead devout, unostentatious lives, but later masters encouraged more mystical experience, or withdrawal from the world, and from their teachings arose the different Ṣūfī orders.

The growth of Ṣūfism. It is often assumed that Ṣūfism is Iranian, Shīʿī, more or less heterodox and populist. But although in 14th-century Egypt Ibn Khaldūn dismissed Ṣūfis as Shīʿī pantheists, in 12th-century Persia they were violently attacked by Shīʿī apologists, who saw them as instruments of orthodox propaganda. They have traditionally been accused of heterodoxy from all sides. On one thing Shīʿī and Sunnī writers, and many Ṣūfī authors, unite: the moral depravity of the others. The accusation is too common in religious polemic for it to be taken literally. The mystical tendencies in much Ṣūfism, which ranked secret knowledge higher than the Sharīʿa and, like the Malāmatiyya in 11th-century Baghdad, who proclaimed the supremacy of the individual conscience above the Law, which was openly flouted, encourage misinterpretation. So does the inevitably erotic character of much allegorical Ṣūfī poetry, which while seeking to preserve its sense from the profane, represents a genuine attempt to convey the elusive character of mystical experience. European mystics, like St Teresa of Avila, express themselves similarly; but it is probable that simpler-minded Ṣūfis made the common mistake of failing to distinguish between different sorts of ecstasy – drink, hashish or sex.

The great early mystics, some of whom suffered for their opinions, were mostly orthodox and were Mesopotamian, not Iranian. The tincture of Shīʿism which came to infect certain orders does not appear before the 14th century and only becomes important in the 15th; for example, the Bektashis only became thoroughly heterodox after their refoundation by Balim Sultan in the 15th century. Populism is a disputed question. It is often assumed that in the 12th to 15th centuries Ṣūfism was encouraged by governments to canalize popular piety and cloak grievances, and there is no doubt that Ṣūfī works, like Aflākī's 14th-century hagiography of the early shaykhs of the Whirling Dervishes at Konya, are concerned to show the all-pervasive influence of the order, from the sultans of Konya down to the dregs of society.

The orders thought of themselves first as mystical brotherhoods. This implied the recognition of a founder to whom the order was linked by a chain of tradition which went back, usually to Abū Bakr or to ʿAlī; and the prime authority of a shaykh over his followers; as well as the acceptance of particular rites; the legitimacy of this was defended by the philosopher and theologian, al-Ghazzālī, who died at Ṭūs in east Persia in 1111 AD. But some orders never settled, in particular the Kalandāriyya or Wandering Dervishes who are still occasionally to be seen, bearded, carrying staves and begging bowls and festooned with cooking pots, in Persia.

Allegiance to an order did not entail either Sunnism or Shīʿism or adherence to a particular school of law. This lack of organization is the feature furthest from Christian monasticism. The Ṣūfī was tied to his order by nothing but personal links, and nothing prevented him from seceding to found his own. For this reason it is mis-

Left: the Madrasat al-Firdaws at Aleppo (pre-1236–37), seen from the *qibla*. There were students' cells on each side of the courtyard behind the colonnade.

Opposite: plan and section of the mausoleum-*khānqāh* of Salār and Sanjar al-Jāwilī, Cairo (1303–04). After Creswell.

taken to see the growth of Ṣūfism in Islam as a result of Christian or Buddhist influence. The combination of asceticism and mysticism, sometimes with a distaste for the world and its works, is a phenomenon characteristic of most evolved religions.

The formation of Ṣūfī orders did not immediately entail communal life, for which there is virtually no evidence before the 12th century, when again Syria appears to have been in the forefront. Bāyazīd al-Bisṭāmī, the founder of the Bisṭāmiyya, died in 875 AD, but the earliest building at his tomb in north Persia is a mosque with minaret dated 1120; Khanykoff in the last century noted a *miḥrāb* dated 1262, but the remains of the earliest Ṣūfī abode there are not earlier than 1303–13. As such abodes became an established part of Islamic life, dwellings followed more rapidly upon the appearance of a new order.

The slow growth of the idea that Ṣūfīs should be housed in special buildings perhaps explains the confusing diversity of names for them: *ribāṭ* (originally a hospice for those fighting the Holy War on the frontiers of Islam, but later principally with the sense of a hospice for pilgrims, widows or orphans); *zāwiya* (an angle); *khānqāh*/*khānegāh* (see below); *takkiya*/*tekke* (principally used in Ottoman Turkey); and *buqʿa* (retreat). The terms are disconcertingly interchangeable; though *zāwiya*s were often smaller and more informally organized, they were on the same legal footing as the others, and it is quite common for buildings described as *khānqāh*s in their *waqfiyya*s to be called *ribāṭ*s or *buqʿa*s in their foundation inscriptions. The impossibility of drawing a precise distinction is shown by Ibn Baṭṭūṭa's remark that in Cairo there were *zāwiya*s called *khānqāh*s where the rites took place in a domed chamber.

In Syria and Egypt some of the earliest *khānqāh*s are associated with the Sunnī revival of the 12th century. Saladin himself endowed the first *khānqāh* in Egypt, the Dār Saʿīd al-Suʿadāʾ (1173–74) in Cairo, of which there are no recognizable remains. Nūr al-Dīn, according to Ibn al-Shiḥna, founded a large *khānqāh* at Aleppo, near the moat of the Citadel and next to the Dār al-ʿAdl in 1148–49. Known as the Old Khānqāh, it contained a hall for the shaykh, a dome for the Ṣūfīs, an *īwān* and a *masjid*, with an entrance from the courtyard down to a cistern fed by an aqueduct. The street porch was added in the late 14th century, just before Tīmūr sacked Aleppo. It passed into the hands of the Suhrawardiyya whose founder died in 1234–35. This account is interesting because it demonstrates how a *khānqāh* could pass from the hands of one order into another; moreover, in spite of the general esteem in which the Suhrawardiyya was held, there was no way of guaranteeing that its *waqf*s were competently administered.

If *khānqāh*s were to be instruments of Sunnī orthodoxy some guarantee of their orthodoxy was required. Ibn al-Shiḥna cites the inscription of an emir of the Sultan al-Malik al-Nāṣir Yūsuf (1246–60) of Aleppo, who left his palace as a *khānqāh* in 1252, on condition that only Arabicized, pious, orthodox Ṣūfīs were to reside there. And at Jerusalem the only indisputable *khānqāh* foundation of the early Mamlūk period, founded by Sanjar al-Qaymarī (1295), bears a *waqfiyya* inscription including endowments for a professor of Shāfiʿī law, a shaykh for the teaching of *ḥadīth*, and Koran readings, all to be given in the adjacent Aqṣā mosque.

One other solution was to attach Ṣūfīs to *madrasa*s. The Madrasat al-Firdaws, for example, at Aleppo (pre-1236–

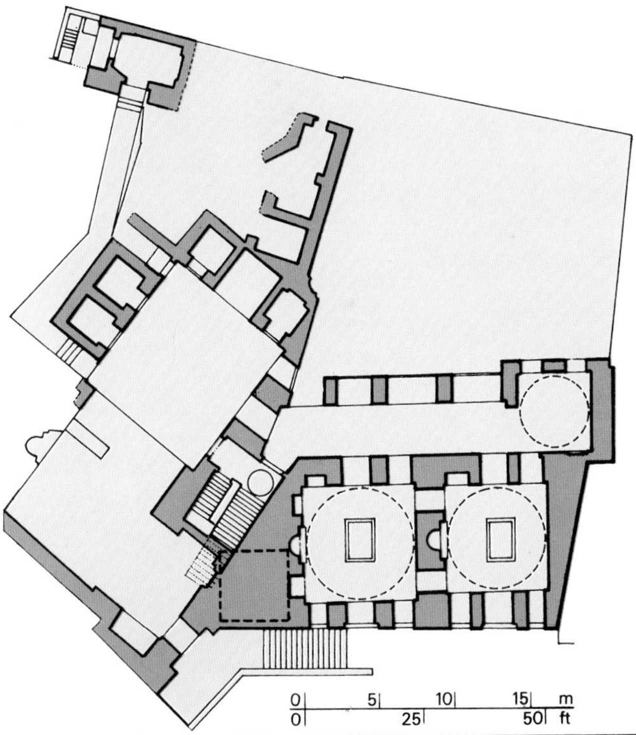

37) is known to have had a *khānqāh* attached to it, though there is scarcely enough room for students. There is an early Cairene combination of *madrasa* and *khānqāh* at the mausoleum of Salār and Sanjar al-Jāwilī (1303–04). Of the *madrasa* virtually nothing remains but stucco decoration and a *miḥrāb* in the blank space in front of the portico to the tombs, but the *khānqāh* is a courtyard with two asymmetrical *iwān*s and two stories of stone-faced cells, those on the ground floor being lit by carved stone grilles. Later a third story of cells of brick faced with carved stucco was added on one side probably when the *madrasa* was built (Maqrīzī gives the date 1323, though this raises problems).

In this particular case the *madrasa* was added as an afterthought; but in the *madrasa* of Barqūq (1384–86) there was a *khānqāh* included, to judge from the inscription below the dome of the mausoleum, though there is no indication where the Ṣūfīs, as opposed to the students of the *madrasa*, were housed. This combination of orthodox teaching institutions and Ṣūfī establishments was probably much more generalized in Egypt, and the larger 14th-century mosques mostly had groups of Ṣūfīs (*mashyakha*s) under a shaykh, evidently non-residential, and evidently for the instruction and control of the Ṣūfīs.

In the 15th century it became standard practice to appoint Ṣūfīs to the foundation of *madrasa*s and Sauvaget notes that a *mubāshir* (Chief of Commissariat) of the ʿUmariyya Madrasa at Damascus (pre-1422) was a Ṣūfī. Qāyt Bāy, Ibn Iyās says, attached 60 Ṣūfīs to a *madrasa* he

Below : dome of the vestibule of the *madrasa-khānqāh* of the Mamlūk Sultan Barqūq (1384–86). The *madrasa*, a cruciform building with a large, splendidly decorated *qibla iwān*, occupies the whole of the street facade.

The Khānqāh of Baybars al-Gāshenkīr/Chāshnegīr, Cairo (completed 1309). Below the minaret can be seen the projecting facade of the portico to his tomb built on the main street after he became sultan. The *khānqāh* proper lies behind the tomb and is the best preserved in Cairo.

founded in Jerusalem in 1470 two years after its foundation. The effect of what had become a systematic policy on the part of the Mamlūks was to tie Ṣūfis to institutions which were subject to state control and to weaken the bonds which linked them as orders or mystical brotherhoods. By the late 15th century Ṣūfis were no longer even obliged to be resident, and the *khānqāh* attached to the mausoleum of al-Ghūrī (1503–04) in Cairo was merely a hall for assembly, where the Ṣūfis doubtless also received their stipends or their daily rations. The concern for the preservation of orthodoxy also explains perhaps one very striking feature of *khānqāhs* in Syria and Egypt, that it is very rarely possible to discover which order inhabited them. The only explanation is that with steadily increasing state control over *khānqāhs* in this period there was no continuity so that shaykhs were appointed and orders were installed or displaced at the whim of a sultan or the demands of the *ʿulamāʾ*. The mausolea attached to Cairene *khānqāhs*, therefore, contain only the tombs of the founder or his family, and not the successive shaykhs of an order, as we find in Mevlevi or Bektashi *tekkes* in Egypt or Turkey.

In spite of the lack of continuity it might appear possible to determine which order a Cairene *khānqāh* was originally built for, since the practices of the orders differ and demand different architectural solutions. However, even the best-preserved Cairene *khānqāh*, that of Baybars al-Gāshenkīr/Chāshnegīr, completed in 1309, is indistinguishable from contemporary *madrasas*.

Organization and practice. At this point various crucial questions arise: how did *khānqāhs* differ from *madrasas*? how were Ṣūfis recruited? how did the orders preserve their individuality? and what generally distinguished Ṣūfi practice from that of the *ʿulamāʾ*? In spite of the history of Ṣūfism under the Mamlūks, the *ʿulamāʾ* regarded themselves as a class apart. Thus, Sibṭ ibn al-ʿAjamī states in the 15th century that while the *ʿulamāʾ* may indeed live in *khānqāhs* (presumably while traveling) and benefit from their *waqfs*, Ṣūfis should not live in *madrasas*. *Khānqāhs* were, nevertheless, teaching institutions, for study of the Koran and *ḥadīth* and often with a chair of law attached to them, though they may not have had the pretensions to intellectual excellence of the great *madrasas* of Islam. They often had considerable libraries: for example, the splendidly illuminated Koran in 30 parts dated 1313 from Hamadān which is one of the treasures of the National Library in Cairo was made *waqf* in 1325–26 to the *khānqāh* attached to the mausoleum of Bektimür al-Sāqī in the southern cemetery of Cairo. As well as subjects which *madrasas* did not teach, *khānqāhs* also "taught" mysticism, partly by means of close study of the founder's works and partly by a close association between the neophyte and the shaykh of the *khānqāh* who became his spiritual director.

The shaykh drew his own teaching from the *silsila* or chain of tradition going back to the founder of the order. This is one reason for the proliferation of Ṣūfi orders in the 13th to 15th centuries, when the novice had to rely upon individual interpretations, often by several shaykhs, instead of the canonical interpretation of the Law given in *madrasas* by qualified professors.

In principle there was no official recruitment: a shaykh might attract a handful of novices wherever he happened to be living, which became his *zāwiya*; after his death his students would carry on his teaching under a successor he had appointed and some pious benefactor might provide the institution with an endowment. Many of these *zāwiyas*, particularly in country areas, never survived the shaykh's death. But the charisma of the greater Ṣūfi mystics attracted royal patronage. Such was the case with Jalāl al-Dīn Rūmī, the founder of the Mevlevi dervishes, and the Seljuk sultans of Konya. Tīmūr's family too was proud to acknowledge its dependence upon Ṣūfi shaykhs; and the practice was also adopted by both the Mamlūks and the Ottomans, each of the Ottoman sultans having his favorite order. Royal patronage gave an order a privileged status vis-à-vis other Ṣūfī orders, and defended it against charges of heresy which the conservative-minded jurists constantly brought against Ṣūfī practices. But royal protection could scarcely guarantee the integrity of an order, which was all the more fragile since any *khānqāh* had as many visiting Ṣūfīs as permanent residents.

Each order had certain ritual practices designed to reinforce the spiritual direction of the shaykh and the novice's own studies. These included communal recitations of the Koran or sermons, though some orders discouraged public recitations; the recital of litanies; some form of retreat, which was either part of the novitiate or could be imposed at any time by the shaykh and varied from service in the kitchens to more extreme practices like being hung upside down for a period in a well; and sometimes more elaborate rites with dancing and music, designed to induce ecstasy. These aroused the greatest disapproval among the *ʿulamāʾ* and also among orders less enthusiastically inclined. However, the dances of the Whirling Dervishes or the performances of the Rifāʿiyya (the Howling Dervishes) including snake-eating, self-mutilation and walking on live coals, have done much to color Western ideas of Ṣūfī practices.

Once admitted to a *khānqāh*, a Ṣūfī was given rations and was required to reside there. This condition was initially very strictly applied. Thus, the *waqfiyya* inscription of the *khānqāh* of Sanjar al-Qaymarī at Jerusalem (1295) prescribes that the Ṣūfīs should reside there continuously, except for good reason. Of the 30 Ṣūfīs on the foundation, 10 were to be married and 20 celibate: the distinction implied is probably between professed Ṣūfīs and novices, who would naturally be younger as well as more numerous. Ṣūfism did not necessarily entail celibacy, of which Islam has never made a particular virtue, and it was indeed common for the headship of a *khānqāh* to be a hereditary position. Some duties required celibacy, but there were no celibate orders.

Unfortunately, with a few exceptions, the distinguishing practices of the Ṣūfī orders have not been described, more attention having been given to their theological positions, for which architecture, naturally, is of little use as evidence. But for the existence of detailed *waqfiyyas*, we should know little of life inside *khānqāhs*. The *waqfiyya* of Rashīd al-Dīn's *khānqāh* at the Rabʿ-i Rashīdī outside Tabrīz (pre-1318) has yet to be studied, but that of the *khānqāh* founded at the tomb of Sayf al-Dīn Bākharzī at Fatḥābād, a suburb of Bukhārā, by the shaykh's grandson (dated 1326 with two additions dated 1332 and 1335) is particularly valuable.

The practical requirements of Ṣūfī life imposed certain architectural conditions in *khānqāhs*: living quarters for staff, professed Ṣūfīs and visitors; kitchens, common rooms, and cells for retreats. These requirements are so similar in many respects to those of Buddhist *vihāras* or Christian monasteries that it might be natural to see

The Khānqāh of Tenkizbughā, Cairo (1364). The building stood isolated in the Eastern Cemetery with high walls and a minaret.

Buddhist or Christian architectural influence upon the development of *khānqāh* plans. However, there is no sign of this in the earliest *khānqāhs* extant, in 12th-century Syria, or in 14th-century Cairo where these practical requirements were ignored in favor of a standard, *madrasa*-like cruciform plan.

Funerary foundations. Most of these institutions were founded *for* orders, the founders of which lived and died elsewhere. But there are many *khānqāhs* which, like the *madrasa*-shrines of Abu Ḥanīfa at Baghdad and the Imām al-Shafiʿī in Cairo, were built near the tomb of the founder of the order. Not all Ṣūfī shaykhs were so provided, however, so that these are not simply shrines.

Conversely, there are shrines with *khānqāhs* which are not those of famous shaykhs. One of the most informative is the Bektashi complex at the suppositious tomb of Jaʿfar b. Ḥusayn Sayyid Ghāzī (the Sayyid Baṭṭāl Ghāzī of many Arabic and Turkish romances) at Seyitgâzi, southeast of Eskişehir in Turkey. The site is a treat for the religious syncretist. It occupies the acropolis of ancient Nakoleia and abounds in ancient tombs, one of which formed the apse of an early Christian funerary basilica and is an integral part of the building, being known as the tomb of the Sultan Valide (Dowager Empress). The *khānqāh*, built round an irregular courtyard, consists of four different blocks. To the right of the entrance gateway there is the funerary basilica, while to the left there is a range of domed kitchens, bakeries and assembly rooms, all with large ovens or chimneypieces, with stabling and cattle sheds below them. At the far end of the courtyard are the staff quarters, including the shaykh's lodging with a parlor, and rooms for his deputy and a guardian of the cemetery which lies outside the enceinte beyond that wing. The space between the living quarters and the funerary basilica is occupied by the octagonal "tomb" of Sayyid Baṭṭāl Ghāzī, with the founder's tomb in a corner, four *samā'khānes* for the Bektashi rites, a mosque with a minaret and various cellar rooms, presumably for retreats. The only element apparently lacking is accommodation for the novices, ordinary Ṣūfis and domestics.

These very precise identifications are possible because the Bektashi still inhabited the *khānqāh* when Wulzinger surveyed it. The disposition reflects the complicated ritual of the reformed Bektashi order of the 15th century, including rites resembling Baptism, Penance and the Eucharist, but the various structures of the foundation identified here very probably took shape over time and were not all built for these purposes. Although the Bektashi ascribed the rebuilding of the tomb sanctuary to the Seljuk Sultan Kaykā'ūs I in 1207–08 and proudly recounted its frequentation by the early Ottoman sultans of the 14th and 15th centuries, all this was probably unhistorical. There are no buildings predating the reformation of the order under Salim Sultan: the "tomb" dates from 1493, and the adjoining buildings which form the sanctuary and the *khānqāh* are no earlier than 1511.

Virtually nothing of the *khānqāh*s founded by Tīmūr and his family at Samarkand, at Shahr-i Sabz or at Herāt survives, but it may be assumed that, as with the royal *khānqāh*s of Mamlūk Cairo, they were not self-governing institutions and that the royal founders interfered in their running. Three private institutions in 14th-century Persia are, however, worthy of mention, particularly for their beautiful stucco decoration. The first, Pīr-i Bakrān, in the Iṣfahān oasis, is surrounded by a Jewish cemetery, and the monument was still known as Esther Khātūn (the tomb of Esther is traditionally supposed to be at Hamadān) when Herzfeld visited it in 1923.

Bisṭām/Basṭām on the northern fringe of the great Persian central desert, the Dasht-i Kavīr, though of the same period, is somewhat different, since it was the center of the Bisṭāmiyya order and had a Seljuk nucleus with a minaret dated 1120.

At Naṭanz there remains the impressive porch of a *khānqāh* associated with Shaykh 'Abd al-Ṣamad al-Iṣfahānī. This is the prolongation of a mosque facade. The mosque bears inscriptions dated 1304–05 and 1309–10, and is an irregular four-*īwān* construction, with several entrances which suggest that, like the Great Mosque at Iṣfahān, it served as a thoroughfare for the surrounding bazaars.

*Khānqāh*s which attach themselves to the burial place of a Ṣūfī shaykh need little explanation, since they are obviously a recognition of his charisma by his followers or by the population among whom he lived. But the Tīmūrid and Mamlūk foundations raise a problem. Why should rulers who boast of their orthodoxy so frequently choose *khānqāh*s as their funerary foundations? I have suggested that one reason was a desire to control the development and expansion of the Ṣūfī orders and to make them, like *madrasas*, subject to outside control; but this explains neither their frequency nor their funerary associations. There is no real answer. Many rulers and their emirs knew Ṣūfī shaykhs and were impressed sufficiently to desire, like Tīmūr, to be counted among their friends or followers, or even to be buried, as he was, beside them. Although there is nothing in Islam comparable to the Emperor Charles V's abdication and retirement into the monastery of Yuste, this concern probably reflects the characteristic attraction of the contemplative life to men of action.

This account has necessarily been confined to Ṣūfism in its more orthodox forms or, as in the case of the Bektashiyya, the form in which it was officially accepted by the Ottoman state. But many Ṣūfī establishments went far beyond the bounds of orthodoxy. Clavijo, on his way to Tīmūr's court in 1403–04, passed through Delilerkent, a town to the east of Erzurum, where he found a building full of dervishes and people who had come to be cured of various ailments.

"The dervishes who live on alms wander about naked or in the most tattered garments, spending the nights singing with tambourines. Above their dwelling is a standard of black wool surmounted by a crescent and at the foot of it there are animal horns – of deer, sheep and goats. Such is the custom in such communities, and they carry them about with them when they go through the streets of the town."

These strange practices are corroborated by a miniature attributed to the late 16th-century Persian painter Muḥammadī which represents dervishes clad in animal skins and wearing antlers dancing in ecstasy. There is a strong Anatolian tradition of Ṣūfis connected with deer, personified by the semi-legendary shaykh Gedik Baba, and if the crouched figure of a deer on the porch of the Çöreği Büyük Tekke at Niksar (early 14th century) is anything to go by, this tradition may well go back to the early 14th century. But what orders practiced these rites is not known.

The Mosque of Sultan Ḥasan in Cairo

VISUAL STORY

Sultan Ḥasan came to the throne of Egypt in 1347 at the age of 13. Early in 1351 he was deposed in favor of one of his younger brothers and spent three years in seclusion, or captivity, improving himself with reading and writing. He was restored to the throne in 1354 and led an uneventful existence till his assassination in 1362.

All the Mamlūk sultans, from Baybars I onwards (d. 1277), built a great deal in Cairo. From the time of his successor, Qalā'ūn (d. 1293), their buildings tended chiefly to be pious foundations associated with their domed mausolea, very often providing an excuse for them, since the early Islamic prejudice against conspicuous tombs of any sort was still strong among orthodox Muslims. The foundations are what are called *complexes*, buildings of different function united under one roof. Qalā'ūn's mausoleum, for example, had a *madrasa* and a large hospital (1284–85) attached to it.

Sultan Ḥasan's father, al-Nāṣir Muḥammad (reigned, with interruptions, 1299–1341), was a great builder, both on his own account and on behalf of his emirs. Sultan Ḥasan succeeded in emulating him. His mausoleum was the first to be attached to a *mosque*; in its enormous size, its plan and above all in its decoration the mosque of Sultan Ḥasan is a very remarkable monument indeed.

The mosque (seen *below* from the south, after Roberts) was built at the western foot of the Citadel of Cairo on a large open space, now the Maydān Rumayla, the site of the official residence of an emir, and the curiously irregular outline of the mosque probably follows the foundations of the earlier building. It was begun in 1356 and, though work on it continued without interruption, it was still unfinished at the time of Sultan Ḥasan's death (1362). The endowments had been partly guaranteed, but the mosque and its *madrasas* probably never functioned at full strength.

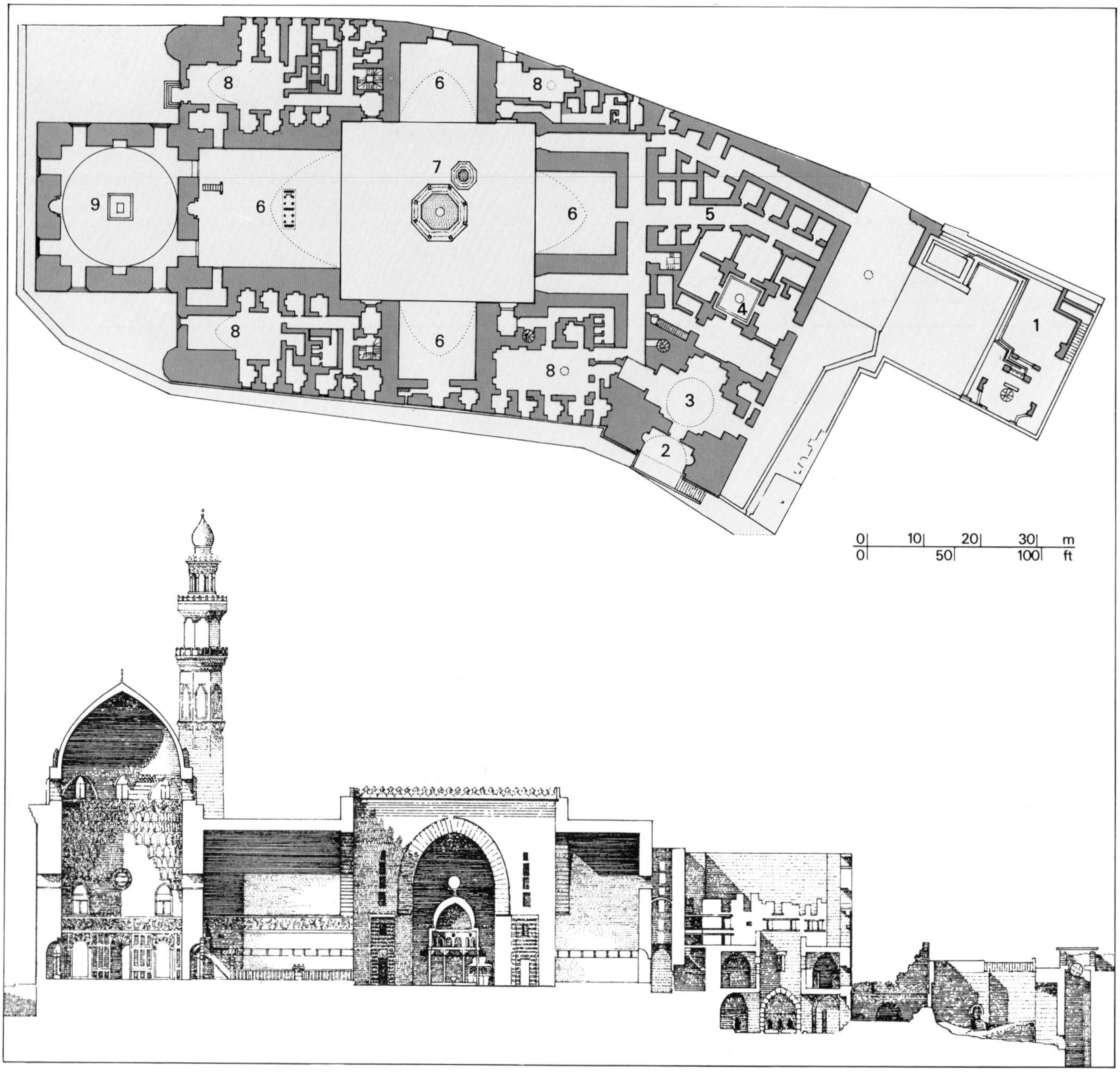

The mosque of Sultan Ḥasan was built on rising ground. Its irregular exterior and the varying thickness of its walls are evidently an attempt to combine the maximum of street frontage with the requirement that the mosque should be orientated towards Mecca. The plan is in three parts. At the northern end is an enormous water tower (1) (*sāqiya*) and, among other ruins which are no longer identifiable, a *qaysariyya*, the rent from which would go to the upkeep of the mosque. In the center is a block of three components all on the same axis and at an angle to the mosque. It consists of a grand entrance (2), a "vestibule" (3) and an ablution courtyard (4) (*miḍā'*), though this last is at ground level and does not communicate. The third part is the mosque proper, at a higher level, linked to the vestibule by a long narrow corridor (5) at an oblique angle to it.

The mosque consists of four *īwāns* (6) round a central courtyard (7) arranged in a cruciform plan, like the restoration of the Great Mosque in Iṣfahān (1121). The cruciform *madrasa* in Cairo, particularly in association with the four Muslim schools of law (*madhhabs*), appears to be an independent, late development and Sultan Ḥasan is the first cruciform mosque; each corner is filled by a *madrasa* (8), one for each *madhhab*, a logical development of earlier cruciform *madrasas* in Cairo. The *madrasas* in the four corners had to be squeezed into the space available, but their plans are all roughly similar – an *īwān* for teaching, a small central courtyard with a fountain, four- or five-story blocks of rooms for the students, and an ablution courtyard.

Immediately behind the *qibla īwān* is an enormous square mausoleum (9) with six large windows at ground level giving on to the Maydān Rumayla. Both plan and section are after Herz.

The great mosque was originally intended to have four minarets, two at the corners of the mosque on the *qibla* side, and two above the entrance porch. Only the southwestern minaret (*above*) is original now. In 1362, three months before Sultan Ḥasan's death, one of these collapsed in the course of erection (its emplacement can be seen on the section) and the second was never built. The two-minaret porch (*above right*, after Roberts), here imitated from the Gök Medrese in Sivas (*below right*) (1271–72) was widely adopted in 14th-century Mongol Persia. Two-minaret porches, were, however, rare in Cairo: the Mosque of al-Nāṣir Muḥammad on the Citadel (1317, restored 1334–35) was a major exception.

The porch is now more than 37 meters high. It was originally even higher since the street has risen to conceal the rocky plinth, 1–4 meters high, on which the whole mosque was built. Even without the two minarets, which it was intended to carry, it is by far the tallest porch in Cairo. Its design is very much an innovation in Cairene Mamlūk architecture.

Much of the decoration is unfinished. It gives us an interesting idea of how the masons worked. The really large elements, like the faceted side niches, were cut to size before they were erected. High relief decorative elements or friezes were only blocked out in outline and then a pattern was scratched on them to indicate the further decoration to be completed by the journeyman craftsman. The imitation of the Gök Medrese is by no means exact; it is certainly not the work of a native Sivas craftsman; but it is one of the very rare imitations of a foreign monument in the whole of Islam.

Decoration of the mosque. One highly interesting innovation is a frieze of chinoiserie lotus, chrysanthemum and trefoil scroll.

To discourage marauders, Barqūq removed the stairway up to the porch from the street and blocked up the entrance, leaving the great bronze doors of the mosque (detail, *below left*) still in place. In 1415 the Sultan al-Mu'ayyad bought the doors unreasonably cheap for his own mosque-mausoleum at the Bāb Zuwayla. In Islamic architecture the sincerest form of flattery has generally been not imitation but theft.

The vestibule, more than nine meters square and with a dome more than 25 meters high, is in many respects the most enigmatic element of the building. Its pointed dome is on pendentives, heavily disguised by rows of stalactites which continue upwards to disguise the drum (*above right*). Much use is made of bicolored stone, but the overall dimensions are more compact, and it is therefore probable that the "vestibule" is a non-Cairene plan imposed upon Sultan Ḥasan's mosque by a foreign architect. The only known analogue, the tomb of Ṭughrābek/Turābik Khānum (*below right*, after Pugachenkova), now thought to be the tomb of two rulers, Ḥusayn and Yūsuf Ṣūfī (1361 or earlier), is at Urgench in Khwārizm, which in the mid-14th century came under the control of the Golden Horde and which regularly furnished Mamlūks to Egypt. This combines a stalactite porch with a domed vestibule, and even has a tomb placed on the axis of the building behind the *miḥrāb*. The decoration of the "vestibule" of Sultan Ḥasan is less elaborate but more appropriate to a brick building faced with plaster or ceramic mosaic.

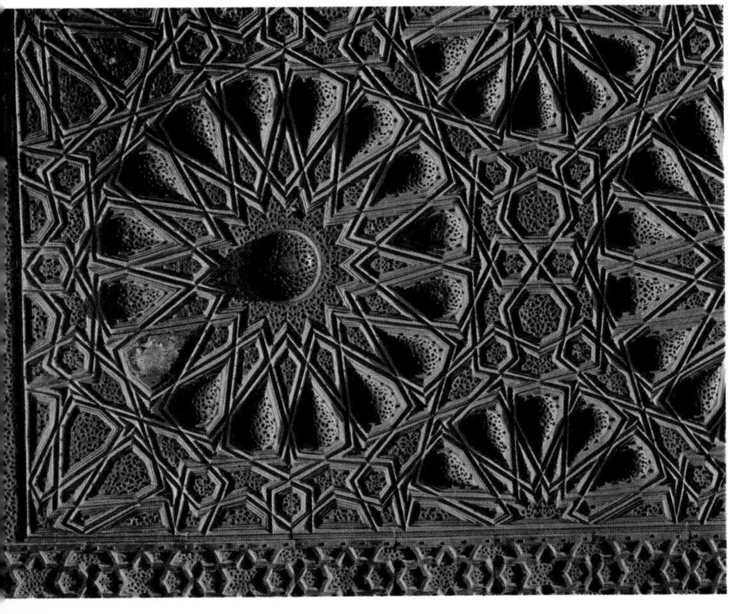

It was boasted in the later 14th century, justly it turned out since someone took care to measure it, that the SE *īwān* (*top left*) was larger than that of Sasanian Ctesiphon (the Ṭāq-i Kisrā) and it is scarcely surprising therefore that the mere wood required for the centering cost as much as a normal mosque. It contains a marble *minbar*, much praised by contemporaries, and also a tribune (*dikka*) for the official deputed to repeat the daily prayers at the *miḥrāb* by the Imām (the *muballigh*) which would have been inaudible to anyone near or in the courtyard. The marble tribune, one of the finest in Cairo, is evidently the work of the same craftsman who failed to complete the porch.

Above right: the ablution courtyard of the Madrasa of Sultan Barqūq (1386), very cramped by comparison.

Below: Roberts gives a better impression of the height of the mosque than any camera can capture. The smaller domed construction in the courtyard (probably 14th century) is now in the mosque of al-Māridānī (1339), Cairo.

The decoration of the mosque consists of a broad carved stucco band just below the springing of the plastered vault, a low dado of marble paneling on the side walls, and a magnificent marble revetment on the *qibla* wall right up to the stucco band. The stucco band uses the medallion motifs which occur on the porch and in the "vestibule" (*top*). The marble paneling was most probably added after Sultan Ḥasan's death. Antique green, yellow, red and pink marbles are used, and red and green porphyry, the panels being formed by columns sliced lengthwise and then set in lightly carved frames of whitish marble. The two pairs of columns at the *miḥrāb* (*above*) are Crusader Gothic.

Above: one of the mosque lamps that hung from the plastered stone vault; 34 still survive from more than 200 specially ordered for the mosque.

In 1362 Sultan Ḥasan was defeated by rebellious Mamlūks. The sultan took refuge in the Citadel of Cairo, where he was arrested and assassinated in mysterious circumstances. He never occupied his mausoleum.

The mausoleum attached to the mosque, the largest royal mausoleum in Cairo, 21 meters square and with a dome at present 48 meters high, has the walls entirely covered with marble paneling, with the addition of a large marble mosaic medallion in the center of each wall. In the center of the mausoleum is a raised marble cenotaph (*below*) on a flat platform. The tomb never housed anyone distinguished.

5. Palaces and Domestic Architecture

Palaces in Islam were miniature cities with the monarch as autocrat surrounded by his ministers and court officials, stables, barracks, the inevitable harem, dependants who were given apartments of their own, as well as armies of servants, slaves and court craftsmen. The population of the Mamlūk palace at the Citadel of 14th-century Cairo could easily have been more than 20,000. Access was as difficult as exit and palaces like those of the Fāṭimids in 10th- to 12th-century Cairo or the Alhambra even had their private cemeteries. Diversions were few – military parades, polo, hunting and intrigue – but by the 10th century Islamic courts mostly had elaborate ceremonial to enhance the ruler's splendor and occupy the day.

It is, however, too simple to view Islamic palaces as the Versailles or the Renaissance courts of their day. Consumption was indeed tremendous, but the gold and silver, the rock-crystal and the ivory, the brocades, the painting and the automata described by court chronicles with uncritical enthusiasm were little more than stage properties. Their descriptions of feasts where poets extemporized appropriate verses and the best musicians and dancers performed are lifeless, and court patronage in the Renaissance sense lacked a dimension; on the contrary, through the descriptions of stifling luxury one glimpses an infinite boredom. Ceremonial was less a distraction than tedium elevated into ritual.

Palace architecture, which was often very flimsy, gives little idea of all this. Nor, architecturally, is palace design particularly inventive, principally because of the paramountcy of the taste of the ʿAbbāsid Caliphate, which led to imitations of the fabled constructions of Baghdad as far as Transoxiana and the Maghrib, even when climatic conditions were very different. Only with the extinction of the Caliphate in 1258, and the subsequent preeminence of Egypt, did national styles appear; and after the Ottoman conquest of 1517 even these became subordinate to Istanbul fashion.

Above: a view of the Alhambra, Granada. The outer walls were restored in 1238 on its reconquest by the Naṣrids.

"Desert castles." The palaces of the early Umayyad capitals – Damascus, Fusṭāṭ, Jerusalem or Ḥarrān – have all disappeared without trace beneath centuries of later buildings. Instead, there are "desert castles" in Syria and Palestine which scholars long attributed to nomadic aversion to town life, consecrated in Muhammad's warning of the temptations of life in the great oases. However, recent discoveries of early palaces (Dār al-ʿImāra) at Kūfa and Wāsiṭ, both Umayyad capitals of Iraq, have shown that the Umayyads, quite naturally, frequented towns as well as the country. That at Kūfa, set back to back with the Umayyad Great Mosque there (probably built by al-Ḥajjāj c. 694–97), is perhaps ʿAbbāsid but may follow the plan of the Umayyad buildings. It was a square buttressed building approached, as at Persepolis, by a double staircase, with a throne room on the axis, evidently domed, approached by a basilical *īwān* with a grand three-arched facade. The palace was set in a square buttressed enceinte with traces of arcades surrounding it.

Of the Umayyad so-called "desert castles" relatively few were royal palaces; virtually none were castles; and some were simply the contemporary equivalent of Roman or Byzantine rural villas. But all were surrounded by outbuildings, usually villages, with mills, granaries and oil-presses, and all, even the apparently isolated bath at Quṣayr ʿAmra, show evidence of all-the-year-round habitation, perfectly possible in Syria and Transjordan given some means of conserving the abundant winter rains.

The most spectacular of all is Khirbat al-Mafjar outside Jericho, probably built between 739 and 744 but destroyed in an earthquake in 747–48. It has been ingeniously reconstructed from the abundant remains. The palace, set in an irregular enclosure of about 150 acres, was entered by a gateway leading to a forecourt dominated by a domed pool with an octagonal surround crowned by a stone parapet. The projecting entrance to the palace in the center of a facade of two-storied porticoes was a vaulted passageway with sedilia backed by carved stucco panels all along set in a composition recalling a Roman triumphal arch but with a domed pavilion on its upper floor. The passageway had lunettes filled with stucco busts in beaded medallions and a vault covered with a peopled vine scroll. The palace court was surrounded by a colonnaded portico, evidently with a wooden roof. The right-hand range was a single room with a colonnade down the center; the left consisted of five narrow rooms, the central one with a *miḥrāb* and a square buttress outside, evidently to take a minaret. On the axis was a *sardāb* with a polychrome mosaic floor and a tank of cold water. Behind this was a recess. Two monumental staircases, very rare in Islamic architecture, led to a piano nobile (principal floor), surrounded by a gallery with stucco balustrades and a belvedere on the axis containing a stone window overlooking the courtyard weighing more than three and a half tons. In the far right-hand corner there was a door leading across an empty courtyard to the bath, but the facade side was filled by a small mosque, entirely bare of decoration.

An aerial view of the unfinished palace of Mshaṭṭā, Jordan, probably begun by the Umayyad Caliph al-Walīd II (743–44). Only the central section was built above foundation level. The splendidly carved facade (see chapter 1) is now in the Islamisches Museum, East Berlin.

Despite the amazingly rich decoration there are signs that Khirbat al-Mafjar was still unfinished when it was destroyed in 747–48. Such was also the case with two Transjordanian palaces, Qaṣr al-Ṭūba and Mshaṭṭā, an area frequented by the dissolute Caliph al-Walīd II (743–44), who may well have built them. Qaṣr al-Ṭūba, to judge from the foundations, consisted of two identical parts, each with a grand entrance, but connected inside by a corridor which could be shut off. Only two brick barrel vaults remained in Creswell's time, and he suggested that many of the other rooms, with walls too thin to support vaulting, might have been open-air courtyards for al-Walīd's Bedouin followers; but it is much more probable that they were to have flat timber roofs. The unfinished palace of Mshaṭṭā is particularly important for its plan, which consisted of three separate strips within its buttressed enceinte: the only parts begun were in the central strip where the foundations of an entrance block, including a mosque with a square *miḥrāb*, were laid, and a throne room was probably completed – a triple apse approached by a three-aisled *īwān* with a three-arched grand facade.

The fate of these Umayyad villas after the fall of the dynasty is unknown, but no more palaces appear to have been built in Syria till the 9th century, when palaces at Raqqa, recently excavated by the Syrian Department of Antiquities, follow the fashions of Baghdad and Sāmarrā. Elsewhere it is unclear how far climatic conditions allowed the development of villa economies. However, the desert fortress of Ukhayḍir (dated by Creswell 775–76) in central Iraq may well be typical of 8th- to 9th-century rural castles

Opposite: plan of the Jawsaq al-Khāqānī palace at Sāmarrā. After Creswell.

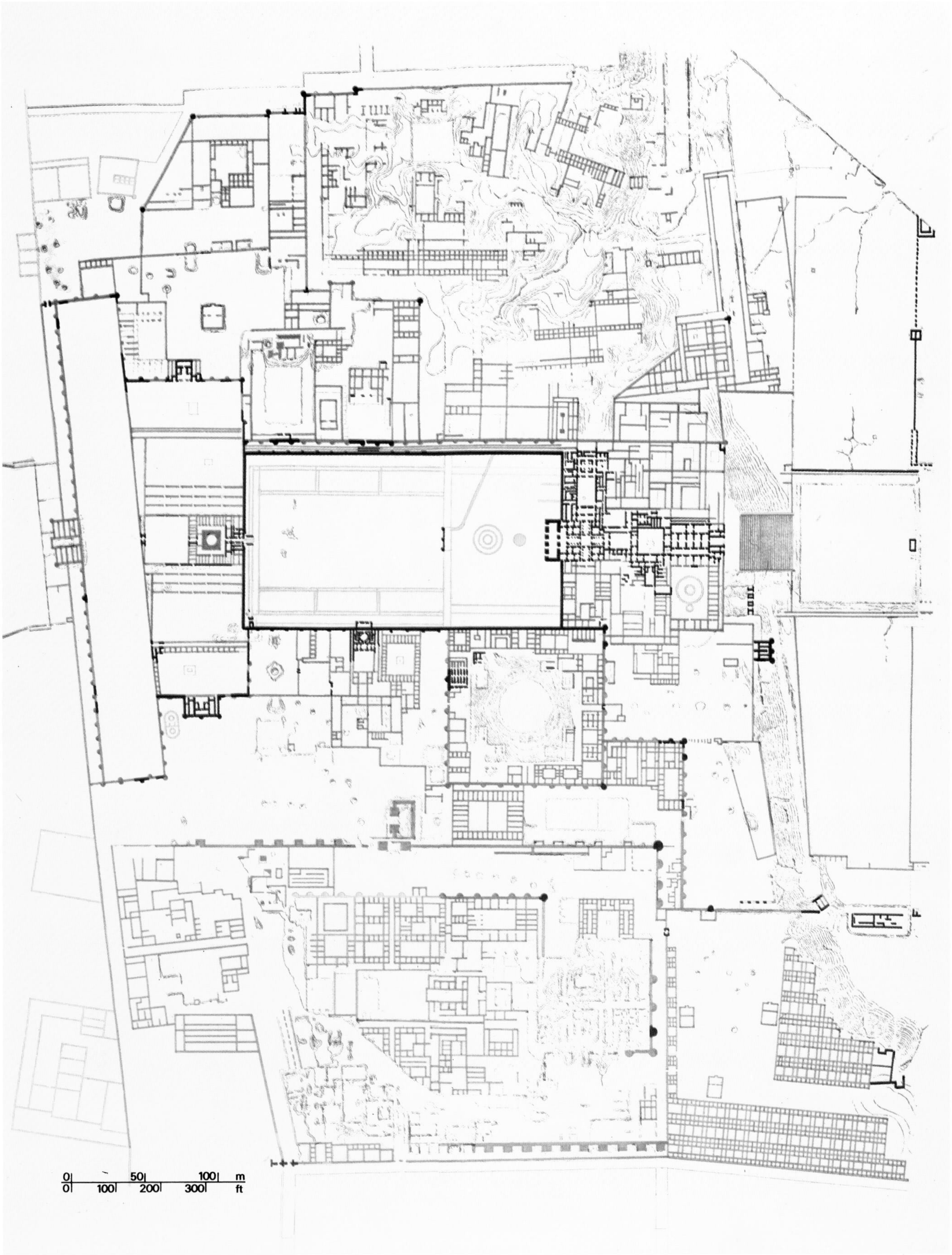
0 50 100 m
0 100 200 300 ft

The main entrance to the palace of Qaṣr al-Ḥayr al-Gharbī between Damascus and Palmyra built by the Umayyad Caliph Hishām in 727. The gateway (now in the Damascus Museum) is an adaptation of eastern Roman triumphal arches, but with a belvedere above.

in Iran and Central Asia where Islam came to terms with the local rural aristocracy. Unlike most of the Umayyad villas, Ukhayḍir was a heavily fortified enclosure built of regularly buttressed limestone walls with arrow slits and stepped crenellations far higher than the palace buildings inside. The main gateway with both machicoulis and portcullis led through a barrel-vaulted hall with decoration strongly reminiscent of the Sasanian palace at Ctesiphon to a cour d'honneur; a great *īwān* led to a cross-vaulted throne room with colonnaded porticoes on the other three sides, a structure which is echoed in a separate pavilion on the east side of the palace. The courtyard and the throne room are surrounded by vaulted corridors giving on to blocks of apartments symmetrically arranged: mostly colonnaded courts with an *īwān*, though the block immediately to the right of the entrance is a mosque. The bath was evidently elsewhere in the compound. The plan is very reminiscent of Sasanian palaces, like Qaṣr-i Shīrīn, Sarvistān and Fīrūzābād; but its patent resemblance in organization to Roman palaces in Mesopotamia, like that of the Dux Ripae at Dura-Europos on the Euphrates (probably c. 230 AD), which is actually western Roman provincial architecture, makes it dangerous to think of ʿAbbāsid palace architecture as merely perpetuating Sasanian tradition.

The triple plans of Mshaṭṭā and Ukhayḍir are taken up in the palace architecture of Sāmarrā, the remains of which give the clearest idea of Baghdad in this period. For the most part their vast extent limited excavation to the central strip. The Jawsaq al-Khāqānī/Bayt al-Khalīfa, probably built by al-Muʿtaṣim soon after the foundation of Sāmarrā in 836 AD, covered at least 432 acres, not counting the game preserve, the polo ground and the racecourses beyond the palace. It was approached from the Tigris by a broad staircase or ramp overlooking a pool 127 meters square up to the Bāb al-ʿĀmma, a triple-arched facade with the side niches blind, evidently for guards when the caliph received there. A vast entrance block gave on to a fountain court and then the cour d'honneur, with the caliph's apartments on the left/north and the harem on the right/south with a large bath giving on to the courtyard. The domed throne room was approached by *īwāns* on all four axes, all basilical, to allow light from a clerestory. Beyond there lay an esplanade with canals and pools with a small *sardāb*, eight meters deep with grottoes round a central pool and a square entrance with a frieze of camels. Beyond the *sardāb* was a grandstand overlooking the polo ground and the racecourse in the distance. To the left of the esplanade was a great *sardāb*, with a central shaft 80 meters square housing a cruciform courtyard with a central pool. The rooms of the harem vary little in plan, except for a courtyard south of the throne room with a painted square pavilion housing a pharaonic granite basin now in the Baghdad Museum. They all had piped water and ablutions, and staircases at various points suggest that parts may have had an upper floor.

Baghdad and its derivatives. Palaces were extraordinarily transient. Inadequate as our knowledge of the 9th-century palaces of Sāmarrā still is, it is essential for the interpretation of contemporary accounts of the caliphal palaces at Baghdad, most of which had already disappeared by the early 13th century when Yāqūt described the remains. An 11th-century account of the embassy from Constantine Porphyrogenitus to the Caliph al-Muqtadir in 917, who was responsible for most of these conceits, describes the palaces as they appeared when new. They passed first through the royal stables with marble columns, then through the *ḥayr* with a lion house and elephants on parade, to a kiosk, the Jawsaq al-Muḥdith, with a rectangular pool of polished tin (tinned copper) surrounded by melon beds and dwarf palms with their trunks in carved teak cases bound with gilt copper rings so cultivated that they seemed to be in fruit all the year round and luxurious pavilions with garden seats. Then came the Dār al-Shajara, a palace with a central courtyard containing a massive silver tree in a pool of clear water with movable leaves and mechanical singing birds, worked either by water or the wind, with figures of mounted lancers on either side as if charging one another. This later became a prison. They then passed through the Firdaws, evidently the royal armory, since one hall contained 10,000 gilded shields hung on the walls, and the corridors were stacked with fine and curious weapons. Before they reached the Qaṣr al-Tāj where the caliph received them, the writer says they had passed through 23 palaces.

The Ṭūlūnid and Fāṭimid palaces of Cairo, which had entirely disappeared by the early 15th century when Maqrīzī tried to reconstruct their appearance, were certainly influenced by Baghdad fashion. The latter in Nāṣir-i Khusraw's time (1047) consisted of ten residences connected by underground passages, pavilions and reception halls (*qāʿas*) with a throne room used for feasts containing a throne with a golden balustrade with silver steps behind it. Maqrīzī mentions the stables, the kitchens, the pantry, the wardrobe, the armories and even a section for flower arrangements for special occasions. He also gives a detailed description of the Fāṭimid treasures, of which a full list had survived: we should see them mostly as curios. The library, 100,000 volumes, was housed in wooden paneled cupboards in one of the halls of the Old Hospital, with works on law, Tradition, grammar, history, alchemy and astronomy and a particularly important collection of illuminated Korans by renowned calligraphers. It had only two copyists and their assistants, however, so his estimate of its size is certainly exaggerated.

A provincial idea of these irretrievable splendors survives in the ruins of the Qalʿa of the Banū Ḥammād in the mountains south of Bougie in Algeria, which was from 1052 the virtual capital of Ifrīqya for 100 years. It included a palace, the Dār al-Baḥr, with a fine bath and courts overlooking a large pool, and an isolated, towerlike pavilion, the Manār, with a basement from which a ramp led up to the piano nobile, a square room, originally with a dome, since there are the remains of squinches. There appears to have been a grand staircase, perhaps with a stalactite porch, and the dome was very probably a royal audience hall, though since only the ramp has windows, and these were arrow-slits, it must have been extremely dark.

There is little development from the palace plans of Sāmarrā, only simplification. The Ghaznavid palace at Ghazna may be the work of Sultan Ibrāhīm (1059–99) since numerous marble fragments inscribed in his name have come to light during recent trial excavations. He evidently built a palace at Nīshāpūr also, since American excavations there in the 1930s brought to light a monumental terracotta frieze from a large secular building. The Ghazna palace was trapezoidal, its form determined by surrounding buildings apparent from air-photographs of the site. The rectangular court was dominated by an axial *īwān* leading to the throne room, but it also contained a rectangular mosque, set at an angle, with a *miḥrāb* dated 1112 in the name of Masʿūd III who radically restored the palace. The most important find was 44 white marble panels, out of a calculated total of 510, carved with a Persian verse inscription, 250 meters long, of which no more than ten complete lines remain, painted in blue and red (wherever red occurs the probability is that it was a bole base for gilding) and celebrating the glories of the Ghaznavids and their architecture.

Mongol influences. The Mongol invasion provided some variety. At Shang Tu (Coleridge's Xanadu) Qubilay Khān built a bamboo palace described by Marco Polo, with gilt varnished columns bound together with silken ropes and a roof of bamboo shingles supported by capitals of dragons rampant. The interior was decorated with

The so-called "Hapsburg Bottle" (pre-1341). The Mamlūk centers for glass enameling were Damascus and Cairo. The decoration on this bottle plainly shows that it was intended for the court, though it is uninscribed. Metropolitan Museum of Art, New York.

Left: the facade of the Çinili Köşk, Istanbul, built by Meḥmed the Conqueror in 1473. The plan of the palace is very similar to a contemporary palace of Uzūn Ḥasan at Tabrīz described by an anonymous Venetian in 1507 (see chapter 1).

Opposite: plan of the Alhambra, Granada. After Burckhardt.

paintings of birds and animals in gilt. Such a hexagonal pavilion is depicted in an early 15th-century miniature of Ögedei's Qarshī (Mongol "palace") at Qarāqorum begun in 1235 and completed by his successor Möngke in the early 1250s. Rashīd al-Dīn's description – a tall palace built by Cathayan craftsmen with every wing a bowshot long and a pavilion in the center – tallies less with the miniature than does Marco Polo's of Shang Tu, and Basil Gray's suggestion that Qarshī-Qarāqorum was built after the plan of Yenching/Old Peking (destroyed 1215) has been borne out by Kiselëv's excavations at Qarāqorum in the 1950s. The palace was, therefore, Chinese. However, it also had toys – gold and silver elephants, lions or horses – which poured wine or koumiss into basins. They may have been made by a Parisian goldsmith, Guillaume Buchier/Boucher, whom Rubruck met at Qarāqorum in 1254, but they would have satisfied Islamic taste equally well. Rashīd al-Dīn, who never saw them, gives a garbled account of them, which probably explains the miniaturist's representation of them like pets being sick.

The only Mongol palace so far excavated in Persia lies at nearly 10,000 feet at Takht-i Sulaymān southwest of Tabrīz, on the shores of a crater lake which had been a cult spot at least as early as the Achaemenid period. The Mongol additions to Sasanian buildings, some dated 1271 by inscriptions on tile friezes decorated with chinoiserie dragons, phoenixes and lotuses, comprise an *īwān* which had to be reinforced during the building, and a complex of two small octagonal pavilions rather incongruously paved with luster-painted tiles. The site is beautiful, but its height gives a very short summer, and the water of the crater lake is arsenious. This and the flimsily built brick *īwān* explain why it cannot have been inhabited long.

The influence of Mongol taste upon Mamlūk Cairo is more apparent in decoration than in architecture. The typical Cairene palace unit was the *qāʿa*, which might be supplemented by a north portico, the *maqʿad*. The earliest extant *qāʿa*, the Qāʿat al-Dārdīr, perhaps 12th century, shows already the main features: a central courtyard (*durqāʿa*), mostly roofed or domed, with a raised *īwān* at either end which often had a wind-shaft (*malqaf*) to catch the cooling north wind in summer. Of the royal *qāʿas* of Mamlūk Cairo, in the palace on the Citadel begun by al-Nāṣir Muḥammad in 1313–15 and restored in 1331–33, with later additions by Sultan Ḥasan (1359–60), virtually nothing survives, and their ruins are buried in the foundations of the 19th-century mosque of Muhammad ʿAlī. They included the Dār al-ʿAdl, a *qāʿa* where the sultans sat in public audience, with a central area covered by a wooden dome, sheeted with lead and revetted with blue tiles. The *īwāns* had marble floors and granite columns brought from Upper Egypt, and the throne was of ebony and ivory.

With the exception of Tīmūr's palace at Shahr-i Sabz described by Clavijo in 1403–04, the ruins of which are still imposing, little is known of Persian or Central Asian palaces in the 14th and 15th centuries. But the Çinili Kösk at Istanbul (1473) is sufficiently like an anonymous Venetian description of Uzūn Ḥasan's contemporary palace at Tabrīz to suggest that it reflected contemporary Persian taste. Built on a high basement containing servants' quarters, kitchens and ablutions, terraced out of a steep hillside, it is a building with a central dome fronted by an open loggia of marble columns with a brick facade inlaid

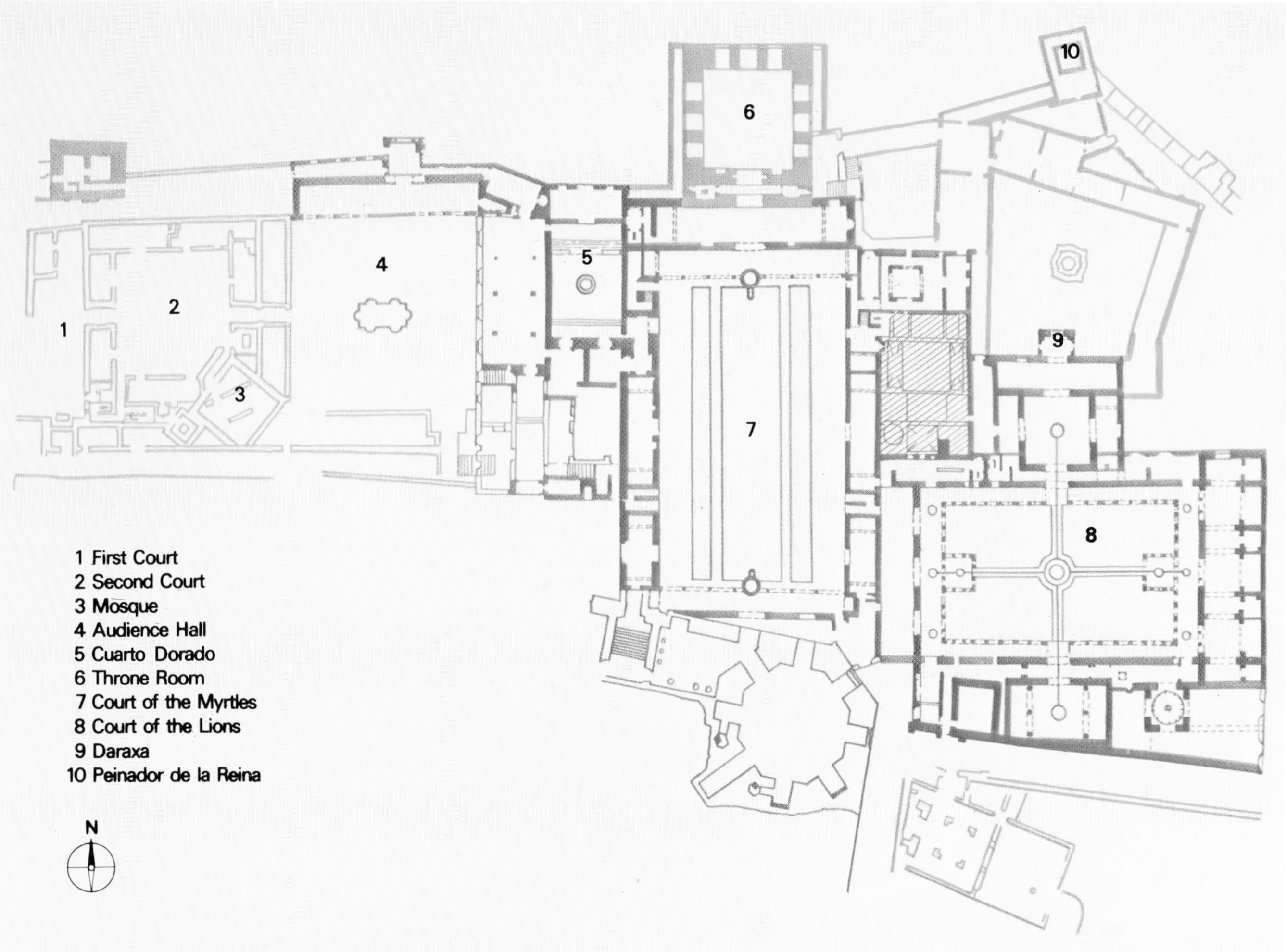

with turquoise and cobalt mosaics. This was reached by a double staircase from what is now a sandy esplanade. Inside, the domed area gives on to four *īwāns*, all with tiled dadoes originally gilded, with rooms of various sizes in the corners, all with fireplaces. The dome now has white stucco stalactite vaults, but if the analogy with Uzūn Ḥasan's palace is pursued, it may originally have been decorated with narrative heroic scenes.

The Topkapi Saray, with the exception of the Treasury (Hazine) which is 15th century, is mostly too late to be considered here. There are, however, two equally striking earlier palace complexes, that of the Shīrvānshāhs at Baku (15th century) and the Alhambra (13th to 15th centuries). Soviet excavations at the Shīrvānshāhs' palace show evidence of prior habitation on a minor scale, as well as careful terracing of the headland on which the palace stands, but little unity of conception, and much of the enceinte may have only been built in the 19th century. The most noteworthy feature of the palace is its masonry – intricate stone vaults, columns with specially carved capitals and bases, stalactite canopies for all major entrances and delicate tracery in their spandrels. This virtuosity explains why Tīmūr included a contingent of masons from Azerbaidzhan when he built the Bībī Khānum mosque at Samarkand (1399–1405). Here at least was a palace built to last.

The Alhambra. Much the same is true of the Alhambra, the structure of which, so well concealed by its fantastic decoration, had gained considerably from knowledge of Gothic engineering. It occupies the Alcazaba (al-Qaṣaba), the earlier Zīrid Citadel of Granada, the walls of which were restored soon after its reconquest in 1238. Its plan, which is the result of two and a half centuries' accretions, may originally have been influenced by an 11th-century palace on the site, that of Jehōseph bar Najralla, but work continued on the complex up to the fall of Granada in 1492, and even afterwards, when part of it was demolished for a palace of the Emperor Charles V (never completed and now mostly ruined). It is now basically a succession of courts, including stables, barracks, *masjids*, baths and gardens, watered by the River Darro and with magnificent vistas of the valley and the snowy Sierra Nevada beyond. The view, as much as its architecture, has made it the most famous of Islamic palaces.

Two ruined entrance courtyards, the second with a mosque, give on to the audience hall, the Mexuar (al-Mishwār), built by Ismāʿīl I (1308–13), restored c. 1365 and again in the 16th century. Beyond this, embassies would pass through the Cuarto Dorado (1313–33) to a

Left: the Court of the Lions (1350–1400) in the Alhambra. The central fountain is supported by 12 bronze lions from the 11th-century palace of the Jewish Vizier Jehōseph bar Najralla. The delicately worked screen walls and the thin columns are masterpieces of structural engineering.

Opposite: the Mirador Daraxa/Dār Ā'isha (after 1350) in the Alhambra. Stucco dècoration of a projecting balcony. The central medallion bears encomiastic verses of the poet Ibn Zamrak.

square throne room, the Sala de Comares (al-Qamariyya), built (pre-1350) in a projecting tower of the walls with windows in deeply recessed niches overlooking Granada. Opposite is the contemporary Court of the Myrtles, an adaptation of the traditional fountain court, with long beds of myrtles lining a rectangular pool. Beyond was a maze of royal apartments, gardens, belvederes and a luxurious bath, culminating in the Court of the Lions (1350–1400), surrounded by deceptively flimsy colonnades and a projecting gabled portico at each end to view the central fountain borne on bronze lions from the 11th-century palace of Jehōseph bar Najralla. This was probably so private that no visitor was ever admitted.

The Alhambra draws heavily upon a Moorish past – grim outer walls with no grand entrance, though even these have been softened by time, and inward-looking apartments. Even its towers or belvederes, like the Daraxa (Dārʿ Ā'isha) (post-1350) or the Peinador de la Reina with paintings showing triumphal processions or royal feasts, most resemble the domestic towers of the medieval Maghrib surmounted by a loggia to catch the evening breeze. Equally Moorish is the ornament – canopies of stalactites dripping like the honeycomb, walls entirely covered with carved stucco as if hung with textiles, Koranic inscriptions and encomiastic verses of poets like Ibn Zamrak; richly painted and gilt coffered wooden ceilings or domes; and low dadoes of *azulejos*, polychrome Moorish tiles, though many of these were restored in the 16th century and later.

The decoration of the Alhambra conceals brilliantly executed architecture. It may also distract attention from important modifications of earlier Islamic palace plans. The characteristic *īwāns* on courtyards have become enclosed and transformed into two- or three-storied loggias, while the courtyards have become compressed into something resembling the Spanish *patio* (as much a descendant of the Roman *atrium* as the Islamic *ṣaḥn*). And with its inaccessible courtyards, its lonely towers and its rich gardens it suggests the *hortus conclusus* of the medieval European romance or its Andalusian parallels rather than the semi-public luxury of earlier Muslim palaces. The Alhambra is not, therefore, typical.

Adjacent to the Alhambra was the Generalife, perhaps built by Ismāʿīl I (1308–13). Later works have transformed it into a terraced garden crowned by two-storied pavilions at either end of a long narrow pool. However, a fire in 1958 revealed the foundations of a palace and, most important, showed that the garden court was originally similar to the Cuarto Dorado in the Alhambra. The Generalife's fame as a garden owes little, therefore, to the founder's conception. Few Muslim rulers admired nature, and the 16th-century Moghul Emperor Bābur's delight in the wild flowers and the birds of Central Asia, Afghanistan and India is exceptional. Although gardens evoke copious allusions, mostly to scented flowers – narcissi, hyacinths, jasmine and roses – in the Classical authors, Islamic gardens must have been disappointing. The water gardens of the ʿAbbāsid caliphs at Sāmarrā never had enough water, and the gardens of

their palace at Baghdad must have been a combination of orchard, market garden and sparse parkland. It is often said that Persian garden carpets were inspired by delight in gardening; but it could equally well be argued that here art was meant to supply the evident inadequacy of nature.

Private houses. The blank street facades and inconspicuous entrances of houses in many Islamic cities have often led Western observers to ascribe a desire for privacy to Islam. But Ward-Perkins justly remarks that the 3rd- and 4th-century houses of Umm al-Jamāl in the Hauran, with their irregular plan disposed around an inner courtyard, are virtually indistinguishable from more recent architecture in the area, or as far north as Siirt or Mardin in Upper Mesopotamia. The Hellenistic, Parthian or Sasanian houses excavated at Ctesiphon or Ashur are the prototypes of Islamic courtyards and open *īwāns*; and in many other areas the persistent influence of Roman provincial architecture, itself obviously influenced by indigenous traditions, can still be felt. House plans differ in Islam no less than in Europe, and the domed *trulli* of the Aleppo area, like those of Apulia, are not less typical than the houses of Sāmarrā, Fusṭāṭ, Sīrāf or Merv.

Sāmarrā is particularly interesting, since it was built on uninhabited land. Predictably, the houses (9th century) have standard plans, and, predictably too, they have an innovation: the inverted T-shaped *īwān*. As with other excavated medieval Islamic houses, their occupants are unknown, and it is not even possible to say whether they were family houses or tenement blocks. Herzfeld describes them as uniformly one-storied, entered directly from the street, with an outer courtyard surrounded by storerooms, servants' quarters and domestic offices, and an inner courtyard, evidently the harem, where male visitors might not penetrate. Some courts side by side suggested summer and winter residences. They all had baths, piped water, and often *sardābs* and their own wells. A house might contain up to 50 rooms, their windows glazed with large glass disks, or there might be basilical halls. Facades were never decorated, and the really lavish stucco decoration, which often included profiled niches, was reserved for the inner rooms.

At Sīrāf the early medieval houses were of the *insula* type. However, since the main street did not run at right angles, some were recessed, doubtless to accommodate street markets. They were entered on the axis, generally up a short flight of steps. With the exception of a single *īwān*, all the other rooms were closed (10th and 11th centuries). Yet another house had a grand entrance with a molded profile on the street. This at least had an upper story, possibly with a gallery all round, while a row of piers outside the south wall on the sea side suggests perhaps a projecting loggia. Most had gutters to take rainwater direct to sewers, and some houses had sewers running under the entrance into the main sewer in the street.

If the medieval houses of Sīrāf had pre-Islamic prototypes they have not yet been identified. But Herzfeld characterized certain house-plans in Khurāsān and Seistān as indigenous: a vaulted entrance block with a domed room on either side, a courtyard and an axial *īwān* with a

Plan of a house at Sīrāf (9th to 12th centuries). After Whitehouse.

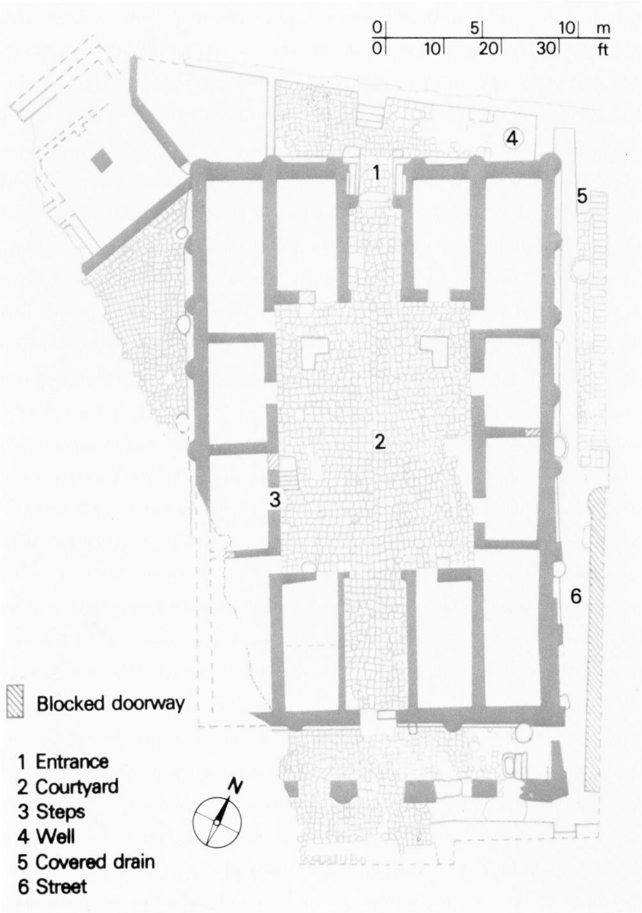

dome on either side of that. Mud-brick medieval houses recently surveyed by Fischer in Afghan Seistān are clearly derivatives of this plan, though many of his types have tunnel-vaulted towerlike entrances on to a yard surrounded with lower flat-roofed buildings on all three sides, which may reduce the central space merely to a well.

Pugachenkova has published remains of some isolated 9th- and 10th-century houses outside Merv, which were probably villas of the landowning rural aristocracy (*dihqāns*). They were mud brick on a basement surmounted by high striated walls with a marked batter, evidently for the winter rains to run off without damaging the fabric. Haram Kushk had a roughly cruciform plan, with corner rooms, two of them domed, and a staircase up to a ruined piano nobile. At Sulu Kushk, on the other hand, only the piano nobile with domed rooms in each corner was apparent. So cramped were these villas that the central court has either been eliminated or is merely a two-story well, probably domed.

Baths. Despite the claim of al-Ya'qūbī (died 905) that *ḥammāms* were a Persian invention, there is no doubt that they were directly copied from the baths of the Roman provinces, for example the harbor baths at Ephesus with splendid public rooms (late 1st century but with later restorations) or at Antioch (4th century following a 2nd-century plan), the reception rooms being often at 90 degrees to the axis with niches or alcoves at either end. The large provincial Byzantine baths continued to function long after the Muslim conquest and this perhaps explains the extreme conservatism of early Islamic baths, in which the only perceptible changes are the suppression of the frigidarium and the extension of the apodyterium into a large audience hall.

Later Islamic baths vary extraordinarily little in plan: apodyterium, tepidarium and caldarium. The hot rooms have hypocaust heating, with a separate entrance for the stoker outside, domes with oculi, glazed to conserve the heat, washbasins, and fountains or jar-stands to provide drinking water. No palace, and no large house, was without one.

The most remarkable Islamic baths so far known are Umayyad, in particular the bath at Quṣayr 'Amra in Transjordan (generally dated 711–12 or 715) and that at Khirbat al-Mafjar (probably 739–44). The bath at Quṣayr 'Amra is an oddly isolated construction, protected by a V-shaped outer wall pointing up a wadi, evidently to minimize the danger of floods, fed by a reservoir, from which the water was drawn by a horizontal waterwheel (*sāqiya*). The main hall has three niches opposite the entrance, the central one square with a painting of an enthroned ruler with an alcove paved with a marble mosaic enhanced with glass tesserae at either side. The main hall was evidently paved with marble. Off this there was a small apodyterium, a tepidarium and a caldarium, all with pierced vaults with their exterior profiles left bare, exactly like the late 2nd- or early 3rd-century hunting baths at Lepcis, which were evidently frequented by furnishers of wild beasts to the Roman amphitheaters. The plans are different but not the conception.

The Umayyad bath at Quṣayr 'Amra, Jordan, probably built for Caliph al-Walīd II in 743–44. The three barrel vaults are of the audience hall which occupies the major part of the construction. The surrounding area, which has yet to be thoroughly surveyed, shows traces of medieval settlement, and the bath was probably therefore not an isolated building.

The entrance hall is covered with paintings, mostly indecipherable until their recent restoration by Spanish craftsmen, but including a painting of "Six Kings," perhaps the enemies over whom Islam had triumphed. But the most impressive paintings are in the tepidarium with *Grandes Baigneuses*, so ample as to explain the relegation of painting by some of the strictest Muslim jurists to baths, and the Zodiac of the caldarium. The very Hellenistic Zodiac, executed in a style characteristic almost of 2nd- or 3rd-century Palmyrene painting, was evidently a feature of Roman or Byzantine baths, to judge from a much cited passage of John of Gaza or allusions in Philostratus' *Life of Apollonius of Tyana.* But the Zodiac of Quṣayr 'Amra is exceptional in three ways: it was executed from a drawing; the drawing showed the constellations as they appear on a globe, that is, from above, not from below, so that it appears inside out; and although the Pole Star in the center should give the northern hemisphere, the constellations are partly those of the southern, arranged in concentric circles below it instead of as they appear in the sky.

The bath recently discovered at Qaṣr al-Ḥayr East (probably 728 AD) has yet to be published in detail, but it can scarcely excel the sumptuousness of that at Khirbat al-Mafjar, of which the hall is a major feature. It is a basilica roughly 30 meters square, with 16 piers dividing its aisles;

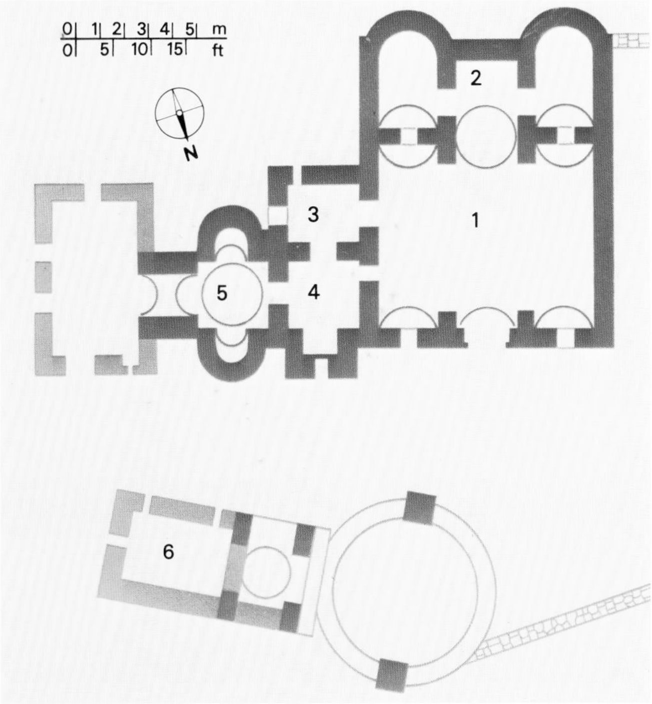

Above: a plan of the baths at Quṣayr ʿAmra. After Creswell. Note the main hall (1), vestibule (2), apodyterium (3), tepidarium (4), caldarium (5) and reservoir (6).
Below: a reconstruction of the *dīwān* at Khirbat al-Mafjar (probably 739–44). After Hamilton.

on the west side, facing the grand entrance, it has three apses, the crown of the central one being of radically coursed stones with a massive stone hook and chain at its apex. In the southwest corner there was a private entrance from the palace, but most of the south side was occupied by a raised pool with three apses, either a nymphaeum or a natatio, as in Imperial Roman baths like those of Caracalla (212–16 AD). The whole floor is covered by rectangular panels of polychrome marble mosaic, giving the impression of masses of separate carpets, but with a continuous mosaic from the entrance right up to the apse which bears the hook and chain. At the northwest corner of this hall there is a small but very highly decorated room, surmounted by a dome on pendentives lit by eight windows with stucco grilles and perhaps a small lantern at the apex. It ends in a raised platform set in a semicircular apse, paved with a brilliantly illusionistic marble mosaic representing a spreading tree with animals grazing or attacking beneath it, surrounded by a fringe of tassels. (Carpets at this period did not exist, but the modeling of the tree anyway suggests tapestry weaving.) The purpose of the large hall has been the subject of fruitful speculation by Ettinghausen, but it may be simply a late revival of the bath-palace like Tiberius' Villa Jovis (14–37 AD): luxury fit for a caliph as dissolute as al-Walīd II (743–44) but not necessarily implying any elaborate Muslim ceremonial. Water was provided by an aqueduct running for part of its length across bridges. The latrines are separate and resemble Roman latrines in being large, communal and provided with seats. However, in the present state of our knowledge, these grand Umayyad baths, with their audience halls far more impressive than the baths themselves, apparently mark a final stage in the history of late Antiquity rather than an innovation in Islam.

A detail from the horseshoe-shaped platform of the mosaic floor of the *dīwān* at Khirbat al-Mafjar. The themes and treatment are characteristic of 6th-century mosaics of the Great Palace of Byzantium or mosaics from contemporary Antioch.

6. Shrines and Mausolea

Shrines

Many mosques are now regarded as holy, particularly their *miḥrābs* or *qibla* walls, but there is no legal sanction for this. Shrines are exceptional because they are recognized as sacred, and admission is restricted to the faithful. Though Sunnīs are generally more tolerant than Shīʿīs, the principal Sunnī shrines, at Mecca and Medina, like the great Shīʿī shrines of Persia and Iraq, are known in the West principally from descriptions by travelers who have penetrated them in disguise, or from converts. Nevertheless a picture can be gained from the Muslim sources, which is particularly fortunate since much of these great shrines – at Mecca, Medina, Qumm, Mashhad, Qādhimayn outside Baghdad, Najaf and Kerbelā – is 17th- to 19th-century reconstruction, and the architectural changes have modified ritual, as they did at Mecca and Jerusalem between 700 and 1200.

The purpose of shrines. Not all shrines are architectural: isolated trees, springs, hill-tops and even one of the piers of the 14th-century Çoban bridge east of Erzurum are all visited and votive rags left in the hope that prayers may be answered. But architectural shrines, as listed, for example, in the guide of al-Harawī (died 1215) are very varied. (1) Tombs or shrines of Koranic Prophets, mostly of the Biblical tradition – Noah, Joshua, Lot, Abraham, Ruben and even the Koranic equivalent of Christ, ʿIsā – but including the Seven Sleepers (Aṣḥāb al-Khaf) and a composite figure, Khiḍr, who appears to stem from both Elijah (Ilyās) and St George. (2) Tombs of Companions of the Prophet, like Khalīd ibn al-Walīd, whose tomb is at Ḥomṣ in Syria. (3) Shrines associated with the Shīʿa – ʿAlī, Fāṭima, Ḥusayn and their descendants, the Shīʿī Imāms. (4) Saints, especially the early Muslim mystics, and jurists like the Imām al-Shāfiʿī or Abū Ḥanīfa, founders of two of the principal schools of Islamic law. (5) Heroes of the early wars of Islam, like Sayyid Baṭṭāl Ghāzī, among whom he includes Nūr al-Dīn and Saladin, the latter doubtless for his reconquest of Jerusalem from the Crusaders. (6) Sites important in the lives of the Prophets, for example the various stations of the pilgrimage at Mecca, sometimes with relics; the most widespread are heads, or footprints. (7) Miraculous sites like Mt Jūdī in the extreme southeast of Turkey near Jazīrat ibn ʿUmar/Cizre on which, according to the Babylonian-Muslim tradition, the Ark landed after the Flood. (8) Famous figures in Arab history, like the poet of the Jāhiliyya, Imru'l-Qays, whose tomb al-Harawī located, rather implausibly, at Kayseri in Anatolia.

The Biblical tradition and the cult of the Prophets were recognized from the first, though they were not thought to mediate between man and God. However, the notion of a communion of saints was never accepted, nor the ideal of sanctity as exemplary virtue. Hence the diversity of figures later venerated in Islam: martyrs for the faith; the founders, real or supposed, of Ṣūfī orders or their distinguished followers; shaykhs venerated for their charisma; and semi-magical figures, esteemed as rain-makers, as at the Jewish-Muslim Tomb of Daniel at Sūsa/Shūsh in southern Persia or on the Citadel of Konya where in the Church of St Amphilochius, which had become a mosque by the 16th century, Plato/Eflātūn was propitiated lest, by oversight, he allowed Konya to be flooded. Moreover, apart from the *ḥajj*, there was no general obligation to make pilgrimages to saints' tombs in early Islam: the purpose of visits was usually the granting of an immediate favor, children for the barren or a husband for an unmarried daughter.

Previous page: the shrine at Mashhad. The gilt dome over the tomb of the Imām Riḍā was added in the 18th century.

Not surprisingly, perhaps, the same person is revered at different sites. Massignon traced shrines of the Seven Sleepers all over the Islamic world, from Turkestan to Spain. There are shrines of Joshua/Yūshaʿ at Maʿarrat al-Nuʿmān in north Syria and at Baghdad as well as at Kafr Ḥārith on Lake Galilee where the Jews, and the Druse, hold him to be buried. There are sanctuaries of Abraham at Urfa-Ḥarrān, at Aleppo, both on the Citadel and in one of the cemeteries, at Mecca and at Hebron, where his tomb is venerated with those of Jacob, Sarah and Leah. And the head of Ḥusayn severed at Kerbelā in 680 appears to have had innumerable resting places before a shrine was built for it at ʿAsqalān/Ashkelon in 1091 from which it was transferred finally to Cairo in 1154. In the case of Abraham these multiple shrines commemorate different episodes in his Koranic biography. However, it is difficult to account for two heads of St John the Baptist/Yaḥyā ibn Zakāriyya, one in the Great Mosque at Damascus and the other now in the Great Mosque at Aleppo. Even minor figures are revered in different places: the tomb of the mystic, ʿAbd Allāh Anṣārī, was still being visited at Aleppo in the Mamlūk period, though he died at Herāt in 1089 and was buried at Gāzur Gāh.

From this two conclusions emerge. Few shrines are revered for their relics; most are of persons. Secondly, multiple shrines may well be Islamic cults at spots with a long pre-Islamic tradition of sanctity. North of Tripoli in the Lebanon, for example, there is a small *khānqāh* of the shaykh al-Badawī, founder of an Egyptian Ṣūfī order. It is much visited for its spring, full of carp, which has evidently been venerated since prehistoric times as a shrine of the Phoenician goddess Atargatis. But it is also visited by local Christians, who identify it with a shrine of St Antony of Padua (*Padua* and *Badawī* are close in the local pronunciation). This may be simply an amusing mistake, but it also suggests a continuous cult.

However, there is no invariable rule of succession, despite the fine 12th-century mosques curiously situated inside the enceintes of the Temple of Jupiter at Baalbek and of Bel at Palmyra and making full use of their splendid pagan surroundings. The shrines mentioned by al-Harawī are often now unidentifiable, even when they are mentioned by later authors, and some, disconcertingly, have changed their names. The tomb of Joshua on the Nablus-Jerusalem road, he mentions, has now become Ezra's

Part of the shrine of Abraham at Urfa (ancient Edessa), believed to commemorate the casting of Abraham into a fiery furnace. There are now few 12th-century remains; but around a large rectangular pool full of venerable carp is a complex of early Ottoman buildings, including the mosque shown here.

tomb (ʿUzayr). The church of Haghia Sophia contained numberless relics, including the tomb of St John Chrysostom, at the conquest of Constantinople in 1453, but subsequently the fact that it had been the greatest church in Christendom was lost to popular consciousness. Instead, a number of arbitrary cults survived: the doors, believed to be of wood from the Ark, encouraged *fātiḥa*s (the opening verses of the Koran) to Nūḥ/Noah; a sacred well "with the cover of the well of Samaria" cured Turkish palpitations; while the Sweating Column, which is always covered with a thin film of moisture, which Christians had attributed to St Gregory, was transferred to Khiḍr who also helped Justinian's architect to orient the building correctly and rebuilt the dome, which fell the day Muhammad was born and which was only rebuilt with Mecca sand, water from Zemzem and Muhammad's spittle.

The *ḥajj* was a duty incumbent upon all adult Muslims of sound body and mind and anyone who failed to make it during his lifetime was entitled to allot one third of his estate to a nominee, one of his heirs, who would then make the *ḥajj* in his stead. The pilgrimage also had to be performed at the right season. The Holy Places could, of course, be visited at any time, but this only counted as a minor act of piety (*ʿumra*). Nevertheless, wars and distance must often have made these requirements impossible to fulfill, and rulers, in particular, could rarely risk leaving their kingdoms. By the 12th century the custom of pilgrimage by proxy was accepted, and carefully drawn-up certificates, beautifully written and sometimes decorated with the principal shrines of Mecca and Medina, were presented as testimony that the pilgrimage had been performed.

Mecca, like Qumm or Mashhad in Persia, is *ḥaram*: only those in a state of ritual purity may enter the Kaʿba area. Hunting was forbidden and the innumerable blue pigeons infesting the courtyard could not be molested. No indigenous plants could be cut down nor any indigenous animal killed except mice, serpents, gray-backed crows (all of ill-omen), mad dogs, fish or noxious insects. Most important, the Kaʿba gave sanctuary to criminals (except for run-away slaves), though since the authorities were not obliged to feed them they could eventually be dislodged. The same was true at Mashhad where for a three-day period criminals were safe, if starving. However, sanctuary does not define a *ḥaram* since elsewhere it was rather strangely applied. Telegraph offices in Persia had it, and the caravansaray al-Khān on the Sinjār-Mosul road in northern Iraq has a porch with reliefs of a dragon-slayer (Khiḍr or St George) and an inscription (mid-13th century) guaranteeing lodging for all, travelers or residents, even those fleeing from justice: it must, if taken literally, have made the *khān* a place of ill repute.

The Kaʿba. For the Kaʿba I principally use Ibn Jubayr's description (1183), despite his disapproval of the local Muslims and their practices, since it has subsequently been transformed out of all recognition. Outside it was rectangular on a raised platform covered with a silken veil bearing the name and titles of the ʿAbbāsid Caliph al-Nāṣir (1180–1225). This veil, the *kiswa*, continued to be sent yearly after the fall of the ʿAbbāsid Caliphate in Baghdad (1258) by the Mamlūk sultans of Egypt, who regarded it as a privilege to be jealously guarded. On the east side was a door plated with silver-gilt in a gilt frame. The interior was irregular, because the shrine contained a black stone, believed to be the cornerstone of Abraham's Temple and to bear his footprint.

A modern poster showing the Kaʿba at Mecca, the principal shrine of Islam and the focus of the Pilgrimage. Its size has been exaggerated in accordance with its sanctity in Muslim eyes. To the right is an enclosure following the elliptical line of a pre-Islamic enceinte. In the center are the buildings of the well of Zemzem and the *minbar* from which the Friday Sermon is given. Below are illustrations of buildings on some of the stations of the Pilgrimage.

The roof of the Kaʿba was supported by three teak columns, the floor and the dadoes were paneled with marble, while the upper part, which appears to have been undecorated except for a gilt frieze, was hung with a green veil. There were four windows and an oculus in the roof filled with Iraqi (stained or painted) glass. In Ibn Jubayr's time the Kaʿba was open on Mondays and Fridays and daily during the month of Rajab. It was entered by a large wooden ladder on wheels, but access was restricted to the Shaybī shaykhs, its traditional guardians, and to the privileged. The later ʿAbbāsid caliphs, and the Mamlūk sultans after them, established the custom soon after their accession of sending richly decorated metal keys for the door of the Kaʿba. This was evidently a demonstration of their authority over the Holy Places and corresponded to the rich jewels and other gifts made to the Kaʿba by the earlier caliphs in the 9th and 10th centuries, even though *waqfs* to it aroused the disapproval of the *ʿulamā'*. It was evidently important that the upholders of Sunnī orthodoxy should make their own preeminence clear, because, rather surprisingly, the traditional proprietors of the shrine, the Sharīfs of Mecca, claimed descent from ʿAlī.

The Kaʿba was surrounded by a broad granite processional way. Behind it was the Ḥijr, the remains of an early enceinte, which had been restored just before Ibn Jubayr's visit by the Caliph al-Nāṣir (1180). It was rather more than a semicircle paved with mosaic and split marble paneling.

In spite of the ancient importance of the Well of Zemzem its importance in the ritual of the *ḥajj* was only slowly established. It was used for ablutions, for drinking and for washing out the Kaʿba three times a year, a ritual in which it was a privilege to be allowed to participate. Under the ʿAbbāsids it was covered with a dome on teak columns with grilles between, from which the faithful obtained water drawn up from the well by buckets. Ibn Jubayr noted various domes: one a pavilion over the well itself with a circular cistern from which water flowed into a trough surrounded by marble benches for the faithful while making their ablutions; and the Qubbat al-Sharāb or Qubbat ʿAbbās, where Zemzem water was placed to cool in large earthenware crocks every evening for the pilgrims to drink. This second dome was apparently a survivor from an early Islamic ritual in which a drink made from grapes or dates watered with Zemzem water was served after the *ṭawwāf* (circumambulation). There was also a third domed building containing Korans, candlesticks and other objects made *waqf* to the Kaʿba.

The Friday prayer was attended with great ceremonies. A *minbar* on wheels was placed against the Kaʿba and a procession of the preacher clad in black, the traditional color of the ʿAbbāsids, and preceded by two standard bearers with black flags advanced. Before climbing to his seat he was girded with a sword by the Chief Muezzin and only then was the call to prayer given, first from the roof of the Well of Zemzem, which was flat with a wooden balustrade, and then from the seven minarets of the enceinte. During the prayer the standards were fixed to rings on the *minbar*. Prayers were led by the Chief Imām before the Maqām Ibrāhīm, but since the Kaʿba was the place to which all Muslims turned when praying it did not matter which way the congregation faced. In fact, each of the four Schools of Law had its own imām with his lodgings in the courtyard, together with accommodation for a *muballigh* who repeated the prayers in a loud voice to those too far away to hear them.

The earliest Muslim enclosure of the Kaʿba was perhaps the work of ʿAbd al-Malik (late 7th century), with arcades of teak columns and gilt capitals. Under the ʿAbbāsids these were replaced by marble columns, and by Ibn Jubayr's time the courtyard was surrounded on all sides by colonnades three bays deep, with an octagonal stone pier to every four columns. The courtyard facades evidently had a cresting of stepped merlons almost touching with a carved stucco frieze below, and the effect was probably somewhat similar to the *ṣaḥn* of the mosque of al-Azhar in Cairo after its restoration in 1130–47 AD. Ibn Jubayr counted 19 gates to the Ḥaram and seven minarets, some of the former bearing inscriptions of the late 8th century, though these may well have been plaques inserted into later masonry. His description of the seven minarets suggests that they had rectangular stone bases with chamfered corners, a cylindrical brick shaft and a globular finial perhaps over a columned pavilion with wooden balconies and balustrades. The building was not, of course, a mosque, yet Ibn Jubayr noted many activities characteristic of mosques – Koran reading, shaykhs teaching, commerce and multitudes of residents, often aged shaykhs who had come to end their days there.

Ibn Jubayr gives other interesting accounts of the ceremonies accompanying evening prayers at the Kaʿba during the pilgrimage months, which show both innovations due to popular piety and a complex pre-Islamic and Islamic tradition.

The Dome of the Rock. Very much the same is true at Jerusalem, where the Ḥaram al-Sharīf, which is no longer closed to foreigners and which confers no sanctuary to criminals, is covered with Islamic monuments of various periods drawing upon Jewish and Christian tradition. The Ḥaram, a vast esplanade with a raised terrace, is almost certainly the site of the Temple of Solomon, at least that rebuilt by Herod the Great in 20 BC and destroyed by Titus in 70 AD, which was left abandoned till the Arab conquest. The first Islamic monument to be erected there was the Dome of the Rock by ʿAbd al-Malik (691–92 AD). Its site was a demonstration to the Jews that Islam henceforth was to replace the Temple; and its monumental inscription inside, the first in Islam, explicitly denies the Incarnation, an assertion of the triumph of Islam over Christianity.

The Dome, originally a double wooden shell, is set on a high drum, 67 feet in diameter, supported on four piers with four columns between each, so as to surround a large irregular rock. This rock in Muslim tradition came to bear the hoofprint of Burāq, the half-human steed on which Muhammad journeyed by night from Medina to Jerusalem, ascending, according to later traditions, to the Seventh Heaven on the way. Between the central cylinder and the octagonal exterior is an octagonal ambulatory with a gently sloping roof. The stone exterior with blind arcading had four entrances on the axes, each with a shallow gabled roof. These were originally faced with split marble paneling. The exterior of the drum was faced by Süleymān the Magnificent with a monumental inscription in Iznik tiles, which have recently been the object of savage restoration, but, to judge from the account of Tschudi (1519), it was previously covered with mosaics of trees, architecture

The Kaʿba today, very different from its medieval form.

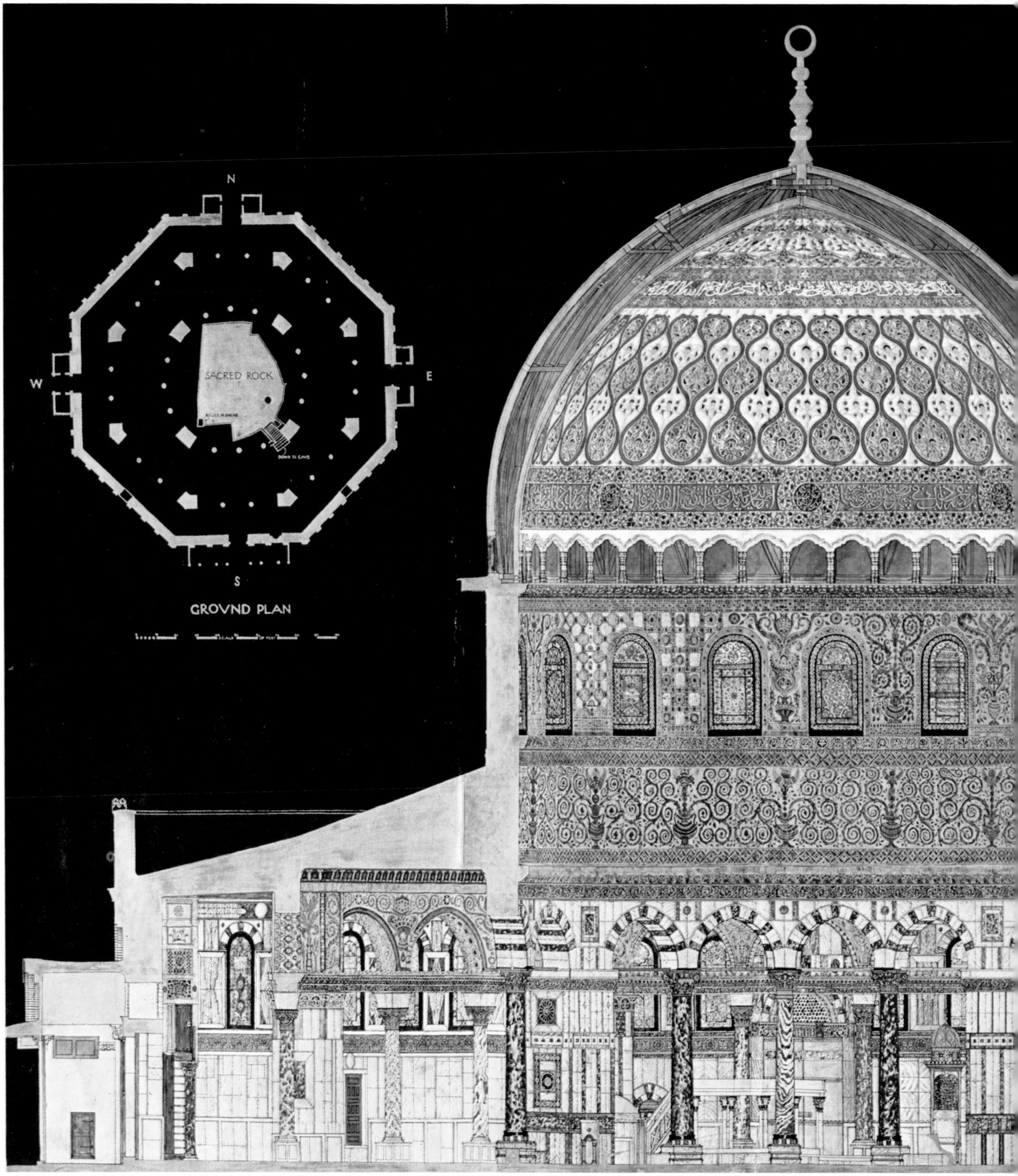

and cherubim. The doorways have wooden lintels encased with repoussé plaques of copper or bronze, probably originally gilt, but the doors had already been replaced by the time of Muqaddasī with carved wooden panels presented by the ʿAbbāsid Caliph al-Muqtadir (908–32 AD).

Inside, the octagonal ambulatory has wooden tie-beams, also encased in repoussé metalwork, once probably gilt as are the capitals of the columns. The inner face of the

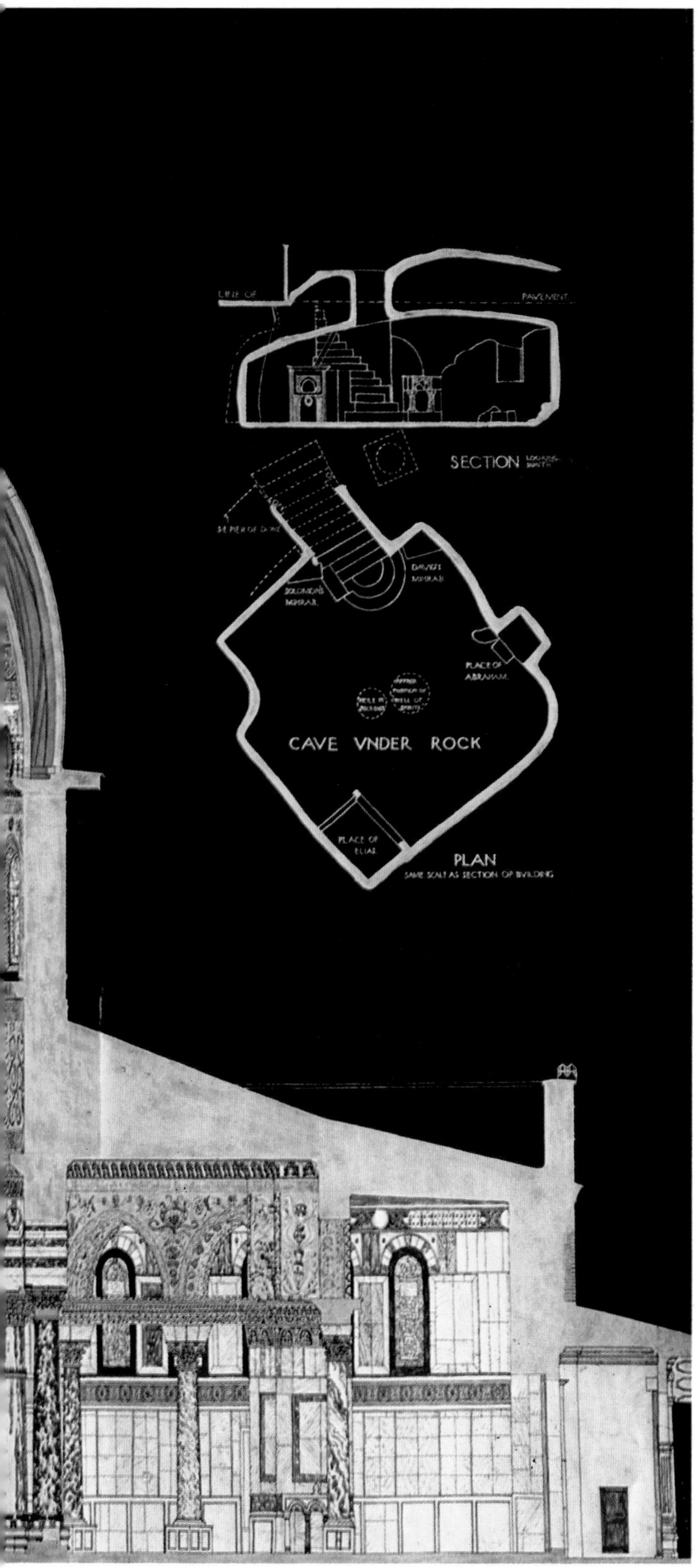

The Dome of the Rock, Jerusalem, erected (691–92) on the Temple mount over a rock from which Muhammad was later believed to have ascended to heaven. The original plan has remained unchanged. The marble paneling and the mosaics of the dome above are original; but the double dome itself was restored in 1022–23. The bicolored arches and the inner decoration of the dome are 14th-century Mamlūk; in the mid-16th century the exterior of the dome was entirely refaced by Süleymān the Magnificent. From the drawing by William Harvey (1909).

octagonal ambulatory, the undersides of the arches and the bodies of the piers are covered with brilliant polychrome and mother-of-pearl mosaics on a gold ground, bizarre in appearance but derivable from the mosaic tradition of pre-Islamic Syria. The richness and variety of the interior and exterior decoration owe much to a series of restorations, but at the time of its foundation there can have been no more brilliantly decorated monument in Syria or Palestine.

Nāṣir-i Khusraw (1047) describes the Bāb al-Silsila, then the most important of the gates of the Ḥaram, as a double tunnel vault with gates of inlaid brass or copper. The gateway was surmounted by a dome, and the outer part of the vaulted passageways was faced with mosaic, doubtless the work of the Fāṭimid Caliph al-Ẓāhir, who also reconstructed the dome of the Dome of the Rock (1022–23) and left his inscriptions on the ribs of the dome. The upper terrace, which is now approached by eight stairways, is mostly a matter of Fāṭimid and Ayyūbid restoration, particularly following upon Saladin's reconquest of the city and restoration of its walls in 1191. The domed pavilions include the Qubbat Yūsuf (1681), built by an Ottoman eunuch who was certainly playing upon the fact that Saladin, like the Biblical/Koranic Prophet, was also called Yūsuf, and the Qubbat Mūsā below the terrace (again a play on its founder's name since Moses has no known association with the Ḥaram), a domed square with a *miḥrāb* and a niche in the facade (1249–50). The most important of these domed pavilions is, however, the Qubbat al-Silsila, which Van Berchem identified with the Treasury (Bayt al-Māl) of ʿAbd al-Malik (691–92) on 12 columns with a projecting *miḥrāb*. This addition perhaps dates from the period 1261–73 when Baybars faced the dome with mosaics, later replaced by Süleymān the Magnificent with tiles (1561–62). By the 13th century this building was believed to be David's, or Solomon's, Judgment Seat, where there hung a chain to separate the good from the bad. The Crusader occupation of the Ḥaram made little difference, and after the expulsion of the Franks in the late 13th century the Mamlūks continued this cult.

In the Ottoman period the Ḥaram was covered with open-air *miḥrābs*, arcades and even hospices for pilgrims. Among installations which suggest a pre-Islamic tradition, however, there are two which are particularly important. The first is an open-air *minbar* "restored" by a 14th-century Qāḍī (1325–88), with a gateway, balustrades and a 12-columned pavilion surmounting it, built largely of Byzantine or Crusader elements and decidedly reminiscent of 12th-century Italian pulpits, though it may well be a Mamlūk construction. Interestingly, however, it appears to have replaced a wooden structure on wheels, from which prayers on the Muslim feasts were said or rogations

Above: general view of Jerusalem from Mount Olivet showing the Dome of the Rock in the center of the Ḥaram al-Sharīf.

Opposite: the Ḥaram al-Sharīf, Jerusalem. The Qubbat al-Silsila, probably to be identified with the Treasury of ʿAbd al-Malik (691–92), is on the right. The projecting *miḥrāb* perhaps dates from the period 1261–73.

made for rain. Secondly there is the Qubbat al-Miʿrāj, restored or rebuilt in 1200–01, an octagonal structure, originally a domed canopy, which its inscription confuses with a Qubbat al-Nabī, which it may have replaced. Both commemorated the Ascension of Muhammad, but Van Berchem notes its similarity to the medieval Chapel of the Ascension on Mount Olivet and suggests a connection between the two. Insofar as the Ḥaram appears to have a predominant tradition, it is, therefore, the Ascension of Muhammad, commemorated primarily in the Aqṣāʾ Mosque and in the Dome of the Rock, but also, Van Berchem notes, virtually all over the Ḥaram. The individual monuments are, therefore, monuments to a general cult, though they appear to commemorate particular events in the Prophet's life.

Kūfa. At Kūfa in 1184–85 Ibn Jubayr reports that the Great Mosque was filled with relics of ʿAlī and also contained a sacred spring, created by Nūḥ/Noah, a prayer place of Idrīs/Enoch, dwellings of Noah's family and the workshop where the Ark was built, and the tomb of ʿAlī at Najaf nearby which, unfortunately, he had no time to describe. It and the shrines of Ḥusayn and ʿAbbās at Kerbelā are known chiefly from Nöldeke's survey. The *mashhad*s of ʿAlī and ʿAbbās are very similar, a central dome open on all sides surrounded by a rectangular ambulatory with a grand entrance facade and a minaret at either end. The surrounding courtyards have arcades of two-storied cells, mostly given over to commerce, with shallow *īwān*s on the axis of the central domes. Neither is *qibla*-oriented. The *mashhad* of ʿAlī was restored under Ghāzān (1304) and a *madrasa*, a *khānqāh* and a *dār al-siyāda* (lodging for kinsmen of the Prophet) added, and Ibn Baṭṭūṭa describes the Kāshān tile revetments of the tomb, some of which still remain. But the only adjacent building Nöldeke noted was a Sunnī mosque adjoining the shrine.

Mashhad. As in Clavijo's time, it is now possible to enter the Ḥaram at Mashhad; but the atmosphere of concentrated religiosity inside the tomb makes precise observation difficult. It passes for the tomb of the Eighth Imām, Riḍāʾ, allegedly poisoned at Ṭūs nearby in 817 and subsequently buried in a mausoleum made ready by the ʿAbbāsid Caliph Hārūn al-Rashīd. It was rebuilt and rewalled in the early 11th century by Maḥmūd of Ghazna, and restored by the Seljuk Sanjar in 1118, and although the nomadic Ghuzz later sacked Ṭūs they spared the shrine. There were further restorations in 1215 when three Kāshān luster-painted *miḥrāb*s were installed inside the tomb chamber, and again in the reign of Öljeytü (1304–16), which doubtless accounts for the large dome Ibn Baṭṭūṭa saw over the tomb. The wooden cenotaph was plated with silver and approached through an entrance with a silver threshold, hung with silk-embroidered veils, and rich carpets (perhaps still kilims) covered the floor. The principal glory of the shrine is, however, a mosque/*madrasa* built in 1415–18 by Gawhar Shād, the wife of Shāh Rukh (ruled 1406–46), as part of restorations which included a Dār al-Siyāda and a Dār al-Ḥuffāẓ.

The building has recently been mercilessly restored by the shrine authorities, but the shrine is a warren of bazaars, tombs, fountains, grand courtyards, public kitchens and assembly rooms. There are still noteworthy buildings, like the Madrasa-yi Dō Dār (1439), a four-*īwān* construction with some of the last stucco decoration in Persia, and two domes on either side of the *qibla īwān* with fine inscriptions on the exterior of their drums on a cobalt ground. The shrine has a magnificent library, not only of illuminated Korans going back to the 10th century, but also of illustrated manuscripts, including a 13th-century *Pharmacopeia* of Dioscorides.

Ardebīl, Balkh and Ashkelon. The shrine of the Ṣafawid dynasty at Ardebīl, centered upon the mausoleum of Shaykh Ṣafī, built c. 1350, most impressed 17th-century European travelers, but the principal transformation is evidently no earlier than Shāh Ṭahmasp (1524–76), who combined the earlier 14th-century mosque and the mausolea into a single whole by adding a covered forecourt or antechamber and an exterior facade. Under his successors cells and assembly rooms for Ṣūfīs were added, and public kitchens for visitors, while Shāh ʿAbbās I dedicated a collection of Chinese porcelain (some of it

pre-Ming), once housed in a specially constructed room, and a rich library, largely dispersed on the Russian occupation of Ardebīl in 1830.

In Sanjar's reign an evidently suppositious tomb of ʿAlī came to light near Balkh. Its rediscovery in 1481 led to an epidemic of suppositious shrines, particularly in the Herāt area, and the frauds became so numerous that they had to be punished.

The head of Ḥusayn, it has been said, was placed in a *mashhad* built at ʿAsqalān/Ashkelon in 1091 from which it was removed to Cairo in 1154, where Ibn Jubayr visited it (1182–83). It was in a shrine approached through a mosque and had a similar (domed?) chamber to either side of it. The head was enclosed in a silver casket draped with precious materials and surrounded with silver and gold candlesticks holding long white candles, characteristic of any great shrine, and lit by gold and silver lamps. The shrine, though completely rebuilt and stripped of its medieval splendor, is still highly venerated in Cairo.

Samarkand. Among these grand shrines is that of Quthām ibn ʿAbbās on the southern slopes of Afrāsiyāb at Samarkand, with the mausolea erected near it known as the Shāh-i Zinde. A cousin of Muhammad, he traditionally came to Samarkand in 676 and died there. Under the ʿAbbāsids his tomb was venerated and the legend grew up that he did not die but was miraculously engulfed in a cliff, hence the name Shāh-i Zinde, the Living King. By the 12th century there was a *madrasa* attached to the shrine, and, as recent excavations have shown, an important cemetery. According to Ibn Baṭṭūṭa, the shrine was so famous that the Mongols dared not touch it; his description of it just before its restoration in 1334–35 is therefore important. Above the tomb was a dome roofed with lead on four piers, each with two engaged columns of marble, black, green, red or white. The walls were of gilt polychrome marble and the tomb was covered with an ebony cenotaph inlaid with gold and precious stones with silver bands at the corners. It was visited on Mondays and Fridays, both by the Samarkandīs and by nomad Turks who brought to it presents, money and sacrificial offerings.

The tomb consists of a pilgrims' hall (*ziyāretkhāne*) with grilles giving on to a dome or *qubba* with the vast, five-tier cenotaph of four platforms surmounted by a gabled top, all of gilt and lajvardina medallions on cobalt or turquoise carved ceramic plaques. The walls of the tomb have painted decoration imitating star and cross tiles, and in 1934 remains were found of raised gilt medallions outlined in red on an olive ground; there was no trace of marble.

Smaller shrines. Apart from these grand complexes, which are mostly accretions of buildings over several hundred years, there are various 14th-century "saints'" shrines in Persia and Central Asia which deserve consideration. Such were evidently the buildings at the Seljuk mosque by the grave of Bāyazīd Bisṭāmī at Basṭām (1299–1313) and that of Aḥmad Jāmī at Turbat-i Jām; the latter includes a large forecourt containing a cemetery and the remains of a large Mongol mosque, as well as a richly painted domed chamber, a *khānqāh* and various secular mausolea. Comparable is the "tomb of Najm al-Din Kubrā" (1321–33) at Urgench with a grand underglaze-painted tiled cenotaph, or the shrine of Aḥmad Yassawī at Gorod Turkestan/Ḥaḍrat-i Turkistān restored by Tīmūr in 1397.

The most interesting of this group, architecturally speaking, is Gāzur Gāh outside Herāt, the tomb of the mystic ʿAbd Allāh Anṣārī, which must have become the focus of a cemetery soon after his death in 1089. However, apart from a *madrasa* there, no longer extant, founded by a Ghūrid vizier in the late 12th century, and the burial there of the last Ghūrid ruler, Maḥmūd (killed 1212), there were no signs of royal interest till 1425, when Shāh Rukh built a large rectangular enceinte, with a colossal tiled and painted axial *īwān*, a cistern now popularly known as Zemzem, and a *khānqāh* outside it which has since disappeared. The tombstone of ʿAbd Allāh Anṣārī is surrounded by a marble kerb and shaded by an ancient pistachio tree. In front of the tomb is a raised platform (*ṣuffa*) dated 1477–78 with six plain black Tīmūrid cenotaphs, four of them dated between 1445–46 and 1461–62. Evidently Shāh Rukh's works encouraged his successors at Herāt to use it as their family cemetery.

For each great shrine of Islam there are 300 local shrines, from that recently discovered at Sīrāf, the cult at which remains to be established, to suppositious shrines of Imāms at Mosul – the Imām Yaḥyā (cenotaph dated 1239–40) and the Imām ʿAwn al-Dīn (cenotaph dated 1248); both bear inscriptions in the name of the ruler Badr al-Dīn Lu'lu', but neither the buildings nor the cenotaphs are oriented and *miḥrābs* of two alabaster slabs are at right angles in the southeast corner of each. This gives the game away: as shrines, Herzfeld rightly remarks, they needed no *miḥrābs*. They must, therefore, have been Christian shrines taken over in the 13th century and adapted to Muslim needs.

It would be easy to attribute the growth of Muslim shrines to infection from other religions or to adaptations of pre-Islamic cults, but, as we have seen, this is by no means always the case. Even if the practices of many visitors to shrines were apparently so unorthodox as to arouse the disapproval of the 13th- and 14th-century jurists, they can mostly be traced no further back than the first centuries of Islam. What is particularly noteworthy, however, is that Sunnī rulers have been as active in restoring Shīʿī shrines as Shīʿīs themselves. This may, of course, have been public gestures to pacify Shīʿī elements among their subjects rather than a personal cult. But it also shows the distinction between Sunnī and Shīʿī and the persons they revere to be complex and elusive, perhaps even more so than in the religious differences and cults of medieval Europe. It is not the clear-cut division so many Westerners have supposed.

Mausolea

Any distinction between mausolea and shrines, which mostly have a mausoleum as their nucleus, or between mausolea and funerary *madrasas* or *khānqāhs*, is inevitably arbitrary. But mausolea are so numerous and Islamic disapproval of them has been so deeply rooted that they demand separate treatment. Why the *ḥadīth* and the later jurists should disapprove so violently is unclear. It may partly have been fear of idolatry (even in the 14th century Ibn Taymiyya, the famous jurist, condemned mausolea because they distracted men's minds from God), or partly doubts about the propriety, or even possibility, of prayers for the dead. No prayers were to be said before tombs and the practice of visiting cemeteries on feast days was frequently condemned. In the orthodox view burial was of the simplest: the body wrapped only in a shroud was placed without a coffin in a vault or in the open ground in a cemetery, well away from human habitation (cemeteries in *The Thousand and One Nights*, for example, are typically places of evil repute frequented by robbers or, worse still, ghouls). Tombs were not to be marked, and those of the early caliphs were forgotten soon after their death. All over Islam these strict ordinances were quickly disobeyed: there is a tombstone in the Islamic Museum in Cairo dated 652; and Monneret cites ironically the *tombstone* of the Egyptian mystic, Dhu'l-Nūn al-Miṣrī (died 859), which boasts of his uprightness in refusing to permit a (domed) mausoleum over his grave. Nevertheless, mausolea alone were never pious foundations: in this at least the jurists had their way.

The shrine of ʿAbd Allāh Anṣārī at Gāzur Gāh built by Shāh Rukh in 1425. The picture shows a detail of the tilework in the northern *īwān* behind the mystic's tomb.

The rebuilding as the Great Mosque at Medina of the burial-place of Muhammad and his wives under the Umayyad Caliph al-Walīd in 706–10 set a precedent followed by many of the early Islamic dynasties. The 15th-century Medina historian Al-Samhūdī states that the tombs of the wives of the Prophet, which had been in enclosures of palm branches with an entrance covered by a goat-hair curtain, were demolished when the mosque was built. Muhammad's tomb itself was enclosed in an irregular masonry screen and deliberately set at one side so that the faithful should not confuse it with the rectangular Kaʿba at Mecca and should not turn to it during prayers. The screen, which had a padlocked entrance, did not reach up to the roof of the mosque but was covered with an awning

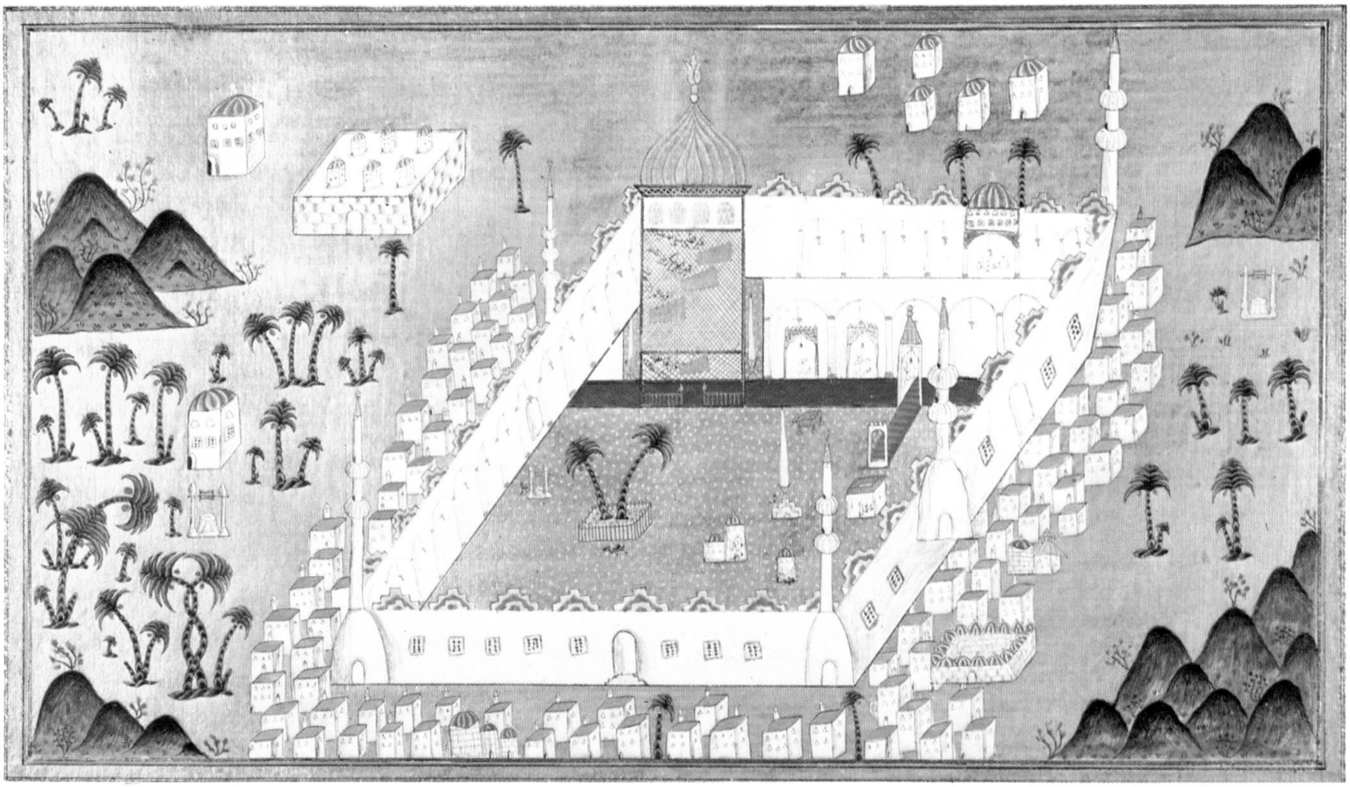

The Great Mosque at Medina, originally built by the Umayyad Caliph al-Walīd I (709). In the far left-hand corner is the shrine with the graves of Muhammad, Abū Bakr, ʿUmar and Fāṭima below. Chester Beatty Library, Dublin, MS. 447 (late 18th century).

of waxed cloth. However, the opening in the roof was masked by an open brick well almost five feet high. The Mamlūk Sultan Baybars replaced this by a low wooden screen (1269–70), and Qalāʾūn added a light dome covered with lead sheeting (1279). In 1476–77 Qāyt Bāy built a masonry dome covering Qalāʾūn's lath and plaster construction, though even this did not apparently reach the roof of the mosque, and there was no conspicuous dome above the tomb till the Ottoman restorations of the 17th century. Nevertheless, in spite of this curiously gradual development of the structure of Muhammad's tomb, Samhūdī's account makes it clear that even in the Umayyad period there was an attempt to emphasize the tomb from the exterior.

This was not exceptional: indeed, in early Islam there was a marked predilection for mausolea. The earliest, as Yūsuf Rāghib has shown, were at shrines – those of Daniel at Susa in Persia, and of Abraham, Sarah, Leah and Jacob at Hebron in Palestine. But there was apparently a monument to Ḥusayn at Kerbelā in Iraq, described variously as a dome (*qubba*) and a *saqīfa* (any roofed construction, for example a shed) by 680 AD, and a shrine of ʿAlī at Najaf "discovered" by Hārūn al-Rashīd (786–809) who ordered a plastered baked brick substructure, evidently with two entrances, covered by a red clay dome surmounted by a green pot, which later went into the ʿAbbāsid Treasury. However, these Shīʿī shrines, which may have been deliberately encouraged by the ʿAbbāsids to pacify their Shīʿī subjects, were not at suppositious tombs; and it is significant that, but for the shrine of the Imām Riḍāʾ (died 818) at Ṭūs (now Mashhad) in east Persia, where Harūn al-Rashīd had apparently erected a mausoleum for himself, all the early funerary structures recorded in the sources are in Syria or Mesopotamia, where there was a deeply implanted pre-Islamic tradition of domed mausolea. This indeed was to determine the characteristic Islamic mausoleum structure.

House burial continued to be regarded as something of a privilege. This explains the dynastic mausolea inside palace enceintes, in particular the Turbat al-Zaʿfarān (the Saffron Tomb – saffron was commonly used to anoint the cenotaphs of tombs visited on feast days) inside the Fāṭimid palace enceintes, in particular the Turbat al-Zaʿfarān (the Egypt in 1170–71. The Buwayhid dynasty evidently had a family cemetery at Najaf-Kūfa at the shrine of ʿAlī in which ʿAḍud al-Dawla (946–83) and his successors were buried. The decisive example, however, was that of the ʿAbbāsid caliphs, who were all buried in a cemetery attached to their palace at Ruṣāfa in east Baghdad. Their mausolea were enclosed by a strong brick wall by al-Mustanṣir (1226–42) with *waqfs* to keep it in good repair and survived more or less undamaged into the 14th century when Ibn Baṭṭūṭa visited them. The royal cemetery at the Alhambra with the remains of canopy tombs was largely destroyed to make room for the chapel of Charles V's unfinished palace. The best-preserved cemetery of this type is the *khalwa* (necropolis) of the Merinid rulers at Chella, outside Rabāṭ in Morocco (late 13th to 14th

The Khānqāh of Qurqumāz, Cairo (1506–07). The mausoleum is the large stone building in the foreground. Stone domes with highly decorated exteriors are characteristic of late 14th- and 15th-century funerary foundations in Cairo.

centuries). The entrance gives on to a forecourt fronting an enclosed *masjid*, a series of canopy tombs and a two-storied rectangular *zāwiya*.

Particularly in Egypt, tombs were enclosed in small courtyards (*ḥawshs*), which now stretch for miles outside Cairo forming veritable bungalow cities of the dead; such *ḥawshs* are also described at pre-Mongol Shīrāz and, for example, in the cemetery which grew up round the tomb of ʿAbd Allāh Anṣārī (1006–88) at Gāzur Gāh outside Herāt in Afghanistan. In Upper Egypt some tombs had small blind enclosures scarcely larger than the burial, but there were more elaborate tombs consisting of a barrel vault enclosed in a blind rectangle of walls paneled like the facade of a house. Many of the tombs bore dated marble plaques, which were removed 50 years ago after a flood without any record of their provenance. However, these are all 9th or 10th century in date, whereas most of the existing tombs cannot be much earlier than the 12th or 13th century.

Such *ḥawshs* originally contained only burials, but they rapidly acquired annexes: rooms for the family when visiting, for the keeper or for Koran readers; cenotaphs, sometimes no more than mounds, bearing plaques; *miḥrābs*, monumental entrances, canopy tombs over well-carved marble cenotaphs, or even completely enclosed domed burial chambers. The most elaborate of these is the Ḥawsh of the ʿAbbāsid Caliphs in Cairo established by the Mamlūks after the destruction of the Caliphate in Baghdad by the Mongols in 1258. This has both a monumental entrance and a *qibla* wall with seven *miḥrābs*, as well as a domed mausoleum with a single entrance (c. 1242–43). This was exceptional. Tombs surrounded by marble kerbs recur in the 14th and 15th centuries – at the shrines of Bāyazīd at Basṭām and Aḥmad Jāmī at Turbat-i Jām or at Gāzur Gāh near Herāt, where these are all shaded by ancient pistachio trees, or the tomb of Bābur (died 1530) at Kābul where a garden of plane trees and Judas trees has been planted (now restored). In 15th-century Persia, as in Islamic Spain, *rawḍa* (garden) is a common term for tomb: however, the trees at these famous tombs, even if almost as old as the tombs themselves, are scarcely enough to justify the description of "garden" and it must be a euphemism, probably for a tomb open to the sky.

The earliest extant Islamic mausoleum, the Qubbat al-Ṣulaybiyya above Sāmarrā, may be as late as 869, but the strong literary evidence for a tradition of domed mausolea even in Umayyad Islam shows that it was no novelty. It is, nevertheless, unique in material, being built of concrete (in spite of the Roman tradition, virtually unknown in Islam), and in its plan. It was a square chamber oriented to the four cardinal points with a dome on squinches enclosed in an octagon open on four sides, itself surrounded by a barrel-vaulted octagonal ambulatory strengthened by transverse arches, open on every side; the mausoleum must, therefore, have appeared as an elaborate canopy tomb, a type of mausoleum which, perhaps as a gesture to the most literally minded of Islamic jurists, is extremely persistent in Islam.

In Sunnī Islam it is customary to lay the corpse on its right side facing Mecca (in most of Shīʿī Islam bodies are laid with their feet towards Mecca, allegedly in order that they should face it when they stand at the Last Judgment). This practice naturally led to the orientation of mausolea and to the closing off of the axial bay to house a *miḥrāb*, though it was not used for prayers. But development was slow. Thus the "Samānīd" mausoleum at Bukhārā (pre-943) has four entrances and no *miḥrāb*. And the recently discovered Arab Ata mausoleum at Tīm in Uzbekistan (977–78) has a single entrance with decorated moldings and a framing inscription; but though the burial is parallel to the *qibla* wall, there is no *miḥrāb*, an addition which, outside Egypt, only begins to appear in Persian mausolea of the 11th century, for example, in the Duvazdāh Imām at Yazd (1037). Even so, many Egyptian and Syrian 12th-century tombs still contain no *miḥrāb*.

Twelfth-century domed mausolea in Persia or Central Asia are richly decorated with terracotta on the exterior or with stucco inside, and the comparatively inconspicuous decoration of early Cairene and Syrian monuments has naturally led scholars to assume that mausoleum architecture in Persia and Central Asia is a novel contribution to Islamic architecture. This cannot really be. The ʿAbbāsid Caliphate in Baghdad had primacy in taste as well as authority, and the Egyptian and Syrian tombs are therefore more likely to be in the Metropolitan tradition than tombs from furthest Transoxania or Afghanistan, which have survived because they were well away from the destruction of the great invasions. The Mausoleum of the ʿAbbāsid Caliphs in Cairo (c. 1242–

43) is, therefore, of crucial importance as an index of Metropolitan taste, though the new caliphs were only buried there after 1260–61. Its interior decoration, with arched stucco panels in each wall, relief medallions and a dome with six-lobed stucco medallions of foliate decoration decreasing regularly in size towards its apex, painted in dull yellow and red on a blue ground, is of a richness suited to the august puppets who were to be buried there. The less impressive exterior, more in the tradition of Cairene 12th- and 13th-century facade decoration, should not be taken as evidence for the appearance of the caliphal mausolea at Baghdad; but the exceptionally sumptuous interior cannot have been chosen for the new caliphs by accident.

Tomb towers. There are pre-Islamic tomb towers at Palmyra (2nd to 3rd century) and in Khwārizm, the latter perhaps Zoroastrian; but the first dated, and most extraordinary, of all Islamic tomb towers, is the Gunbad-i Qābūs (1006–07) near Gurgān in northeast Persia, ·61 meters high, crowned by a conical roof, with a flanged plan and a marked batter to emphasize its height. Its foundation inscription describes it, indeed, as a *qaṣr* (from Latin *castrum*, a fortress), but in the sense of an enormously high building. Grave robbers may have destroyed traces of the burial (there was apparently no crypt), but the picturesque story that Qābūs was buried in a glass coffin slung by chains from the rafters of the tomb is obviously a legend.

Nearer to the mainstream of development are square or polygonal mausolea on a plinth: the Gunbad-i ʿAlī (1056) at Abarqūh, with the first known stalactite cornice, and two recently discovered octagonal brick tomb towers at Kharraqān on the medieval Qazwīn-Hamadān road, an area evidently used by the Seljuks in the later 11th century as summer pastures. They are only 29 meters apart and are signed by the same craftsman. The earlier, dated 1067–68, has a single entrance, is roughly *qibla*-oriented though without a *miḥrāb*, and has staircases in two of its eight exterior buttresses. The later, dated 1093, has a *miḥrāb* and only one staircase. Both had double domes, the outer dome being ribbed, but their appearance is difficult to reconstruct since the tops of the buttresses have all been destroyed. The earlier tomb (in lieu of a *miḥrāb*) has each of its eight niches decorated with paintings of mosque lamps hung on chains with medallions of birds, mostly peacocks, singly or in pairs, above.

It has been justifiably remarked how advanced these early Persian tomb towers are. The Gunbad-i Qābūs type persists in central Persia into the 14th century, for example the mausoleum attached to the Great Mosque at Basṭām, but with the flanges less pronounced and the height reduced. Historically, the most interesting later mausoleum of this type is that at Radkān East (1281) in the steppe north of Mashhad where the Mongol viceroy of the western dominions, Arghūn Āghā, had died in 1275 and was buried. This may be a coincidence, but it may also be, to judge from Rashīd al-Dīn's biography of Arghūn Āghā, that he was buried in this tomb tower.

The Sāmānid mausoleum at Bukhārā (pre-943). It is brick faced with decoratively coursed bricks and terracotta plaques, but is not oriented.

At some undetermined period tomb towers began to include a crypt. The "Tomb of Tughril" at Rayy, datable 1140 by a cast-iron plaque now in the Museum of Art of the University of Michigan, certainly has a hollow floor. But in the case of tombs at Marāgha – the Gunbad-i Surkh (1154) and the Gunbad-i Kābūd (1196) – and at Nakhichewān – the tombs of Yūsuf ibn Kuthayyir (1161) and Muʾmina Khātūn (1186–87) – the entrance shafts to the crypts are above ground in the stone plinth of the brick superstructure. In these tombs staircases have been eliminated since they no longer have substantial corner buttresses, and their hemispherical domes were generally covered by conical or pyramidal roofs. Much simpler brick patterns than the Kharraqān mausolea are enhanced sparingly by turquoise ceramic inlay, particularly on cornices or over entrances; while at least in the tomb of Muʾmina Khātūn at Nakhichewān the inside has traces of painted plaster.

While brick tomb towers, mostly cylindrical, were erected in Azerbaidzhan well into the 14th century, mausolea, mostly stone, found a new lease of life in 13th-century Seljuk Anatolia, where they are so numerous that only a few can be mentioned here. One of the earliest (conceivably 12th century), at Erzurum, is a domed cylinder enclosed by an ambulatory with projecting gables, each containing a window set in a carved hood with animal or human figures. Another early stone mausoleum (probably c. 1200) is the octagonal Halifet Gazi mausoleum at Amasya, with a crypt and a room above reached by stairs to an entrance which is a compendium of Seljuk decorative motifs crammed into the minimum space. At Konya at the Alaeddin Mosque (restored 1220), just above the ruined Seljuk palace, there is one decagonal tomb containing the tiled cenotaphs of various royal burials from at least 1192 onwards, and an octagonal tomb, apparently unfinished, though it bears an inscription dated 1219, which was evidently also intended for the royal cemetery, since only one Seljuk sultan, Kaykā'ūs I, whose mausoleum is at the hospital he built at Sivas in 1217–18, is buried outside Konya. At Tercan, west of Erzurum, there is an eight-lobed anonymous tomb, the Mama Hatun Kümbed (1200–20), uniquely set in a circular enceinte with a richly decorated entrance, the decoration of which is more appropriate to brickwork than stone-carving, with 12 niches inside, some with burials, and a staircase up to a terrace.

The tomb tower at Radkān East, Khurāsān (1281). The burial was in a crypt in the basement and there were blind staircases in the upper walls. Tomb towers of this type first appear in Persia in the mid-11th century.

Few mausolea in Seljuk Anatolia are incorporated into *madrasas* or other funerary foundations, and most are isolated constructions in cemeteries or far from towns. However, there were also *īwān* burials, often with a crypt below, most spectacularly in the family tomb attached to the *khānqāh* of Ṣāḥib Ātā/Fakhr al-Dīn ʿAlī (1280s) at Konya, which is a domed *īwān*; at Ahlat/Khilāṭ on Lake Van the two forms were sometimes combined, the crypt being half-open and the height of an *īwān* and the tomb chamber above reduced to a narrow drum below the dome, for example in the "Emir ʿAlī" tomb (14th century). Nevertheless, most of the Ahlat tombs continue the Anatolian tradition of crypt and upper chamber. Two are particularly fine – the Ulu Kümbed (1273) with pendent arcading on the exterior and the mausoleum of Erzen Khātūn (1396–97) with broken-arched arcading and traces of plaster inside, painted with chinoiserie lotuses. The fashion was by then on the wane: the Bayindir tomb at Ahlat (1481) is a colonnaded canopy over a built-up crypt. The Ahlat cemeteries are particularly rich in domed mausolea of various types, as well as in beautifully carved 13th- and 14th-century rectangular stone stelae. But the town was ravaged by earthquakes and almost two centuries of campaigning (1300–1500), and too little else remains standing for us to know the people for whom the mausolea were built or to determine exactly how they developed.

Ottoman royal tombs are a much simplified derivative of Anatolian tomb towers – free-standing polygonal constructions, sometimes preceded by a portico, with low, saucerlike domes covered with lead sheeting on the exterior. Their exteriors are mostly paneled with marble, but their interior decoration was often sumptuous. Such was the Yeşil Türbe, part of a large foundation of Çelebī Meḥmed I (1413–21) at Bursa, and characteristically in a private cemetery. Its exterior was originally covered with turquoise tiles. Inside it has dadoes of bright green hexagonal tiles with gilt decoration, as well as a monumental polychrome ceramic *miḥrāb* and the brilliantly colored ceramic cenotaph of Meḥmed I. All this was probably executed a few years after the completion of the building in 1419–20.

The striking appearance of the Persian and Anatolian tomb towers has prompted the suggestion that they are characteristic of *nomadic* peoples, like the Seljuks, who controlled Persia and Central Asia from 1140 onwards. But the tomb towers are first of all Persian, and the Sīrāf monuments show that there was a tradition of tomb towers by the 9th or 10th century. Moreover, they never displaced the domed squares of Central Asia, or of Egypt and Syria,

The octagonal Halifet Gazi mausoleum (c. 1200) at Amasya in Anatolia. The entrance is a compendium of Seljuk decorative motifs crammed into the minimum space.

which remained in closer contact with the ʿAbbāsid capital at Baghdad, and they appear to be the work of local craftsmen ignorant of Metropolitan trends.

Isolated monuments. There are also monumental mausolea standing apart from funerary foundations. The most impressive is that of Sanjar, the last of the Great Seljuk sultans, on the old citadel of Merv, probably built about 1152. It has a double dome, approximately 30 meters high, on a base 27 meters square with walls up to 6 meters thick. The transitional zone is concealed on the exterior by a gallery with curiously archaic stucco decoration drawn almost entirely from the 9th-century Sāmarrā repertoire. The inner hemispherical dome is decorated with radial brick star patterns, but traces of painted decoration suggest a 14th- or 15th-century restoration. A Soviet dig in 1937 demonstrated that the mausoleum was adjacent to the Seljuk Great Mosque of Merv and opened into it through a grille in its west side. This doubtless explains why it had no *miḥrāb*. The tomb became famous in Islam.

In Cairo there is also a colossal isolated mausoleum, though it must stem from another tradition, the Qubbat al-Fadāwiyya (1479–81), which had considerable influence on the design of large domes in Ottoman Cairo. But in Egypt the only dome of comparable size, that over the grave of the Imām al-Shāfiʿī (1211), appears to have been deliberately erected beside the *madrasa* founded there by Saladin in 1178 when he restored the Imām's tomb and covered it with a splendid paneled teak cenotaph. The dome, Maqrīzī says, was erected by al-Malik al-Kāmil for his mother, whose cenotaph, dated 1211, is still to be seen; and one of his sons, as well as the Ayyūbid ruler al-Malik al-ʿAzīz ʿUthmān and his mother, was also buried there. Evidently in response to an outburst of legal criticism from the *ʿulamā*ʾ against the construction of mausolea, al-Malik al-Kāmil decided to attach his family mausoleum to a building the fame of which was apparent to all his contemporaries and beyond all criticism. This was to have important implications for the great domed mausolea of Mamlūk Cairo, all with domed tombs large enough for scores of Koran readers, not to mention groups of Ṣūfis whether resident on the foundation or not.

In Cairo, moreover, Layla ʿAlī Ibrāhīm has noted attempts to endow mausolea with dynastic importance, perhaps originally because succession in the Mamlūk dynasties was not necessarily hereditary. Al-Ṣāliḥ Najm al-Dīn Ayyūb, the last Ayyūbid ruler of Egypt (killed at the Battle of Manṣūra in 1249), bought as slaves the Baḥrī Mamlūks, mostly Qipchāq, Pecheneg or even Kievan Russians, refugees from the Mongol invasions on the steppes of south Russia, from 1227 onwards, gained their unswerving loyalty and used them as his crack regiment. His death was kept secret to avoid civil strife but his widow, Shajarat al-Durr and the first Mamlūk ruler, built him a mausoleum (attached for propriety to the *madrasa* he had founded) in which he was buried in 1250 after a funeral

Entrance to the Mama Hatun Kümbed (1200–20), an anonymous mausoleum at Tercan, eastern Turkey. It is a stone version of the brick tomb tower with a dressed stone enclosure.

procession in which his clothes and weapons were solemnly placed in the mausoleum. Henceforth, Maqrīzī says, oaths of fealty were taken there after the Mamlūks' official manumission at the Citadel on the conclusion of their training, "in order that the Law [Turkish law, not the Sharīʿa] should be maintained there as it had been in the sultan's lifetime." This interesting practice was later transferred to Qalāʾūn's tomb (1284–85) by his son, al-Ashraf Khalīl, who paid the tomb the respect of dismounting before it when he returned from Syria to Cairo, and Ibn ʿArabshāh's account of the Gūr-i Mīr at Samarkand describes exactly similar practices at the tomb of Tīmūr.

Cemeteries. Two famous cemeteries, the Shāh-i Zinde at Samarkand, and the southern and eastern Mamlūk cemeteries of Cairo, also shows signs of organization. Admittedly, the nucleus of the Shāh-i Zinde was a shrine, that of Quthām Ibn ʿAbbās, and it was given greater unity by a gateway added by Ūlūgh Beg in 1428. However, the personages buried there in Tīmūr's time are surprisingly diverse: first, perhaps, ladies of Tīmūr's family, but quite soon his emirs and even distinguished scholars, like the astronomer Qāḍī-Zāde Rūmī (died c. 1436). The earliest of these mausolea is apparently that of Khwāja Aḥmad (datable 1340–60), the work of a craftsman, Fakhr-i ʿĀlī, with a porch largely covered with deeply incised turquoise tiles, with a few panels of relief tiles in turquoise, cobalt and white. A second tomb (1360–61) of an anonymous lady, "whose chastity God preserved," has a similar revetment, and a few similar fragments incorporated haphazardly into other tombs suggest that there may have been yet another like it. Similar tiles are known outside Samarkand only in the mausoleum of Būyān Qūlī Khān at Bukhārā (1358), but terracotta tiles carved in a similar technique occur in the area as early as the southern tomb at Uzgend (1186). Later these carved tiles gave way to underglaze painting in thick slip colors – white, yellow and reddish on a cobalt ground; their last occurrence is the Amīrzāde mausoleum (1386), where the carved tiles are combined with stalactite squinches magnificently decorated and gilt.

The mausoleum of Yūnus al-Dawādār (1382), Cairo. The ribbed dome on its incongruously narrow drum demonstrates the Cairene tendency steadily to increase the height of mausolea.

There was one further development, ceramic mosaic, though this is the rarest of the techniques used to decorate Tīmūr's own monuments. The mausoleum of his favorite sister, Shīrīn Bika Āqā (1385–86), has a porch entirely faced with tile mosaic in turquoise, white, brownish-yellow and green, all on a cobalt ground. The interior is particularly interesting, with a high dado of deep green tiles with gilt chinoiserie designs of phoenixes, and wall paintings above of rivers, trees and magpies, a favorite bird of Tīmūrid court painters, and one of the commonest birds of the Central Asian steppes. The mosque and tomb (1405) of Tūmān Āqā, one of Tīmūr's favorite wives, opposite the entrance to the mosque at the shrine of Quthām ibn ʿAbbās, were similarly decorated.

Of the southern cemetery of Cairo perhaps the most interesting mausolea are those attached to the Sulṭāniyya (probably 14th century), two double stone domes similar in construction to the ribbed domes of the Gūr-i Mīr at Samarkand or of Gawhar Shād at Herāt. The most imposing mausolea of the eastern cemetery, stretching almost in a straight line from north to south, are 15th century, built well away from Cairo in the desert. They range from the funerary *khānqāh* of Faraj ibn Barqūq to the graceful complex of Qāyt Bāy (1472–74), the carved dome of the mausoleum rising in the center of buildings which included a *madrasa*, a *maktab-sabīl*, various reception rooms or adjacent tombs, as well as lodgings, a watering trough and a *khānqāh*, rather further away but all enclosed by a wall with monumental gates. Most interesting, perhaps, are the later 15th- to 16th-century domed tombs without any attached foundation, clustering around the larger royal complexes. This recalls a phenomenon frequent all over Islam: great tombs become popularly identified with great saints, so that even the wickedest ruler's tomb may be surrounded by modest burials of people misled into the hope of gaining grace by proximity to him in death.

Tomb furniture. One final topic deserves mention, tomb furniture and interior decoration. Although there was a

The main way of the Shāh-i Zinde, the medieval necropolis of Samarkand. On the right is the porch of the mausoleum of Shīrīn Bīka Āqā (1385–86) with the walls of an octagonal canopy tomb (now roofless) beyond. On the left is the dome of the mausoleum bearing the signature of Ustādh ʿAlī Nasafī (14th century).

Above: the eastern Mamlūk cemetery, Cairo. On the right is the mausoleum and *khānqāh* of al-Ashraf Barsbay (1432).

Right: tiled cenotaph in the mausoleum of Sayyid ʿAlā al-Dīn (1342) at Khiva. Rich chinoiserie decoration for cenotaphs is typical for Central Asia in this period.

constant tendency for funerary domes to rise higher, inside tombs plaster vaults often hang down. Although some tombs have rich interior painted or tiled decoration, this is exceptional: very often the *miḥrāb* will be decorated, just because it is a *miḥrāb*, though no prayers could be said there, as in the case of the mausoleum of Qalāʾūn; but it is very rare to have monumental *miḥrāb*s inserted bodily as furniture. The earliest is perhaps Anatolian, in the 13th-century Arabşah Türbe, an anonymous tomb at Kharput, which contains a fine black and turquoise mosaic *miḥrāb*, but that of the Yeşil Türbe at Bursa is undoubtedly the grandest. Otherwise, it is mostly the Mamlūk tombs of Egypt and Syria which show the richest decoration – marble paneling, wall painting, carved wood and carved and painted stucco.

The only characteristic piece of tomb furniture is the cenotaph, a paneled wooden boxlike construction, often bearing an inscription richly decorated and generally placed in the center of the mausoleum, without respect to where the burial vault actually is. The earliest surviving wooden cenotaphs are that of the Imām al-Shāfiʿi in Cairo, built by Saladin (1178), that of Saladin in his tomb at Damascus (1195), still there but displaced by a marble slab contributed by Wilhelm II in 1898, and the Fāṭimid or Ayyūbid cenotaph from the shrine of Sayyidnā al-Ḥusayn in Cairo, now in the Islamic Museum there. In Mamlūk Cairo wooden cenotaphs were later replaced by a rectangular marble dais resembling a throne, often with ornamental knobs at the corners. In Persia there were still some 14th-century wooden cenotaphs, though the latest well-preserved example of 1326 comes from Bukhārā from the tomb of Sayf al-Dīn Bākharzī. Meanwhile tiled cenotaphs were also gaining popularity, with a whole spectrum of types, both dais plus cenotaph and cenotaph alone. There was other tomb furniture. But of the carpets, the rich hangings and the enameled and gilt glass lamps described by so many late medieval travelers nothing remains in place.

Further Reading

Most of the material used for the present book was in the form of scattered articles, often in inaccessible languages. It has not been thought useful to incorporate these into a general bibliography. The volumes suggested here give some idea of the present, if not the future, of Islamic archaeology.

Bartol'd, V. V., *Die geographische und historische Erforschung des Orients mit besonderer Berücksichtigung der russischen Arbeiten* (Leipzig, 1913).

—— *Turkestan down to the Mongol Invasion* with an additional chapter translated by C. E. Bosworth (3rd ed., London, 1968).

Bosworth, C. E., *The Ghaznavids* (Edinburgh, 1963).

—— *The Islamic Dynasties* (Edinburgh, 1967).

Broadhurst, R. J. C., trans., *The Travels of Ibn Jubayr* (London, 1952).

The Cambridge History of Iran, vol. IV, *The Period from the Arab Invasion to the Saljuqs*, ed. R. N. Frye (Cambridge, 1975); vol. V, *The Saljuq and Mongol Periods*, ed. J. A. Boyle (Cambridge, 1968).

The Cambridge History of Islam, ed. P. M. Holt, A. K. S. Lambton and B. Lewis, I–II (Cambridge, 1970).

Cohn-Wiener, E., *Turan. Islamische Baukunst in Mittelasien* (Berlin, 1930).

Corpus Inscriptionum Arabicarum: Aleppo, E. Herzfeld, 3 vols. (Cairo, 1954–55); *Anatolia*, M. van Berchem and Halil Edhem (Cairo, 1910); *Egypt*, M. van Berchem, completed by G. Wiet (Paris, 1903; 1929–30); *Jerusalem*, M. van Berchem, 3 vols. (Cairo, 1927); *N. Syria*, M. Sobernheim (Cairo, 1909).

Creswell, K. A. C., *Early Muslim Architecture*, I (Oxford, 1932); II (Oxford, 1940); Penguin abridgment of the two volumes (Harmondsworth, 1958); 2nd edition of I in two parts (Oxford, 1970).

—— *The Muslim Architecture of Egypt*, I (Oxford, 1952); II (Oxford, 1959).

della Valle, P., *Viaggi*, 3 parts in 4 (Rome, 1650–63).

Dieulafoy, J., *La Perse, la Chaldée et la Susiane* (Paris, 1887).

Encyclopedia of Islam (2nd ed., Leiden and London, 1960–).

Gabriel, A., and Sauvaget, J., *Voyages archéologiques dans la Turquie orientale*, I–II (Paris, 1940).

Gibb, H. A. R., *Mohammedanism: an Historical Survey* (London, 1949).

Gibb, H. A. R., trans., *The Travels of Ibn Baṭṭūṭa A.D. 1325–1354*, 3 vols. (Hakluyt Society, Cambridge, 1958, 1961, 1971).

Goodwin, G., *A History of Ottoman Architecture* (London, 1971).

Hamilton, R. W., *Khirbat al-Mafjar: an Arabian Mansion in the Jordan Valley* (Oxford, 1959).

Herzfeld, E., *Geschichte der Stadt Samarra* (Berlin, 1948).

Hourani, A. H., and Stern, S. M., ed., *The Islamic City* (Cassirer, Oxford, 1970).

Inalcik, H., *The Ottoman Empire. The Classical Age 1300–1600* (London, 1973).

Lambton, A. K. S., *Landlord and Peasant in Persia* (2nd ed., London, 1969).

The Legacy of Islam, 1st edition edited by T. W. Arnold and A. Guillaume (Oxford, 1931); 2nd edition edited by J. Schacht and C. E. Bosworth (Oxford, 1973).

Le Strange, G., *Palestine under the Moslems* (London, 1890).

—— *Baghdad under the ʿAbbāsid Caliphate* (Oxford, 1900).

Lewis, B., *The Assassins. A Radical Sect in Islam* (London, 1967).

Marçais, G., *L'Architecture musulmane d'Occident* (Paris, 1954).

Morier, J., *A Journey through Persia, Armenia and Asia Minor to Constantinople in 1808 and 1809* (London, 1812).

Niebuhr, C., *Voyage en Arabie et en d'autres pays circonvoisins*, French translation, 2 vols. (Amsterdam-Utrecht, 1776–80).

Pope, A. U., ed., *Survey of Persian Art*, 4 vols. (Oxford, 1939).

Reinaud, J., *Description des monumens musulmans du cabinet de M. le Duc de Blacas*, 2 vols. (Paris, 1828).

Rodinson, M., *Muhammad* (Harmondsworth, 1974).

Sarre, F., *Denkmäler persischer Baukunst* (Berlin, 1901–10).

Sarre, F., and Herzfeld, E., *Archäologische Reise im Euphrat- und Tigris-gebiet*, I–IV (Berlin, 1911–20).

Setton, K. M., ed., *A History of the Crusades* (Philadelphia, Pa., 1958–62).

Siroux, M., *Caravansérails d'Iran et petites constructions routières* (Cairo, 1949).

—— *Anciennes voies et monuments routiers de la région d'Ispahan* (Cairo, 1971).

Sourdel, D., and Sourdel-Thomine, J., *La Civilisation de l'Islam classique* (Paris, 1968).

Sourdel-Thomine, J., and Spuler, B., ed., *Propyläen Kunstgeschichte. Die Kunst des Islam* (Berlin, 1973).

Texier, C., *La Mésopotamie, l'Arménie et la Perse*, 2 vols. (Paris, 1842–52).

Wulzinger, K., and Watzinger, C., *Damaskus. Die islamische Stadt* (Berlin-Leipzig, 1924).

Acknowledgments

Unless otherwise stated all the illustrations on a given page are credited to the same source.

Aerofilms, 54.

Association Netherlands USSR Friendship Society, 51.

Dick Barnard, 21 bottom right, 23 bottom left, 44, 45 bottom, 46 top right, 97 left, 102, 104 bottom right, 117 bottom left.

Bibliothèque Nationale, Paris, 29 bottom.

Bodleian Library, Oxford, 17, 41.

British Library Board, 73 bottom, 76 bottom, 77 bottom left, 78 top left.

Chester Beatty Library (photo Rex Roberts), 129.

Clarendon Press, Oxford, 108.

Courtauld Institute, by permission of R. G. Searight, 15 top.

Elsevier, 56 top, 86 left, 117 bottom right, 126, 127.

Werner Forman Archives, London, 40, 53, 63.

John Freeman, 2, 11, 12, 67, 101, 103 top right, 105 bottom, 124 (by kind permission of John Harvey).

Freer Gallery of Art, Washington, 31.

Roger Gorringe, 20 top, 20 bottom left, 22 bottom right, 55, 56 bottom, 65 bottom, 76 top, 80 top, 109, 113, 115 bottom, 117 top.

Susan Griggs, 123.

Robert Harding Associates, 19, 20 bottom right, 21, 22 bottom left, 49, 107, 119, 131, 135.

Michael Haynes, 61, 65 top, 133 bottom.

Hermitage, Leningrad, 22 top.

Holle Verlag, 18 top, 46 bottom, 78 bottom, 86 right, 87 left, 90 right, 112, 116, 132.

Angelo Hornak, 43, 48 bottom left, 57, 64, 74 bottom, 75 top left, 81, 83, 85 left, 91, 96, 104 bottom left, 105 top right, 106 top right, 110, 136 left.

Lovell John, Oxford, 26, 29 top, 35.

Metropolitan Museum, New York, 30, 111.

Musée du Louvre, 73 top, 79 bottom left.

Museum of the History of Science, Oxford, 93.

Nauta, 90 right, 114.

J. M. Rogers, 13, 15 bottom left and right, 23 bottom right, 24, 33, 45 top and middle, 46 top left and middle, 47, 48 top left and right and bottom right, 50, 59 bottom, 60, 70, 71, 74 top left and right, 75 top right and bottom left and right, 76 middle, 77 top left and right and bottom right, 78 top right, 79 top and bottom right, 80 bottom left and right, 84, 87 right, 92, 97 right, 98, 99, 103 top right, 121, 122, 128, 130, 132, 134, 136 right.

Ronald Sheridan, 104 top left.

Graham Speake, 42.

Spectrum, London, 23 top, 39, 115 top.

Staatliche Museum, Berlin, 18 bottom, 85 left.

Alex Starkey, 10, 37, 59 top, 68, 89.

University Library, Groningen, 25.

Ton van der Heyden, 32, 103 top left, 104 top right, 105 top left, 106 top left and bottom left and right.

Roger Viollet, 14.

The Publishers have attempted to observe the legal requirements with respect to the rights of the suppliers of photographic materials. Nevertheless, persons who have claims are invited to apply to the Publishers.

Glossary

ʿAbbāsids The dynasty of caliphs who ruled at Baghdad from 750 to 1258 tracing their descent from ʿAbbās, the uncle of the Prophet. From 1258 to 1517 a line of caliphs descended from an ʿAbbāsid refugee succeeded one another in Cairo, but under the strict control of the Mamlūk sultans. The rule of the Baghdad ʿAbbāsids, and their development of administration, town and court life, law, literature and the sciences, have been regarded as a classical period in the history of Islam.

Achaemenids Persian dynasty, 539–330 BC. Its most noteworthy rulers were Cyrus II (559–529 BC), Darius I (522–486 BC) and Xerxes I (485–465 BC) under whom the Persian Empire extended from Libya to the Aral Sea. Their capital was at Persepolis which, under Darius III, was destroyed by Alexander the Great in 330 BC and the dynasty overthrown.

Al-Idrīsī (?1100–63) The author of an important geographical work on the *Seven Climes* (1154) for Roger II of Sicily. It contains one map for each clime (i.e. climatic zone); the maps of later manuscripts suggest that those in the autograph were colored.

Al-Maqrīzī (1364–1442) Distinguished Egyptian scholar, public official (*muḥtasib*) and author. Chiefly important as a historian of Egypt (Fāṭimids to Mamlūks) and as the topographer of Fusṭāṭ and Cairo, which he describes in their actual state and in reconstructions of their pristine splendor.

Amṣār (plural of *miṣr*) Military encampments founded for the Arab troops upon the first conquest of Islam. Though intended to keep the troops away from the conquered peoples, they rapidly became towns of their own with a population of clients (*mawālī*) and unconverted natives as well as the garrison of Arab troops. Famous *amṣār* include Fusṭāṭ in Egypt, Qayrawān in Tunisia, Baṣra and Kūfa in Iraq.

Apadana Columned basilical audience hall of the Persian kings: that at Persepolis is the most famous. On the Arab conquests others were turned into mosques, like the Masjid al-Ṭawr (the Mosque of the Bull, from its Achaemenid capitals in the form of kneeling bulls) at Qazwīn described by the early Islamic geographers.

Apodyterium See **ḥammām**.

Artuqids The Turkish rulers of the Diyarbekir area in SE Turkey from the late 11th to the early 15th century. They controlled major copper and iron mines and were important in the trade between Iraq and the Caucasus which was only marginally affected by the Crusades and Muslim counter-Crusade in the 12th and 13th centuries. Their copper coins bear many ruler portraits, signs of the zodiac or planets and heraldic animals. They were considerable patrons of the arts, in particular al-Jazarī's famous *Book of Automata*, which probably describes machines he had made, written in 1205 for the ruler of Diyarbekir.

Ashʿarī Orthodox theological school founded by Abu'l-Ḥasan al-Ashʿarī (873–74 to 935–36) combining the literal reading of the Koran of the **Ḥanbalīs** with rational argument (**kalām**), an approach developed by later theologians. Its most important political consequence was the doctrine that a Muslim remained a believer even when in a state of grave sin, hence that even a wicked caliph must be obeyed.

Assassins An **Ismāʿīlī** sect established by Ḥasan-i Ṣabbāḥ who seized the mountain fortress of Alamut near Qazwīn in 1090, then a series of other fortresses, proclaiming open revolt and assassination to attain success. In 1094 a major split in the **Fāṭimids** of Egypt occurred and Ḥasan b. Ṣabbāḥ proclaimed himself supreme head of all Ismāʿīlīs. In 1256 Alamut was captured by Hülegü and the Ismāʿīlī Imām killed. Missionaries from Alamut were also active in N Syria seizing castles including Maṣyāf on the Orontes (1140–41), and it is from the Syrian branch that most of the Crusader legends of Assassins, hashish and superhuman cunning derive. By 1273 the **Mamlūks** controlled the Syrian Assassin fortresses, but the community continued to exist and the loosely termed "ʿAlawīs" of present-day Lebanon and N Syria probably include Ismāʿīlī elements.

Bull-headed capital at the Persepolis apadana.

Astrolabe The basic astronomical instrument used and developed by the Arabs to measure altitudes, determine the hour of day and cast horoscopes. The body, suspended by a ring, is circular and composed of several interlocking disks with a central axis on which turn the "spider" (*ʿankabūt*), representing the vault of the fixed stars revolving around the earth at rest, and the *alidad*, a flat ruler determining sines, cosines, tangents and cotangents. Astrolabes were valid only for a single latitude till al-Zarqalī/Azarchel (1068–91) produced generally valid astrolabes.

Atābeg The title given by Seljuk and Mamlūk rulers to the **emir** appointed guardian of a crown prince. In the 12th century certain *atābegs* took advantage of the weakening of the Great Seljuks to make themselves independent, e.g. in Fārs, Syria and northern Iraq, while in Mamlūk Egypt, on the death of the Sultan al-Malik al-Nāṣir Muḥammad in 1341, there ensued a series of short reigns entirely controlled by successive *atābegs* in the names of his sons who had not attained their majority.

Ayyūbids The dynasty of Ṣalāḥ al-Dīn b. Ayyūb (Saladin) ruling between the late 12th and the mid-13th centuries over Egypt, Muslim Syria and Palestine, most of Mesopotamia and the Yemen. Kurdish by origin, Saladin was perhaps the most talented general ever to fight the Frankish Crusaders whom he defeated at Ḥattīn (1187). After his death in 1193 the dynasty concentrated on Egypt and Syria, and Mesopotamia gradually split up into minor states which fell to the Anatolian Seljuks and later to the Mamlūks and the Mongols. But at Ḥamā' there remained a small principality whose penultimate ruler was the celebrated historian Abu'l-Fidā (1310–1331). Under their patronage *madrasas* and *khānqāhs* were founded all over Egypt and Syria.

Bartol'd, V. V. (1869–1930) Probably the most outstanding Russian Orientalist to date. Arabist, Persian scholar and Turcologist, his major work is historical (*Turkestan down to the Mongol Invasion*, 1928; 1958; 1968) but his mastery of epigraphy and realization of the importance of archaeology and historical geography to Islamic history make all his works essential for the student of Persia and Central Asia.

Bedouin Pastoral nomads tribally organized, of Arabian stock, mostly now inside Arabia. The most famous of their tribes, from whom Muhammad claimed descent, was the Quraysh at Mecca who in the mid-7th century were extensively involved in trade. The exploits of the pre-Islamic Bedouin, mostly animists by religion, are the theme of much early Islamic literature.

Bektashi A Turkish **Ṣūfī** order, the legendary patron of which, Ḥājjī Bektāsh, probably lived in Anatolia c. 1240, though the order only gained its definitive form under Salim Sulṭān in the early 16th century. Its heterodox aspects – Shīʿism with Ismāʿīlī tendencies, curious rites suggesting confession and the Eucharist, and the participation of unveiled women – may be later accretions. Some of the earliest Bektashi **tekkes** were in the Balkans, and Bektashi influence upon the Ottoman Janissaries is perhaps connected with the Balkan origins of the Janissary troops.

Beluch/Balūch/Balōč Iranian nomads organized in tribes, now largely confined to Balūchistān (Persia east of Kirmān to Sind in Pakistan). Kirmān fell to the Arabs in 644 but the Beluch were not subdued till the arrival of the Ghaznavids and then the Great Seljuks whose centralized government made raiding, their principal occupation, unprofitable and encouraged migration eastwards. Their history before 1500 is, however, extremely obscure.

Berbers The native population of the North African coast from the oasis of Sīwa in Egypt to the Atlantic, speaking a multitude of dialects and now broken up into many tribes. They were speedily, though not permanently, converted to Islam, and while the ʿAbbāsids used them as crack troops, heterodox dynasties based on Berber opposition to the Arabs occupied North Africa except for the orthodox Almoravids in the 11th to 13th centuries.

Bidʿa Innovation. A belief or practice for which the Sunna gives no precedent, generally with the implication that it is arbitrary, if not wrong. However, some innovations have been accepted, for example the codification of law, and innovation, even when unacceptable, is therefore regarded as confused thinking as much as heresy.

Black Sheep A Turcoman dynasty, the Qarāqoyūnlu, which controlled Mesopotamia and much of west Persia between 1375 and 1468, with a subsidiary branch at Baghdad in the 15th century. Their history is a series of pitched battles, advances and retreats and virtually the only Qarāqoyūnlu monuments remaining are a few tombs and gravestones, some in the form of sheep, at Ahlat/Khilāṭ on Lake Van in eastern Turkey.

Buwayhids or Būyids A **Shīʿī** dynasty from Daylam (N Persia) who occupied first the Iranian plateau (Iṣfahān, Fārs, Kirmān and Azerbaidzhan) and then Baghdad and ʿAbbāsid Iraq in the 10th and 11th centuries. They established their supremacy over the caliphs and their viziers and reinforced the **iqṭāʿ** as a means of paying the army, but their most conspicuous influence was in the revival of Persian culture in the very center of orthodox Islam.

Caldarium See **ḥammām**.

Caliph (Arabic *khalīfa*, "vicar," "successor") The supreme head of the Muslim community. Under the Umayyads the Caliph was treated principally as a secular monarch (for with the death of Muhammad Revelation had come to an end) but the ʿAbbāsids emphasized their majesty and spiritual preeminence, which was ultimately all that remained to them with the progressive delegation of power to their **viziers** and the political control of Baghdad first by the Buwayhids and then by the Seljuks (10th and 11th centuries). This authority was further weakened by the proclamation of the Umayyad Caliphate in Spain (928) and of the Fāṭimid Caliphate in the Maghrib and then in Egypt. After the death of the last ʿAbbāsid Caliph in Baghdad (1258), a puppet Caliphate was installed in Egypt by Babyars (1261). It has been customary to dismiss it, but its influence in the Mamlūk state was not negligible.

Caravansaray Abode for travelers, usually with provision for trade. See **khān**.

Cartouche A term taken from Pharaonic archaeology to describe the royal blazons of Mamlūk sultans in Egypt and Syria in the 14th and 15th centuries. They are circular, divided horizontally into three fields, with an inscription of the form "Glory to his Majesty, Sultan . . ." in lieu of a coat of arms. They appear not only on royal buildings but also on objects specially commissioned for them – mosque lamps, bronze chandeliers or wooden doors.

Cenotaph (Greek "empty tomb") Muslims are not buried in sarcophagi or coffins but directly in the ground or in vaults. Graves were, however, often marked by a sarcophagus-like or dais-like cenotaph (*ṣandūq*, *takht*, *tābūt*) of wood or carved stone. Such cenotaphs are found in both mausolea and open cemeteries.

Chancery (Arabic *dīwān al-inshā'*) The department of state concerned with formulating royal decrees, serving for both interior and foreign affairs. Islamic chanceries attracted the most eminent scribes, and because of the grandeur and importance of their documents are particularly important for the evolution of calligraphic hands.

Charisma An uneasy translation of *baraka*, the spiritual power exercised by shaykhs even after their death. Islam rejects the possibility of mediation between God and man and hence rejects the notion of grace. Nevertheless it is widely believed that a shaykh's *baraka* will ensure the granting of minor prayers, e.g. by a childless woman.

Circassian (Cherkes) A group of peoples in the northern Caucasus speaking a variety of N Caucasian languages, Sunnī Muslims of the **Ḥanafī** school who were converted gradually in the 16th to 18th centuries. In Egypt "Circassians" were an important element in the Mamlūk state from the time of Qalā'ūn (1279–90) onwards and came to control it entirely under the dynasty of Circassian Mamlūks (1382–1517), the Burjīs. Their exact race and language are unknown; confusingly they virtually all have Turkish/Qipchāq names though differing from them in, implausibly, claiming Arab lineage.

Cloisonné Polychrome enamels where the colors are kept from running by small compartments (*cloisons*) of metal which fuse with a metal base during firing. The technique is particularly characteristic of Byzantine and Caucasian medieval enamels. The only known Islamic enamels, in particular the Innsbruck Plate, are all cloisonné.

Cour d'honneur An esplanade, normally fronting the throne room of a palace, designed for military reviews and receptions of ambassadors. At Sāmarrā and Ukhayḍir, no less than Versailles, their architectural decoration was particularly grand.

Creswell, Sir K. A. C. (1879–1974) Traveler, archaeologist and architectural historian, one of the founders of modern Islamic archaeology. He was the author of a fundamental corpus of early Islamic monuments (*Early Muslim Architecture*, I–II, Oxford, 1932, 1940; Oxford, 1970), and of a two-volume corpus of the monuments of Egypt from the 10th century to 1326 (*The Muslim Architecture of Egypt*, Oxford, 1952, 1959). But his interests covered the whole of medieval Islamic architecture from Spain to India.

Dār al-Ḥarb In theory, all territory outside the **Dār al-Islām**, the Land of Islam, though states might conclude truces with Muslim states against payment of tribute without actual conversion. The territories which did not recognize Islam were under threat of a missionary war (**jihād**), as were territories like 10th- to 12th-century Syria, which were temporarily recaptured by non-Muslims – Byzantines or Crusaders.

Dār al-Islām The whole territory in which the law of Islam prevails, recognizing the community of the Faithful (**umma**), the unity of the law (**sharīʿa**) and the protected status of the People of the Book (*ahl al-kitāb*, hence **dhimmī**).

Dervish A common term for **Ṣūfīs** of any persuasion, but particularly applied to the wandering Ṣūfīs (Qalandāriyya) whose failure to belong to the established orders excited reproaches of vagrancy, heresy or vice.

Dhimmī The protected minorities in Islam who were tolerated against payment of a poll tax and a land tax. They comprised first Jews and Christians whose scriptures partook of the Covenant of Abraham; then, by extension, Zoroastrians whose sacred books, the Zend Avesta, were probably written down only in the 9th century; then, even further, the Sabaeans, who included star-worshipers at Ḥarrān near Urfa in SE Turkey, Samaritans and the like.

Dīnār The gold unit of the Islamic coinage. The earliest Umayyad type imitated the *solidus* of Heraclius, but with a Muslim legend. But ʿAbd al-Malik's coinage reform of 698–99 established a standard epigraphic type of high fineness (96%–98%) and unvarying weight which was maintained without significant debasement till the 11th century, though the dīnārs of later dynasties tend to vary slightly in appearance.

Dirham The silver unit of the Islamic coinage from the rise of Islam. Initially dirhams imitated Sasanian silver coins while adding a Kūfic inscription giving the governor's name and the mint. Then after some experimentation ʿAbd al-Malik (698–99) introduced a purely epigraphic type which was to become standard. From the 11th century onwards a well-documented "silver famine" led to the issue of base dirhams, and when after the Mongol invasions silver dirhams were again struck, they differed considerably in design and weight from the earlier standard type.

An 8th-century dirham from Spain.

Dīwān The medieval equivalent of a ministry (its meaning was later extended) dealing with taxes, land grants, pious foundations and military affairs, and the means by which royal decisions formulated in the chancery (*dīwān al-inshā'*) were implemented. They each had their archives, few of which have survived, except those of the Ottoman Empire in the Topkapi Saray in Istanbul, now the Başvekalet Arşivi.

Druse/Druze (Arabic *durūz*) Sect stemming from the Ismāʿīlīs mostly inhabiting the Lebanon, the Ḥawrān in Syria and parts of Palestine. The sect originated in the reign of the Fāṭimid Caliph al-Ḥākim (disappeared 1021) who became its Messiah, whom the Druse have been passively awaiting ever since. They are **Ḥanafī**, though their practices are otherwise scarcely Muslim, and their identifiable beliefs are strongly Gnostic.

Emir (Arabic *amīr*) The title given to great military commanders (the *ahl al-sayf* or Men of the Sword), particularly under the Seljuks, Ayyūbids, Mongols and Mamlūks. With the development of the **iqṭāʿ** system they became military governors of large provinces while holding high positions at court – Grand Chamberlain, Keeper of the Wardrobe, Cupbearer etc. The government was carried out by the **vizier** and his staff or the **ʿulamā'**, the *ahl al-qalam* or Men of the Pen.

Enceinte Walled enclosure, either of a fortress or, in Islam, of a mosque, generally those with a central courtyard. Some early mosques – Mutawakkil's in Sāmarrā (847–), Ibn Ṭūlūn's and al-Ḥākim's in Cairo (876 and 1012) – have outer enclosures (*ziyādas*), possibly derived from the *temenos*, the outer enclosure, guarding the sanctity of many Classical temples.

Fātiḥa The opening chapter of the Koran which is therefore often splendidly illuminated. It has come to be recited also as an occasional prayer, particularly on passing the tombs of learned or pious men, though orthodox Islam rejects the idea of prayers for the dead.

Fāṭimids Missionary Ismāʿīlī anti-caliphate in North Africa, Egypt and Syria (909–1170) and tracing its descent from ʿAlī and Fāṭima. They founded Mahdiyya in Tunisia (920), Cairo (969) and by 971 controlled Mecca, Medina and most of Syria and Palestine which they held for nearly 200 years. They were expelled from Egypt by Saladin in 1171, which brought their caliphate to a close; but Yemen and parts of India, which had been evangelized in the 11th century, remained faithful to their doctrine. In Egypt particularly they were magnificent patrons of the arts and architecture.

Fatwā Official decision on a point of law given by a *muftī* or a professor of law in a *madrasa*.

Funduq (from the Byzantine Greek, *pandokheion*) An inn, though *funduq* plans are rarely distinguishable from *khāns*. Foreign merchants, particularly the Pisans, Genoese, Amalfitans, Florentines and Venetians, each had their own *funduq* (Italian *fondaco*), a "factory" which housed the colony and its archives, a church, and the central depots of goods in which they specialized.

Garmsīr (Persian "hot lands") Used to describe the winter settlements of transhumants which in the hot weather they forsook for summer pastures (*sardsīr*, "cold lands"). This semi-nomadism was paralleled by Turcoman/Turkish transhumance (*qishlāq*, "winter quarters," *yaylāq*, "summer pastures"); but *qishlāq* came to mean "winter quarters for an army," hence "barracks," in both Persian and Turkish.

Ghassānids An important Arabian tribe who settled as client kings c. 490 AD in Syria in the eastern sector of the Byzantine Empire. Once there, they became Monophysite, protected the Syrian church, established capitals, of which Sergiopolis/Ruṣāfa in NE Syria is the best preserved, and patronized the great pre-Islamic poets of Arabia. Their power was crushed by the Sasanian invasion of 613–14 and then the Muslim conquest.

Ghaznavids Strongly Sunnī Turkish dynasty founded by a Sāmānid governor, Sebüktegin (977–97), with Ghazna as its capital, ruling over east Persia, modern Afghanistan and finally part of the Punjab till 1187. Its most famous ruler was Maḥmūd I (998–1030), the patron of Firdawsī, who dedicated his *Shāhnāme* to him, and the historian and scientist al-Bīrūnī. The most important archaeological remains, at Ghazna, Bust and Lashkarī Bazar in Afghanistan, are mostly datable to the reign of Masʿūd III (1099–1115), but new discoveries are coming to light every year.

Ghūrids Sunnī Turkish dynasty ruling first over mountainous Afghanistan with a capital at Fīrūzkūh (probably Jām) and then in India. With the decline of the Ghaznavids and the Great Seljuks in the mid-12th century they made themselves independent; the devastation wrought by the ruler ʿAlā' al-Dīn Ḥusayn (1149–61) earned him the nickname of "World Burner." The most impressive architectural patron of the dynasty was Ghiyāth al-Dīn

Muḥammad (1163–1203) whose works at Herāt, Jām, Shāh-i Mashhad and Chīsht (all in Afghanistan) have recently been discovered, brick constructions of fascinating virtuosity. The dynasty collapsed in 1215 just before the Mongol invasions.

Ḥadīth Tradition. As a source of law and dogma in Islam it was held to be second in authority only to the **Koran**, relating to Muhammad's own commentaries on the text which were essential for its proper understanding. It later formed the subject of special study in specialized institutions (*dār al-ḥadīth*), to determine its validity, chiefly by tracing it back via reputable authorities: on this basis much was rejected as unsound.

Ḥajj The Pilgrimage to Mecca which every adult Muslim of sound mind and body must perform once during his lifetime during the final month of the Muslim year, Dhu'l-Ḥijja. The principal rite is the circumambulation of the **Kaʿba** (*ṭawwāf*) but the *ḥajj* came to include the visitation of many sites in and around Mecca associated with Ishmael/Ismāʿīl and the Prophet. It culminates in the Feast of Sacrifices (ʿId al-Adḥa) on 10 Dhu'l-Ḥijja on which every Muslim family that can slaughters a sheep in commemoration of the Sacrifice of Abraham.

Ḥamdānids The Shīʿī Arab rulers of Mosul and Aleppo in the 10th century. The most famous of them all was Sayf al-Dawla who controlled Aleppo from 944 to 967, a brilliant general who fully exploited the strength of his Bedouin clients in fighting against the Byzantines and whose court attracted a dazzling collection of poets and prose writers. The Mosul branch was absorbed by the Persian Buwayhids, and Aleppo early in the 11th century came under the domination of the Fāṭimids of Egypt.

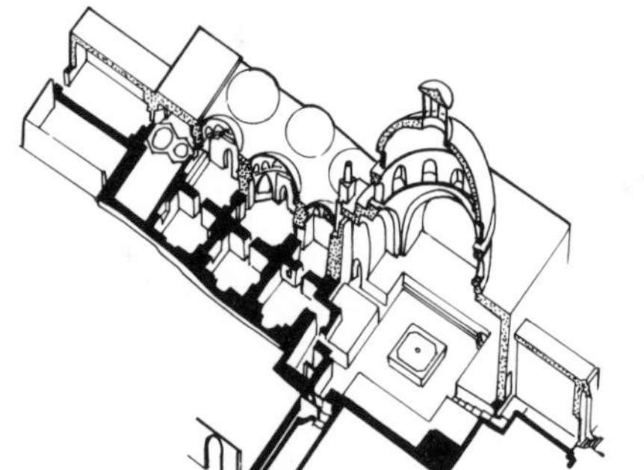

Isometric reconstruction of a 14th-century ḥammam *at Damascus. After Ecochard.*

Ḥammām "Turkish" bath. Roman-Byzantine baths were adopted by the early caliphs to accord with the requirements of ritual purity in Islam. The cold room (*frigidarium*) was suppressed and the dressing room (*apodyterium*) enlarged. This gave on to latrines, a cool room (*tepidarium*) and one or more hot rooms (*caldarium*) heated by under-floor ducts in the Roman manner (hypocausts) from a furnace stoked from the outside. There was strict segregation of the sexes and some disapproval of baths is perhaps reflected in *The Thousand and One Nights* where they are generally assumed to be the haunt of ghouls. They remained, nevertheless, places of social intercourse, and the Umayyad baths at Quṣayr ʿAmra and Khirbat al-Mafjar were attached to splendid audience halls.

Ḥanafīs School of law founded by Abū Ḥanīfa (died 767) which was particularly influential in the Mashriq: the Great Seljuks, the Mamlūks, the Ottomans and probably the Anatolian Seljuks as well were all solidly Ḥanafī. The school is normally regarded as the most favorable to the development of Islamic economics – commercial partnership, the rules governing permissible investment and the theory of *waqf ahlī*, a family trust which was also a pious foundation – all owe much to Ḥanafī influence.

Ḥanbalīs School of theology and law founded by Aḥmad b. Ḥanbal (died 855), hostile both to speculative theology (**kalām**) and to Ṣufī mysticism, though many of his followers practiced both. It was particularly important in 11th-century Baghdad under the Great Seljuks and then in 12th-century Syria. Its influence later declined, though the severity of the celebrated scholar Ibn Taymiyya (died 1328) in Mamlūk Egypt ultimately inspired Wahhābism, the present rite of Saʿūdī Arabia. Ḥanbalism is chiefly known for its literalism, the doctrine that the dicta of the Koran must be believed and obeyed to the very letter.

Ḥaraka Pointing. The use of signs above and below the line to indicate short vowels in Arabic, Persian and Turkish. It is *de rigueur* in all late copies of the Koran. *Ḥaraka* should be distinguished from *tashkīl*, the addition of dots or strokes to differentiate consonants and oblique cases. Such dots might be thought essential for legibility but they were, nevertheless, often omitted by fair copyists.

Ḥaram Sanctuary. Few Muslim monuments count as sanctuaries – apart from Mecca, Medina, Jerusalem and, for Shīʿī Muslims, those towns in Iraq and Persia associated with ʿAlī and his descendants. All of these confer some right of sanctuary as well. Mosques do not; neither were they considered holy places by the orthodox.

Harem/Ḥarīm The private parts of a house or palace inhabited by the women of the family, hence inaccessible to adult males.

Ḥawsh In Egyptian Muslim funerary practice an unroofed enclosure, sometimes with annexed kitchens or reception rooms attached, containing a family's tombs. Some were on a grand scale, like the *ḥawsh* of the ʿAbbāsid Caliphs in Cairo (1242 or later) with seven *miḥrāb*s in its great *qibla* wall. In Egypt funerary enclosures are a survival of Ptolemaic or even Pharaonic practice. They are now uncommon elsewhere, but certainly existed in 10th-century Shīrāz, well away from Egyptian influence.

Ḥayr Walled parkland in which wild animals roamed (Byzantine *paradeisos*) which was an amenity of large Islamic palaces – Qaṣr al-Ḥayr al-Gharbī and Qaṣr al-Ḥayr al-Sharqī in Syria, the Jawsaq al-Khāqānī at Sāmarrā and the 10th-century ʿAbbāsid palace at Baghdad are examples.

Hegira/Hijra The emigration of Muhammad from Mecca to Medina in September 622. The *hijra* era (often indicated by AH) is, however, reckoned from the first day of the lunar year in which it occurred, namely 16 July 622.

Herzfeld, E. (1879–1948) Distinguished German Orientalist. He studied architecture at Berlin then history, archaeology and Oriental languages. He excavated at Assur (with Andrae 1903–06) and at Persepolis and Pasargadae (1905–06). Between 1907 and 1924 he made field trips all over the East, studying Indian, Achaemenid, Sasanian and Islamic antiquities. His most significant contributions to Islamic archaeology were excavations at Sāmarrā with **Sarre**, 1911–13) and at Kūh-i Khwāja (basically a Parthian site) in Seistān (1929). But his contributions to Islamic epigraphy were immense, notably the volume of the *Corpus Inscriptionum Arabicarum* devoted to Aleppo (3 vols., Cairo, 1954–55). His field notes and unpublished papers are now in the Freer Gallery of Art, Smithsonian Institute, Washington, D.C.

Ḥijāz The northwest part of the Arabian peninsula up to the Jordanian frontier, including the two holy cities of Mecca and Medina and celebrated as the birthplace of Islam.

Ibn Baṭṭūṭa (1304–68/9 or 1377) A famous Maghribī traveler whose *Travels* all over the lands of Islam are a prime source for Islamic archaeology. The approximate chronology is as follows: 1325 N Africa, Egypt and Syria; 1326 Ḥijāz, Iraq, Tabrīz, W Persia and Baghdad; 1327–30 Arabia with three pilgrimages; by 1332 the Red Sea and the Persian Gulf; by 1334 Constantinople, the Lands of the Golden Horde, Transoxania, Afghanistan and India; then the Far East, return to the Maghrib by 1349, and a journey across the Sahara to Central Africa from which he returned in 1353.

Ibn Jubayr Andalusian traveler (1145–1217) who, to expiate the sin of drinking wine, made the pilgrimage to Mecca and described it in his *Travels* which are the most graphic and useful account of the shrines of medieval Mecca and

Medina and the rites observed there. His description of Mesopotamia is similarly graphic and rewarding.

Ijtihād (Arabic "reflection") The means by which the early lawyers arrived at legal decisions from the **Koran**, from Tradition (**ḥadīth**) or by deduction (*qiyās*). In principle all such decisions were consistent, but inevitably they led to the multiplication of local idiosyncracies, and the establishment of the main legal schools (**madhhabs**) replaced individual judgment by generally accepted rules.

The īwān *at Ctesiphon, Iraq.*

Īl-Khāns The title taken by the Mongols in Persia from Hülegü (1256–63) to Abu Saʿīd (1316–36). From 1260 they were bitter enemies of the Golden Horde and of their allies, the Mamlūks in Syria and Egypt.

Imām The spiritual leader of the Islamic community, hence in Sunnī Islam, the caliph. In Shīʿī Islam the *imām* was more important because of the requirement that he be heroic or of saintly virtue. In modern terminology, the *imām* is the officially appointed leader of prayers in a mosque.

Imāmī The school of law adopted by the Twelver Shīʿa. It rejects the **jihād**, which can only be proclaimed by the absent *imām* on his return, and does not recognize the legal dicta of the Umayyad caliphs, but its general attitude is fairly close to the Sunnī **Ḥanafīs**.

Iqṭāʿ Non-hereditary grant of land by a ruler (ultimately the sultan) to a soldier or an administrative official in lieu of pay, conditional upon further service. It was particularly developed by the Great Seljuks who had adopted the Sasanian view of the ruler as sole proprietor of his domains, though even in Mamlūk Egypt no more than half the land was made *iqṭāʿ*. It is somewhat comparable to medieval European fiefs, but the comparison must not be strained.

Ismāʿīlī A group of Shīʿīs recognizing Ismāʿīl, the son of the sixth Imām Jaʿfar al-Ṣādiq (died 765), as their Messiah. In the late 9th century they appear as a missionary movement radiating from Iraq to Khurāsān and Transoxania, Bahrein, the Maghrib, Yemen and Sind, though the advent of the Ismāʿīlī **Fāṭimids** caused internal dissensions which were accentuated by extremists like the Assassins in Persia and Syria, and the different communities tended to draw apart. Communities of Ismāʿīlīs survived the Mongols, particularly in Transoxania, but the most important group today are the adherents of the Agha Khan.

Istiḥsān and **Istiṣlāḥ** General principles of equity used by the Muslim schools of law to supplement legal reasoning "by analogy," generally as a justification for revisions of practice in the light of changed circumstances. Istiḥsān, favored by **Ḥanafīs**, is a particular interpretation of the law by a judge's own deliberation. Istiṣlāḥ, favored by **Mālikīs**, justifies such interpretations by reference to the ultimate good of all (Islamic) society.

Īwān Open porch, normally with a pointed barrel vault and fronting a domed chamber, either a throne room (compare the Jawsaq al-Khāqānī at Sāmarrā) or the *miḥrāb* of a great mosque (compare Iṣfahān pre-1092). *Īwāns* were an important element of Sasanian palace architecture (compare the great *īwān* at Ctesiphon), but their origins appear to be Mesopotamian, notably Assur/Ashur in the Parthian period.

Jalā'irids Mongol dynasty which in the break-up of the Īl-Khānate following the death of Abū Saʿīd (1336) established itself at Baghdad (c. 1340) and controlled part of western Persia (Fārs) and Tabrīz. The rise of the **Tīmūrids** put an end to any hopes for Jalā'irid domination of Persia, and then even Baghdad fell to the **Black Sheep** in 1410.

Jāmiʿ (in Persian *masjid-i jumʿa*) The great mosque in which alone the **khuṭba** might be said on Fridays. The early sources use the term *minbar*, and even great mosques like that of Ibn Ṭūlūn in Cairo (876–   ) are described as *masjids*. The first occurrence of *jāmiʿ* in an inscription (1032) is in Fāṭimid Egypt. Thereafter the term gradually gained common acceptance.

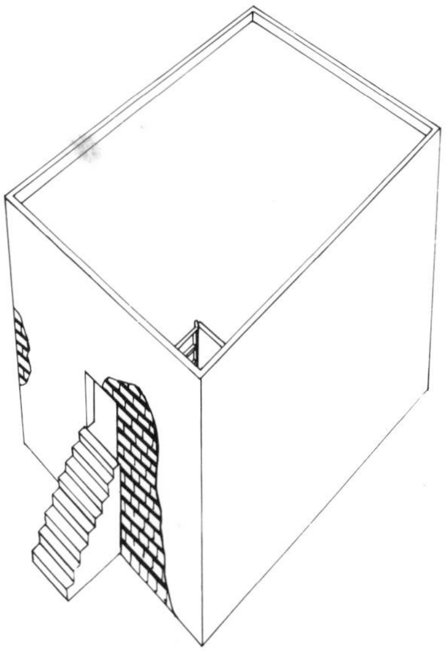

Reconstruction of the original Kaʿba.

Jihād The Koranic duty to impose the peaceful rule of Islam; hence the just war, but as much a collective as an individual duty. Armed conflict against Muslims or protected minorities (Jews, Christians etc.) is prohibited, and it was essentially a means of converting other peoples to Islam, or of defending Muslim states against attack.

Kaʿba Originally a cubic construction covered with a black veil (the *kiswa*) housing a Black Stone, associated in Islam with a sanctuary, built by Abraham at Mecca, though it was evidently the center of a pre-Islamic cult of idols in the form of stones. Almost from the first it was the focus of Islam: not only as the culminating point of the Pilgrimage when it is circumambulated, but also as the point to which all Muslims turn when praying.

Kalām Muslim scholastic theology, devoted to solving problems raised by Koranic interpretation – the ascription of anthropomorphic predicates to God, the freedom of the will, causality etc. – by rational argument and not dogmatic pronouncement. Its most famous proponent was al-Ghazzālī of Ṭūs (died 1111).

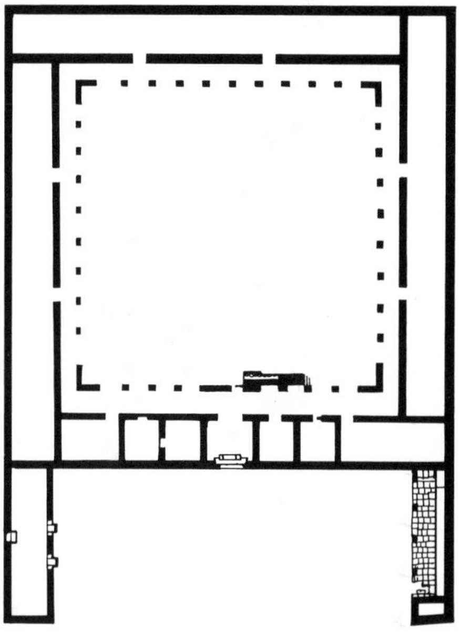

The khan *at Qaṣr al-Ḥayr al-Gharbi, Syria.*

Khān Caravansaray, both urban and rural (in Persia the term *ribāṭ/rubāṭ* is used), providing lodging and some protection for merchants, quarters for government officials and accommodation for trade. Some rural *khāns* are known to have been pious foundations; those in towns were generally not and were a convenient way for local notables to tap the gains from international trade.

Khānqāh An endowed foundation governed by a shaykh with provision for the maintenance of **Ṣūfīs**. *Khānqāhs* were particularly popular as funerary foundations in 12th- and 13th-century Syria and 13th- to 15th-century

Egypt. They are in some respects similar to medieval European monasteries, except that there was no specific rule to govern the order. Often, however, they were so richly endowed that their inmates must have found even spiritual poverty difficult to practice.

Khārijī Secessionists. The party who refused to recognize ʿAlī's treaty with his opponents after his defeat at Siffīn (657), with the result that, in their view, any miscreant *imām* loses his divine authority, becoming an infidel, and may be removed, if necessary by force. In spite of this alarming tenet which won for them at times orthodox opprobium as "heretics," the Khārijīs, in particular their moderate branch, the Ibāḍīs, were closer in spirit to orthodox Sunnism and were mostly quietist.

Khilʿa "Robe of honor" distributed to emirs and ambassadors by medieval rulers as a mark of favor. On the shoulder they bore **ṭirāz**, woven inscriptions in the ruler's name, thus implying that the receiver was his servant. The gift of a *khilʿa* was, therefore, more like an official issue of a dress uniform.

Khuṭba The Friday sermon delivered in the great mosque of a town by the ruler or his legal representative, which it was the duty of all adult Muslims to attend. Now essentially a moral discourse, under the Umayyads and the early ʿAbbāsids its content was primarily political, and the ceremonial which accompanied it was designed to show the prestige of the sovereign in state.

Koran The Muslim scriptures, the uncreated word of God, revealed progressively to Muhammad at Mecca and at Medina. At his death these revelations had to be edited and among various versions that of ʿUthman prevailed. The book is divided into chapters (*sūras*), not arranged chronologically, and verses (*āyas*). The first chapter, the **Fātiḥa**, came to be much used as a prayer of intercession.

Kufic A square, often highly decorated, Arabic script, the origin of which is groundlessly attributed to Kūfa in Iraq. It was much used for early Korans and for architectural inscriptions up to the early 12th century; but it coexisted with rounded scripts even in the Umayyad period and survived the general adoption of *thuluth* or *naskhī* for the coinage, chancery documents and Korans (late 12th century onwards).

Floriated Kufic inscription from Ghazna.

Lakhmids An Arab dynasty of Yemeni origin established in Iraq by the 5th century and controlling much of Syria from its capital Ḥīra, southeast of modern Najaf. Its rulers were Nestorian Christians, courted simultaneously by the Byzantines and the Sasanians and patronizing famous poets from the Arabian peninsula. Although Ḥīra and a castle outside it, Khawarnaq, did not survive the growth of Kūfa under the Umayyads, these buildings, and the poetry the Lakhmids inspired, became for the classical Islamic poets a symbol of their glorious past.

Luster Decoration of pottery. Glazed pottery painted with a mixture of metallic oxides, sulfur and acid, which, refired in a reducing atmosphere, produces a brilliant copper, silver or gold sheen. The technique was originally used on glass (pieces from Fusṭāṭ dated 773 and 779–80), but was adapted to pottery at Sāmarrā or Baghdad by the mid-9th century, and was further developed in 10th- to 12th-century Fāṭimid Egypt, 12th- and 13th-century Syria and late 12th- to 14th-century Persia, with a few revivals in later periods.

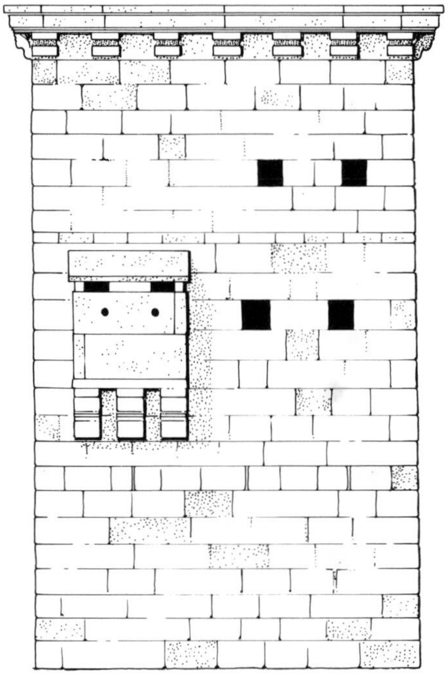

Tower with machicoulis.

Machicoulis Projecting balcony, usually above a gate, with holes through which noxious substances – boiling oil or molten lead – could be poured on to the heads of besiegers. The earliest known machicoulis are Roman and appear to be an adaptation of latrines.

Madhhabs Schools of law, all accepting the preeminence of the Koran and Tradition but differing in the emphasis in individual cases put upon sound judgment (*ra'y*), consensus or common opinion (*ijmāʿ*), analogy or deduction (*qiyās*) and equity (*istiḥsān* or *istiṣlāḥ*) as means of reaching a correct verdict. In Sunnī Islam there are now four main schools: **Shāfiʿī**, **Ḥanafī**, **Mālikī** and **Ḥanbalī**; and in Shīʿī Islam two: **Imāmī** and **Ismāʿīlī**.

Madrasa College for the teaching of theology (Koran, exegesis, Tradition) and canon law. Early *madrasas* recorded in 10th-century Khurāsān were small, normally grouped around a single teacher, and were little different from teaching **zāwiyas** in mosques. Under the Seljuks in Iraq and the Zengids in Syria (late 11th and 12th centuries) *madrasas* became state institutions with salaried staff and students endowed upon the foundation, but the primacy of mosques as educational institutions was never lost.

Maghrib Literally "the West." The lands of Islam, including Tunisia, Morocco, Algeria and Spain, regarded by the classical authors as peripheral to the course of Islamic history despite their considerable cultural contribution.

Maktab (In Cairo *kuttāb*) School for the teaching of the Koran. Primary education in Islam was left to parents, so that *maktabs* were often for orphans. Even imperial *maktabs*, like those founded by Ottoman sultans in the late 15th century, were private, in the important sense that there was no control over teaching and the curriculum. Architecturally *maktabs* are often associated with **sabīls**.

Mālikī The school of law founded by Mālik b. Anas (d. Medina 795–96) in which the principle of compromise was initially extremely important. It is chiefly established in the Maghrib and virtually all Islamic Africa, including much of Upper Egypt.

Mamlūks Two dynasties of freed slaves (Arabic *Mamlūk*, "owned") in Egypt and Syria reigning from 1250 to 1382 (the Baḥrīs) and 1382 to 1517 (the Burjīs or Circassians), of diverse origins but mainly **Qipchāq** Turks. Their regime was essentially military, but they were devout Muslims in public, at least, and their control over Mecca and Medina was as much religious as political. They were probably the greatest builders of any Islamic dynasty.

Maqṣūra Primarily an enclosure within a mosque to protect the ruler or *imām* from attack during prayers. The earliest (7th to 8th century) *maqṣūras* were probably lath and plaster. Later, as at Qayrawān, carved wooden grilles were erected, or even, as in the great mosques of Cordova and Iṣfahān, domed chambers fronting the *miḥrāb*. In Ottoman architecture there is a reversion to theater boxes, often above floor level, from which the governor could survey the congregation.

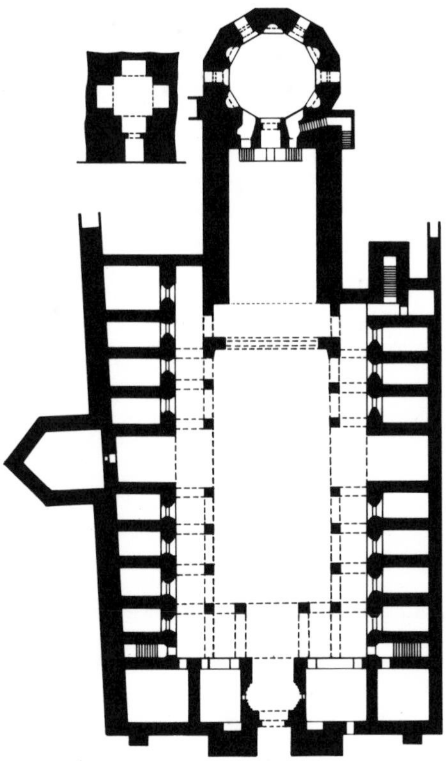

Plan of the Çifte Minare Medrese at Erzurum, E Turkey.

Mashhad (Arabic "a place of witness") The equivalent of the Greek *martyrion* applied to Shīʿī shrines in particular, whether or not their (suppositious) occupant is believed to have died a martyr. The most famous is Mashhad, the tomb-shrine of the Imām ʿAlī Riḍā in NE Persia.

Mashriq Literally "the East." The lands of the Eastern Caliphate, in which Egypt and Syria were generally included as clients and (after 1258) protectors of the ʿAbbāsid Caliphate. The eastern frontier was conventionally accepted as Transoxania/Farghāna/Mā warāʾl-Nahr, despite the presence of substantial Muslim communities in Turkestan and China.

Masjid Place of prayer, prostration; hence mosque. In early Islam there was no special term for Friday mosques (the sources refer to them as *minbars*, and *jāmiʿ* does not occur in inscriptions till the 11th century). However, later *masjid* was restricted to smaller oratories where the Friday prayer might not be said. In modern terminology *masjid* and *muṣallā* (an informal prayer place) are virtually synonymous.

Mausoleum (Arabic *qubba, turba*; Persian *gunbadh*) Monumental tomb; building for a tomb. Mausolea were common to the Hellenistic, Iranian and early Christian traditions, which possibly explains initial Muslim prejudice against them. The Qubbat al-Ṣulaybiyya above Sāmarrā (perhaps 860s) is probably the earliest Muslim mausoleum extant, but there is evidence that mausolea were tolerated from the late Umayyad period onwards (before 750).

Maydān An open space in a town, hence now a square. Few medieval Islamic towns had more than slight widenings at crossroads where markets sometimes grew up. But the rulers' palaces were often approached by a broad esplanade, for example the 9th-century Qarāmaydān before Ibn Ṭūlūn's palace in Cairo.

Mevlevi The order of whirling dervishes, followers of Jalāl al-Dīn Rūmī (1207–73), who spread from Konya through Anatolia and thereafter throughout the Ottoman Empire. The order was pantheistic in tendency and symbolized this in its dances, whirling with the right foot as a pivot to the melancholy music of reed-flutes, violins and drums or tambourines.

Miḥrāb Niche or slab in a place of prayer indicating the **qibla** or direction of Mecca. Its origins are disputed, but by the reign of ʿAbd al-Malik (685–705) a *miḥrāb* was installed underneath the Dome of the Rock and *miḥrābs* subsequently became standard features of mosques, *masjids*, *madrasas* and even tombs. They are customarily highly decorated.

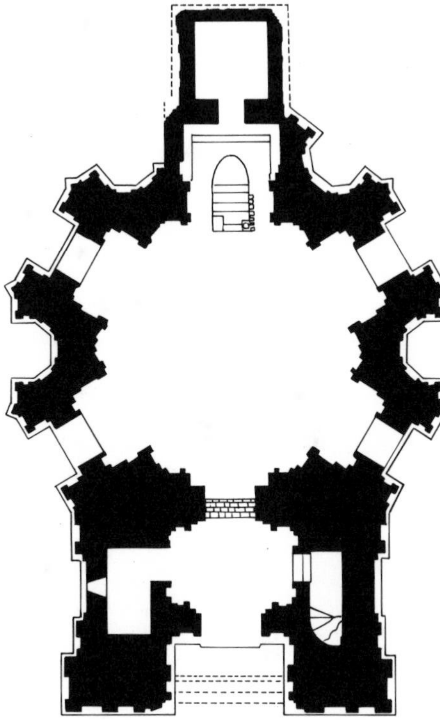

Plan of the mausoleum of Ṭughrābek at Urgench.

Minaret In theory the tower from which the call to prayer was given five times a day, hence an essential element of mosque architecture. Later, though never solitary, they were added to many private foundations – *madrasas*, *khānqāhs* or mausolea. Their origins in Syria were probably square Roman watch towers, and the name minaret (from the Arabic *nār*, "fire") has suggested a derivation there and in Iran from pre-Islamic fire towers for signaling.

Minbar Pulpit from which the Friday prayer in a mosque is given. It owes its development to Umayyad and early ʿAbbāsid ceremonial, but it may have been derived from bishops' thrones like that of the monastery of St Jeremiah at Saqqara (now in the Coptic Museum, Cairo). The earliest extant *minbars* (11th century) are hollow paneled wood constructions. In Mamlūk Cairo and Ottoman Turkey stone or marble was also used, and there is a ceramic mosaic *minbar* at Kāshān (15th century). *Minbars* in *madrasas* were intended not for the *khuṭba* but for sermons (*waʿẓ*).

Miḥrāb *niche at Boṣra, now plastered over.*

Mongols Tribes inhabiting a vast plateau in eastern Central Asia speaking an Altaic language with an alphabet remotely derived from Syriac. In the early 13th century the tribes were temporarily united by Genghis Khan, but after his death (1227) his sons divided up the colossal empire he had subjugated. In the present volume the Īl-Khāns and the Golden Horde, both of them heavily Islamicized by the 14th century, and the *ulus* of Chaghatay/Transoxania are particularly important. Mongolia is now divided between Outer Mongolia (the Mongolian People's Republic) and China (the old Inner Mongolia).

Muezzin The official on the staff of a pious foundation (mosque, *madrasa, khānqāh*) charged with giving the call to prayer five times a day. Most foundations had two, but the mosque-*madrasa* of Sultan Ḥasan in Cairo (1356–62) had a whole chorus of muezzins.

Muḥtasib Legal official appointed to oversee the markets as inspector of weights and measures and controller of prices. He was also a censor of public morals and was empowered to demolish unsafe houses, repair or clean out foul water supplies and keep the streets of *souqs* clear.

Muṣallā Open prayer place in 14th- and 15th-century Persia, with a monumental *miḥrāb* and *minbar*, in which prayers on the two great feasts of the Muslim year were customarily attended by the whole population of a town rather than in the Friday mosque. *Muṣallā* is, however, used by many medieval authors of any prayer place whatsoever.

Muʿtazilī Natural theology, officially adopted by the ʿAbbāsids in 9th-century Baghdad but proscribed in 847 AD. It proposed metaphorical interpretations of Koranic verses referring to God in human terms, for God was the transcendent Creator, even of the Koran, and had granted man total free will. The sinner, on the other hand, went into a state of suspense and could no longer be considered a true Muslim, which entailed that any caliph be perfect or forfeit the obedience of the community. This led the opponents of the Muʿtazilīs to accuse them of Shīʿism since this approximated to Shīʿī belief in the superhuman nature of their *imāms*.

Naṣrids The rulers of Granada 1231–1492 who owed their survival mainly to the faction and strife within the kingdom of Castille. The greatest builder was probably Yūsuf I (1333–54) who built the *madrasa* of Granada in 1349 as well as many additions to the Alhambra.

Naṣūḥ al-Ṣalāḥī al-Matrāqī An Ottoman jurist, according to Ḥājjī Khalīfa's biographical dictionary, the *Kashf al-Zunūn*, who died in 1533. He also accompanied Süleymān the Magnificent on his campaigns in eastern Turkey and Mesopotamia and his account of these, the *Beyān-i Menāzil der sefer-i ʿIrāqayn*, copied c. 1537, contains the earliest detailed topographical illustrations of many Islamic cities.

Nilometer Graduated shaft to measure the height of the Nile flood (before the Aswan dam eliminated it) which irrigated the land and determined the harvest, and hence the taxes on production. A repoussé silver Byzantine plate in the Hermitage (6th century) represents workmen finishing a Nilometer landscape, but the earliest surviving column is that erected by al-Mutawakkil (861–62) at the S tip of Rawḍa off Cairo, in a cylindrical shaft with intake tunnels at three different levels.

Niẓām al-Mulk (1018–92) The grand vizier of the Seljuk sultans Alp Arslān and Malikshāh and author of the *Siyāsetnāme* or *Book of Counsel for Kings*. Under his administration considerable changes in the **iqṭāʿ** were made, order and peace were maintained within the Seljuk dominions, and Niẓāmiyya *madrasas* established throughout the Seljuk Empire.

Ottomans Turkish dynasty originating as a minor principality in western Turkey in the late 13th century. Their first historical ruler, ʿOsmān/ʿUthmān, extended their dominions to Bursa (1326) which long remained their capital. It was transferred to Edirne/Adrianople in the 15th century but in 1453 was moved to Constantinople on its fall to Meḥmed II.

Parthians Western Asian empire (250 BC–226 AD) stretching from Central Asia (Merv/Old Nisa) to the Euphrates with, ultimately, capitals at Ctesiphon, Palmyra, Ashur and in western Persia. The principal eastern enemy of Rome until the Sasanians absorbed the empire in 226 AD.

Post house A stop, probably superficially no different from a caravansaray, along the main routes where official messengers could rest, change horses or hand on messages in relays. The post (*barīd*) was important from the ʿAbbāsid period onwards, but more is known about it from the Mamlūk sources, where carrier pigeons were also used, and from the Mongols since Ghāzān Khān (1296–1304) set up a chain of post houses (*yāms*) linking Persia and Iraq with Central Asia and China.

Qāʿa Central reception hall with one, two or four **īwāns** of Cairene palaces, the central space normally being covered. The Muslim topographers use *qāʿa* in the sense of a complete palace, i.e. reception hall with living quarters and dependencies.

Qāḍī Muslim judge, mostly on points of religious law. It was customary for each **madhhab** to have its own *qāḍī* since a judge is bound to adhere to the decisions of his own school of law. *Qāḍīs*, although important urban notables, rarely received large salaries but instead received most of their income from administering trusts, acting as executors and giving private legal opinions.

Qalandāriyya Wandering dervishes without fixed abode, strangely shaven and beringed, whose coarse garments and unconventional behavior provoked astonishment in Damascus in 1213 and subsequently much disapproval. They practiced physical mortification but were slack in their observances and were held to be immoral, both by the orthodox *ʿulamāʾ* and by other orders of Ṣūfīs.

Qānāt Underground irrigation system carrying water from its source sometimes as far as 50 miles. The channel is normally about 20 feet below ground and *qānāt* diggers are able to alter the incline so as to take the water over low obstacles. Every 20 yards or so the diggers are obliged to come up, so that *qānāt* systems are easily recognizable from the air as lines of hillocks.

Qānūn Customary or administrative law in Islam, recognized by royal decree. The growth of *qānūn* was an inevitable development of commerce and industry and of the conquest of countries whose laws were already codified, like the Byzantine provinces ruled by Justinian's code.

Qaysāriyya (probably from the Byzantine term for an imperial market) A lockup market for the sale and storage of valuable goods – fine cloth, jewelry, spices etc. – often patrolled by night-watchmen. In Turkey such markets are usually known as *bedestens*.

Qibla The direction in which prayers should be said, i.e. Mecca. Applied to the walls of buildings or to **miḥrābs**, the orientation of which, however, may often be faulty.

Qibla *wall at Medina. After Sauvaget.*

Qipchāq Turkish tribes now spread out from the Dniepr to Siberia (south Russia, Soviet Kazakhstan, Uzbekistan, Kirghizstan) but in the 13th to 15th centuries mostly concentrated in the Volga-Don steppes. Speaking a characteristic dialect and mostly pagan, they were imported *en masse* into Mamlūk Egypt and formed the core of the Mamlūk elite.

Qubba (Arabic "dome") Applied to any large domed building, e.g. the Dome of the

Rock in Jerusalem. In the later Middle Ages it came to be applied in particular to (domed) mausolea and is, therefore, one of the common words for tomb. Cf. Persian *gunbadh* (e.g. the Gunbadh-i Qābūs, 1006) and Turkish *kümbet*.

Ramaḍān The ninth month of the Muslim lunar year during which abstinence from food and liquid is enjoined from dawn till nightfall. The end of Ramaḍān is celebrated by the ʿId al-Fiṭr, the Breaking of the Fast, one of the two great festivals of the Muslim year, the prayers for which were held not in mosques, but in **muṣallās**.

Rawḍa (Arabic "garden") Used euphemistically in Spain and Central Asia for "tomb," e.g. the palace cemetery of the Alhambra. Rōḍa/Rawḍa is an island in the Nile off Fusṭāṭ, now part of modern Cairo, which was a favorite residence of the Ṭūlūnid, Fāṭimid and Ayyūbid rulers of Egypt. At its southern tip is the **Nilometer** of al-Mutawakkil.

Repoussé Relief decoration normally executed by beating a metal sheet over a wooden block. Particularly used for the more malleable metals, gold and copper, of which few medieval Islamic objects survive. Gold was too precious, and time and time again plate was melted down to furnish the coinage; copper was not precious enough and it was commoner to melt down old pieces rather than repair them.

Ribāṭ Literally, a place where horses are tied. First, a barracks where fighters in the **jihād** lodged, like the Ribāṭ at Sousse in Tunisia (9th century). Then, in Iran, a caravansaray in the country. Finally, in Mamlūk Egypt and Syria, a hospice, for example that for pilgrims to Jerusalem built by Qalāʾūn (1281–93), the Ribāṭ al-Manṣūrī, or for widows, orphans etc.

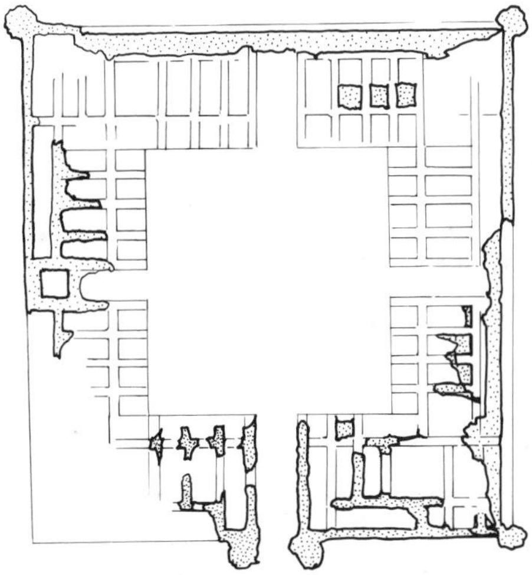

Reconstruction of Ribāṭ Zaʿfarānī. After Herzfeld.

Sabīl Public fountain for the provision of fresh water. The idea was probably adapted from the nyphaeum of Hellenistic and Roman towns, but their recognition in Islam as pious foundations and their elaborate plumbing and decoration in the 13th to 15th centuries are far from the appearance of the earliest Islamic *sabīl* known at Qaṣr al-Ḥayr al-Gharbī (707 AD). See plan, p. 143.

Ṣafawids The descendants of Shaykh Ṣafī al-Dīn of Ardebīl (1252–1334), the founder of the Ṣafawiyya order of dervishes. This was originally puritan and Sunnī, but under Shaykh Junayd (killed 1460) the order assumed its militantly Shīʿī character, which enabled Ismāʿīl I, who seized power in Persia in 1502, to proclaim Shīʿism as the state religion. The Ṣafawid capitals were first Tabrīz, then Qazwīn and later Iṣfahān, but the shrine remained at Ardebīl.

Ṣaffārids East Persian dynasty founded by a coppersmith, Yaʿqūb b. Layth, who controlled all Seistān by 867, then expanded into Kirmān and Khurāsān. His brother's descendants maintained themselves in Seistān till 1163 but the beginnings of the Ṣaffārids are the most interesting, since they were the first Persian Islamic dynasty to base their authority on their Persian lineage.

Ṣaḥn A flat courtyard, normally inside early Islamic mosques, e.g. that of Ibn Ṭūlūn in Cairo (876). Also used, however, of the interior of the *khānqāh* of Sayf al-Din Bākharzī at Bukhārā in its *waqfiyya* dated 1326.

Sāqiya The horizontal water wheel, driven by a buffalo or ass, geared into one or more vertical water wheels, to raise water high enough for adequate pressure to be maintained. This was perhaps an Egyptian invention and was particularly popular in Islamic Egypt. The same principle was used to work oil-presses and sugar-mills.

Sardāb (Persian *sard āb*, "cold water") Sunken grotto in houses or palaces in the Near East for refuge from the summer heat. Those of the 9th-century palaces of Sāmarrā have large central pools, but a *sardāb* recently discovered at Fusṭāṭ, like the modern *sardābs* of Yazd, was simply a cellar, ventilated by a wind-trap.

Sarre, Friedrich (1865–1945) Founder and first director of the Islamic department of the Berlin Museums (now the Museum für Islamische Kunst in West Berlin and the Islamisches Museum in East Berlin). His youth was spent in fieldwork in Anatolia and Persia, from which basic works, including *Denkmäler persischer Baukunst* (Berlin, 1910), emerged. He then dug with **Herzfeld** at Sāmarrā (*Die Keramik von Samarra*, Berlin, 1925), but he was principally eminent as a museum director and as the virtual founder of Islamic art history in Germany.

Sasanians Persian dynasty, 224–637 AD. The principal eastern enemies of the Romans, then the Byzantines, ruling over Persia, Iraq and much of the Caucasus and Central Asia. Zoroastrianism was the state religion, but though many of their palaces (Ctesiphon, Fīrūzābād and Sarvistān) remain, little is yet known of town life and trade under their dominion.

Sauvaget, Jean (1901–50) French Arabist, epigrapher and, above all, Islamic archaeologist: most of his work is based on Damascus and Aleppo, but he repudiated the notion of Islamic history considered in isolation from inscriptions and the standing monuments (including those of late Antiquity), the geographical circumstances or social organization, particularly the compartmentalization of Islamic markets in the mapping of which he was a pioneer. But, as with the Umayyad Mosque at Medina (built by al-Walīd in 709), where there are no remains, he also brilliantly exploited the historical sources to reconstruct its original form. See drawing, p. 146.

Seljuks A Turkish dynasty controlling most of Central Asia and Iraq in the 11th to 13th centuries. The Great Seljuks (1038–57) with capitals in Iṣfahān, Baghdad and Merv associated themselves with the ʿAbbāsid Caliphate in Iraq and assumed the title of Sultan. The Seljuks of Iraq (1118–94) were mostly puppets in the hands of their **atābegs**. Of the minor branches, the Seljuks of Kirmān (1041–1186) and Syria (1078–1117) and the Seljuks of Rūm (1077–1302) have left the most striking monuments, in what is now modern Turkey.

Serif Probably originally a Dutch word. Stroke at the head or base of a letter as in Roman capitals. In Arabic used only for *alifs* and *lāms* (*a*s and *l*s).

Shāfiʿī The legal school founded by the Imām al-Shāfiʿī who died in Egypt in 820. Originally most influential in Baghdad and Cairo, it was adopted at Mecca and Medina (10th century), and in much of Persia and Central Asia. With the triumph of Saladin in Egypt and Syria (1169) it achieved preeminence in the central lands of Islam but was displaced by the Ottoman conquests in favor of the **Ḥanafī** school, except in Egypt, Syria and the Ḥijāz.

Shahāda The basic Muslim statement of faith. "There is no God but God. Muhammad is his Prophet." To this Shīʿīs add "ʿAlī is the friend (*walī*) of God."

Shāhnāme (*The Book of Kings*) A collection of Persian legends from the creation of the world, including the heroic exploits of heroes like Rustam, a version of the Alexander Romance and the more or less historical exploits of the Sasanian kings. This was written down by several authors, but in particular by Firdawsī (940–1021) whose compilation has become the Persian national epic.

Sharīʿa The Law which, in spite of the development of administrative law (**qānūn**) and the acceptance of custom (**ʿurf**), was always regarded as supreme. Although its basis is religious – the Koran and Tradition – the translation "canon law" is too restrictive, since it covered every aspect of Muslim life and was the yardstick by which *qānūn* or *ʿurf* was judged.

Sharīf (plural *ashrāf*) A title accorded to the heads of prominent families entrusted with tribal or urban administration. Soon restricted to kinsmen of Muhammad and their descendants (in Persian the term *sayyid* is more usual). They enjoyed special respect, and Mecca was governed by ʿAlid *sharīfs* from the 10th century to 1924.

Shaykh A title of respect, normally for a distinguished scholar (*ʿālim*). The spiritual head of a Ṣufī community. Finally, the title accorded to various of the governing officials of al-Azhar in Cairo. Although many shaykhs were rich, the association of shaykh with "merchant prince" is modern, and intellectual or spiritual preeminence was not judged to entail material wealth.

Shīʿī A general term for the sects who, against the traditional orthodox view, insisted upon the recognition of ʿAlī as the legitimate successor (caliph) to Muhammad. They exalted the spiritual and moral qualities of their **imāms** and rejected the claims of the Umayyads to power. They were initially most powerful in Iraq: their particular association with Persia was only sealed by the triumph of the Ṣafawids in the early 16th century.

Shuʿūbiyya National sentiment which distinguished between race and religion in early Islam. This was most pronounced in Persia where, from the 9th century, Persian increasingly became the language of literature and the chancery and Arabic was restricted to the Koran and theology.

Silsila Chain of tradition handed down by Ṣūfī shaykhs to their pupils, comprising the individual teachings of a particular order of dervishes.

Siyāsa The equivalent of criminal law, applied by the Mamlūks in Egypt, by the Ottomans and other Turkish dynasties. Although in principle accepted as compatible with the **sharīʿa**, it was not based upon it, and its exercise was the prerogative of the ruler, not the corps of Muslim judges.

Souq (Persian *bazar*; Turkish *çarşi*) A market, in Islam mostly divided up by trades, lined by open booths with *khāns*, depots, baths and *masjids* opening off them. It thus formed the center of the Islamic town.

Stadtplan Highly conventionalized depiction of a town without stereometric projection so that plan and elevation are shown together. Used in all medieval and Renaissance European illustrated topographical works and common up to the late 17th century.

Ṣūfī (Arabic "woolen," with respect to the ascetic life symbolized by the woolen robe) Mystical or ascetic orders in Islam united under the authority of a shaykh who draws his teaching from a "chain" (**silsila**) of his predecessors. Ṣūfism becomes apparent in Islam as early as the 8th century, but, contrary to general supposition, it is not necessarily either Shīʿī or heterodox. Ṣūfīs are often referred to as "the poor" (*fuqarā'*).

Suhrawardiyya Founded by Shihāb al-Dīn Abu Ḥafṣ ʿUmar al-Suhrawardī (1145–1234), one of the strongest Ṣūfī orders of the Muslim Middle Ages and closely connected with the revival of the ʿAbbāsid Caliphate at Baghdad in the early 13th century.

Sultan A political title first accorded to the Great Seljuks by the ʿAbbāsid Caliphs in the 11th century, in the sense of the independent ruler of certain territories. It was theoretically granted *ad hominem* but by the 13th century, even before the end of the Baghdad Caliphate in 1258, many dynasties had assumed it as a right.

Sunnī Orthodox Islam, basing its teaching upon the Koran and its interpretation, *ḥadīth*, traditions reputably associated with Muhammad himself, and the teaching of the four orthodox schools of law (**madhhabs**).

Tafsīr Exegesis of the Koran based upon traditions (**ḥadīth**) firmly ascribed to Muhammad. It was an essential constituent of **madrasa** education.

Ṭāhirids Short-lived east Persian dynasty founded by Ṭāhir b. al-Ḥusayn (775–822) with a capital at Nīshāpūr. They were celebrated for their patronage of Arabic culture but were displaced gradually by the Ṣaffārids (c. 873).

Tatar Originally a Mongol tribe which mainly settled in the Lands of the Golden Horde after the Mongol invasion, on the steppes between the Volga and the Dnepr/Dnieper where they became the ancestors of the modern Tatars. By the mid-13th century, if not earlier, it was Turkish speaking. However, the close association with the Mongols remained since their Muslim and their Western contemporaries both refer to Mongols as Tatars.

Tekke Turkish **khānqāh**, particularly associated with the **Bektashi** and the **Mevlevi** orders, comprising individual cells, kitchens, heated infirmaries, assembly rooms for communal rites and shaykhs' lodgings. These provisions suited the severe Anatolian climate, but they were also dictated by the orders ritual needs.

Tepidarium See **ḥammām**.

Tersāne Ottoman Turkish form of Italian darsena/arsenale from the Arabic *dār al-ṣināʿa* (workshop, particularly an establishment for the construction and equipment of warships). Military arsenals like that on the citadel of Aleppo were generally known as *zardkhānes* ("places for chain mail").

Tīmūrids The dynasty founded by Tīmūr/Tamerlane (1336–1405) who ruled at Samarkand from 1370 onwards. After his death his son, Shāh Rukh, ruled at Herāt till 1447, while his grandson, Ulūgh Beg, ruled at Samarkand till 1449. Thereafter the two branches became separate, though both fell victim to the Uzbeks (1500–10). One of the last Tīmūrids of Samarkand, Bābur, founded the Great Mogul dynasty in India which boasted its descent from Tīmūr right up to the 18th century.

Ṭirāz State factories of fine cloth. They were most probably monopolies because they wove fabrics bearing the sovereign's name which were then used for robes of honor (**khilʿas**), essentially official garments. By extension, *ṭirāz* is then used for the bands of inscription across the facades of many Mamlūk buildings in Cairo, Damascus, Aleppo and Tripoli.

Trulli The local name for the houses of Apulia with "beehive" conical domes built without centering or transitional zones. Their origins are prehistoric, for example the *nuraghi* of Sardinia. In Islam they occur in Mesopotamia, around Aleppo on the Middle Euphrates and at Ḥarrān, near Urfa in SE Turkey. The possibilities of such domes, which are highly appropriate to areas where wood is scarce, do not, however, seem to have been exploited in monumental Islamic architecture.

Turcoman Used in the medieval sources for the Oghuz/Ghuzz tribes of the Turks who were forced westwards by Seljuk and then Mongol expansion. In the 12th century they formed principalities in Azerbaidzhan and Anatolia but were not fully absorbed by the Seljuks of Rūm. On the disintegration of the Seljuk state (late 13th century) they established new emirates, of whom the Ottomans became the most famous, but most of the Turcomans never settled and remained as they are today, nomads.

ʿUlamā' (plural of Arabic *ʿālim*) Essentially scholars who had the traditional *madrasa* education in the Koran and its exegesis (*tafsīr*), tradition (*ḥadīth*) and canon law (*fiqh*). Such scholars were appointed to the judiciary or other posts in the administration and came to form a class of urban notables, the *ahl al-qalam* (the Men of the Pen).

Ulus The kingdoms of the successors of Genghis Khān. The Great Khān remained first at Qarāqorum in Mongolia and later under Qubilay at Peking/Khān Baligh. The *ulus* of Jöchī, the Lands of the Golden Horde, stretched roughly from the Dnepr/Dnieper to the Oxus, its eastern frontier; that of Chaghatāy occupied Transoxania; while Persia, Iraq and the southern Caucasus ultimately became the Īl-Khānate (see **Īl-Khāns**).

Umayyads Caliphal dynasty reigning from 661 to 750, based, in spite of its phenomenal expansion, principally in Syria, Palestine and Egypt. Although their successors, the ʿAbbāsids, enormously expanded Islamic administration, virtually all their reforms were foreshadowed in the period 690–730. On their destruction in 750, a refugee Umayyad Caliphate was established at Cordova in Spain (756–1031).

Umma The Islamic community, originally restricted to Muhammad and his fellow Meccans or Medinans. As a community it was regarded as united in its views on religious, legal and ethical questions, a principle which was all the more important in view of its internal divisions – the Shīʿa and the orthodox *madhhab*s.

ʿUmra Pilgrimage out of due season to Mecca and Medina. This was always a pious work but it was insufficient to satisfy the requirement that every male adult Muslim should, if humanly possible, make the Pilgrimage (**ḥajj**) once in his lifetime.

ʿUrf Customary law, which was often accepted in areas where the ruling *madhhab* was not that of the ruled, as in Egypt under the Mamlūks, where direct application of the **sharīʿā** would have led to conflicts of interest. The principle that *ʿurf* and *sharīʿā* were compatible was steadfastly maintained.

Vizier (Arabic *wazīr*) The principal minister of the ʿAbbāsid caliphs, in charge of the **chancery** and, later, of the other administrative offices of state. Although under the Seljuks, the Mongols and the Ottomans viziers were often the ruler's *de facto* deputies, initially even the Barmecides at Baghdad (late 8th to early 9th century) had very little independence and were essentially subject to the caliph's every whim.

Waqf Land or property perpetually endowed upon a pious institution, the income of which is managed by a legally appointed administrator. The principle is basic to all Islamic pious foundations, though it may well have been derived from the Byzantine *piae causae* which catered for orphans, the poor, the aged and the sick and which were likewise perpetual endowments. One permitted form was the *waqf ahlī* or family trust in which surplus revenue was allotted to the founder's descendants.

Waqfiyya Legally attested document specifying the constitution of a pious foundation, its physical limits and its endowments in detail. Since **waqf** revenues were tax-free, special departments of state were set up to register property and income and contained copies of all current *waqfiyya*s. Virtually none remain, but those surviving are invaluable for the specific details of topography, architecture and practice they give.

White Sheep (Āqqoyūnlu) A confederation of Sunnī Turcoman tribes which first appeared in the Diyarbekir area (SE Turkey) c. 1350 and which for 150 years was important in NW Persia. The most famous White Sheep ruler was Uzūn Ḥasan (reigned 1466–78) with his capital at Tabrīz though he restored *inter alia* the Great Mosque at Iṣfahān. The Venetians even sought his alliance against the Ottomans, but his successors, caught between the Ottomans and the Ṣafawids, gradually lost their territories and succumbed soon after 1500.

Wikāla (literally Arabic "intendancy") Now used in Egypt as a synonym of **khān**, a market building with which it shares many superficial similarities. However, in the Mamlūk period *wikāla*s appear to have been buildings to collect goods so that dues might be levied upon them, and as such must have had equivalents all over the Islamic world.

Zāwiya (Arabic "corner, angle") Used variously by the medieval sources for **khānqāhs**, hospices (see **ribāṭs**) or even small **madrasas**. These divergencies all presuppose, however, an abode for a teaching shaykh around whom pupils (either *madrasa* students or Ṣūfīs) congregated. *Zāwiya*s were often endowed, but, unlike *madrasa*s, neither endowments nor a strict constitution were necessary prerequisites of their existence.

Zaydī Supporters of the revolt of Zayd ibn ʿAlī (740) who were prepared to support any descendant of ʿAlī and Fāṭima who rose up as Imām against the illegitimate rulers of Sunnī Islam; moral offenses invalidated the imāmate and a candidate of greater virtue then had the right to it. Zaydī states were established in the area south of the Caspian and in the Yemen in the 8th and 9th centuries and persisted in the latter.

Zengids Originally **atābegs** of the Seljuk sultans who made themselves independent and gained control of N Iraq, Mesopotamia and much of Syria in the early 12th century. They were among the most efficient agents of the Muslim counter-Crusade against the Franks and laid the essential basis for the successes of Saladin, himself a Zengid client, at the end of the 12th century.

Zindīq Heresy. In so far as it had a specialized sense, it applied to dualist Manichaean heresies which were prevalent in eastern Islam in the 9th and 10th centuries. However, sovereigns who grandly refer to themselves as extirpators of *zindīq* in their inscriptions are not precise and appear to have regarded any opposition to themselves as heresy.

Zīrids A Berber dynasty ruling in N Africa (10th to 12th centuries) with a branch in Spain having Granada as its capital. The former first enjoyed Fāṭimid favor and its capitals at Qayrawān and Ṣabra Manṣūriyya grew prosperous. But its attempt to cast off Fāṭimid overlordship brought savage retaliation (1052): the ruler fled to Mahdiyya where his successors established a powerful naval base, but the rest of his kingdom disintegrated into petty principalities. The last of the African Zīrids died in 1167.

Index

Page reference in *italics* refer to illustrations or their captions.